The Dynamics of Deforestation and Economic Growth in the Brazilian Amazon

A multi-disciplinary team of authors analyze the economics of Brazilian deforestation using a large data set of ecological and economic variables. They survey the most up-to-date work in this field and present their own dynamic and spatial econometric analysis based on municipality-level panel data spanning the entire Brazilian Amazon from 1970 to 1996.

By observing the dynamics of land-use change over such a long period the team is able to provide quantitative estimates of the long-term economic costs and benefits of both land clearing and government policies such as road building. The authors find that some government policies, such as road paving in already highly settled areas, are beneficial both for economic development and for the preservation of forest, while other policies, such as the construction of unpaved roads through virgin areas, stimulate wasteful land uses to the detriment of both economic growth and forest cover.

LYKKE E. ANDERSEN is Chief Economist at the Sustainable Development Department, Institute for Socio-Economic Research, Catholic University of Bolivia, La Paz.

CLIVE W. J. GRANGER is Chancellor's Associate Chair in Economics, University of California, San Diego.

EUSTÁQUIO J. REIS is Director of Macroeconomic Studies, Institute for Applied Economic Research (IPEA), Rio de Janeiro.

SVEN WUNDER is a scientist at the Center for International Forestry Research, Indonesia.

DIANA WEINHOLD is Lecturer in Development Economics, Development Studies Institute, London School of Economics and Political Science.

The Dynamics of Deforestation and Economic Growth in the Brazilian Amazon

Lykke E. Andersen
Clive W. J. Granger
Eustáquio J. Reis
Diana Weinhold and
Sven Wunder

CAMBRIDGE
UNIVERSITY PRESS

PUBLISHED BY THE PRESS SYNDICATE OF THE UNIVERSITY OF CAMBRIDGE
The Pitt Building, Trumpington Street, Cambridge CB2 1RP, United Kingdom

CAMBRIDGE UNIVERSITY PRESS
The Edinburgh Building, Cambridge, CB2 2RU, UK
40 West 20th Street, New York, NY 10011-4211, USA
477 Williamstown Road, Port Melbourne, VIC 3207, Australia
Ruiz de Alarcón 13, 28014 Madrid, Spain
Dock House, The Waterfront, Cape Town 8001, South Africa

http://www.cambridge.org

First published 2002

Printed in the United Kingdom at the University Press, Cambridge

Typeface Plantin 10/12 pt   *System* LaTeX 2ε [TB]

A catalogue record for this book is available from the British Library

Library of Congress Cataloging in Publication data

The dynamics of deforestation and economic growth in the Brazilian
Amazon/Lykke E. Andersen . . . [et al.].
p. cm.
Includes bibliographical references and index.
ISBN 0 521 81197 X (hardback)
1. Deforestation – Brazil. 2. Deforestation – Amazon River Region.
3. Deforestation – Economic aspects – Brazil – Econometric
models. 4. Deforestation – Economic aspects – Amazon River Region –
Econometric models. 5. Brazil – Economic policy. I. Andersen, Lykke E.
SD418.3.B6 D96 2002
333.75′137′0981 – dc21 2002067617

ISBN 0 521 81197 X hardback

Contents

List of figures — *page* vii
List of tables — ix
Preface — xiii
List of acronyms and abbreviations — xviii

1 Introduction — 1
Deforestation and development — 4
Structure of the book — 9

2 Development of the Brazilian Amazon — 11
The geographic focus: the Brazilian Legal Amazonia — 11
Historical perspectives — 13
"Operation Amazonia" and SUDAM — 15
The rise of environmental concern — 18
Improvements in monitoring capacity and enforcement — 20
The distributional impact of Amazon development — 21
Avança Brasil — 33
Conclusions — 34

3 The municipal database — 36
Deforestation: concepts and measures — 37
Socio-economic dimensions — 48
Geo-ecological dimensions — 61

4 The sources and agents of deforestation — 66
Cattle ranching — 70
Small- and large-scale agriculture — 77
Logging — 80
Mining — 83
Hydroelectric dams — 85
Property rights — 86
Secondary forest growth — 88

5 Alternatives to deforestation: extractivism — 91
The data — 93
Mapping extractive value densities — 97
Explaining spatial differences in extraction values — 101
Conclusions and discussion — 107

6 Modeling deforestation and development in the Brazilian Amazon 111
Previous studies 111
Model specification 113
Estimation results 122
Policy simulations 138
Conclusions 149

7 Carbon emissions 152
The carbon inventory model 153
Clearing, carbon emissions, and economic growth, 1970–1985 160
Discussion of the results 163
Conclusions 166

8 The costs and benefits of deforestation 167
The global costs and benefits of Amazon deforestation 167
The value of intact Amazonian forests 173
The value of cleared land in the Amazon 189
Towards a better use of the Amazon rainforest 196
Conclusions 198

9 Conclusions and recommendations 200
Conclusions 200
Policy implications 203

Technical appendix 209
A1 Econometric philosophy 209
A2 Panel model evaluation 211
A3 Random reduction estimation strategy 212
A4 Technical issues with simulations 214
A5 Full model results 216

References 241

Index 257

Figures

2.1 Legal Amazonia, Brazil *page* 12
2.2 Average annual *per capita* GDP growth in the municipalities of Legal Amazonia, 1970–1985 22
2.3 Average annual *per capita* GDP growth rates in the municipalities of Legal Amazonia, 1985–1995 23
2.4 Average annual growth rate of rural *per capita* GDP in the municipalities of Legal Amazonia, 1985–1995 24
2.5 *Per capita* GDP in the municipalities of Legal Amazonia, 1995 24
2.6 Relationship between average pre-move income level of migrants and poverty rates in the municipalities of Legal Amazonia, 1991 27
2.7 Poverty rates in the municipalities of Legal Amazonia, 1970, 1980, and 1991 28
2.8 Life expectancy in the municipalities of Legal Amazonia, 1970, 1980, and 1991 29
2.9 Illiteracy rates in the municipalities of Legal Amazonia, 1970, 1980, and 1991 30
2.10 Infant mortality rates in the municipalities of Legal Amazonia, 1970, 1980, and 1991 30
2.11 Percentage of private area in small farms in Legal Amazonian municipalities, 1975, 1985, and 1995 31
2.12 Share of private area occupied by large farms in the municipalities of Legal Amazonia, 1975, 1985, and 1995 32
3.1 Total crop area in Brazil according to Agricultural Census and PAM data, by year, 1980–1996 47
3.2 Rural population densities in the municipalities of Legal Amazonia, 1970, 1980, and 1996 48
3.3 Rural population densities in the municipalities of Legal Amazonia, 1995 49
3.4 Average annual growth rates of rural population in Legal Amazonia, 1970–1995 50

3.5 Cattle densities in the municipalities of Legal Amazonia, 1970, 1980, and 1995 54
3.6 LANDSAT satellite image from 1991 of a piece of the Transamazônica highway 57
3.7 LANDSAT satellite image from 1991 of deforestation in Rondônia along the Cuiabá–Pôrto Velho highway 58
3.8 Cumulated Area of CUs created in Legal Amazonia, 1959–2001 62
4.1 Land prices and interest rate subsidies in Legal Amazonia, 1968–1992 76
5.1 Value of non-wood extractive products per hectare in Legal Amazonia, 1995/1996 Agricultural Census 97
5.2 Value of non-wood extraction per establishment in each municipality of Legal Amazonia, 1995/1996 Agricultural Census 100
7.1 Carbon contents during a slash-and-burn cycle 155
8.1 Temperature changes over the last 160,000 years 183

Tables

2.1	Historical information on key variables for the North region of Brazil, 1840–1980	*page* 14
2.2	Migrants into Legal Amazonian states, by source region	25
2.3	Average level of income in migrants' municipality of origin, 1991	26
3.1	Municipalities and Minimum Comparable Areas (MCAs) in Legal Amazonia, 1996	37
3.2	Natural vegetation types in Legal Amazonia	39
3.3	Natural forest shares, by state	40
3.4	Gross deforestation based on INPE satellite data, 1978–1995	41
3.5	Comparing deforestation estimates from satellite and land surveys, 1975–1995	42
3.6	Satellite deforestation estimates, 1978 and 1988	44
3.7	Rural GDP *per capita*, by year and state, 1970–1995	52
3.8	Urban GDP *per capita*, by year and state, 1970–1995	52
3.9	Road building in Legal Amazonia, by type and state, 1960–1995	56
3.10	Comparing estimates of paved federal and state roads, 1975–1995	59
3.11	Comparing estimates of unpaved federal and state roads, 1975–1995	60
3.12	CUs and IRs in Legal Amazonia, 1992	64
4.1	Changes in agricultural land-use, 1970–1995	67
4.2	Land-Use Transition Matrix, 1975–1985	68
4.3	Cattle herd, by state and year, 1970–1995	71
4.4	Cattle stocking intensity, 1970–1995	72
4.5	Subsidies to cattle ranching until 1985	73
4.6	Land prices, by state and year, 1970–1995	75
4.7	Existing dams in Legal Amazonia, selected years	86
5.1	High value non-wood extraction municipalities: main characteristics	99

5.2 Economic explanations of spatial variations in extraction values 102
5.3 Biophysical explanations of spatial variations in extractivism values 105
6.1 Estimation results: growth of cleared land 125
6.2 Estimation results: growth of rural GDP 128
6.3 Estimation results: growth of urban GDP 130
6.4 Estimation results: growth of urban population 131
6.5 Estimation results: growth of rural population 132
6.6 Estimation results: growth of cattle herd 133
6.7 Estimation results: growth of paved roads 135
6.8 Estimation results: growth of unpaved roads 136
6.9 Simulated effect of *Avança Brasil* road improvements after ten years 142
6.10 Simulated effect of *Avança Brasil*, by state 142
6.11 Aggregate relationship between new paved roads and cleared land 144
6.12 Simulated effect of land-use regulation after twenty years 148
6.13 NPV of rural GDP lost owing to land use restrictions 149
7.1 Carbon contents for different vegetation types and land uses 154
7.2 Decay parameters for the Carbon Inventory Model 154
7.3 Estimated age structure of fallow areas in Legal Amazonia, 1970–1985 159
7.4 Summary statistics for the average age of fallow areas across municipalities, 1970–1985 159
7.5 Accumulated deforestation in Legal Amazonia, by vegetation type, by 1985 161
7.6 Carbon emissions in Legal Amazonia, by state, 1970–1985 162
7.7 Accumulated GDP in Legal Amazonia, 1970–1985 162
7.8 Biomass sensitivity analysis 164
8.1 TEV of standing Amazon forest at current forest stock levels 172
8.2 Rural GDP, urban GDP, and cleared area in Legal Amazonia, by year, 1970–1995 178
8.3 NPV of cleared land in Legal Amazonia, according to Agricultural Census data 192
8.4 Simulated rural GDP, urban GDP, and cleared area in Legal Amazonia, 1995 194
8.5 NPV of road building in Legal Amazonia, according to estimated model 195
A.1 List of variables 216
A.2 Full estimation results: growth of cleared land 217

A.3 Full estimation results: growth of rural GDP 220
A.4 Full estimation results: growth of urban GDP 223
A.5 Full estimation results: growth of cattle herd 226
A.6 Full estimation results: growth of urban population 229
A.7 Full estimation results: growth of rural population 232
A.8 Full estimation results: growth of paved roads 235
A.9 Full estimation results: growth of unpaved roads 238

Preface

This book truly represents the result of a North–South collaborative effort between the Institute of Applied Economic Research (IPEA) in Rio de Janeiro, the University of California in San Diego (UCSD), the Catholic University in La Paz, Bolivia, The London School of Economics in the UK, and the Center for International Forestry Research (CIFOR) in Bogor, Indonesia. The origin of the project dates back to 1989 when Professor Rudi Dornbusch of MIT organized a conference on economic policy responses to global warming and invited Eustáquio Reis to contribute a paper discussing the policy issues surrounding Amazonian deforestation. The resulting paper, co-authored with Sérgio Margulis, was the original seed of this book. Thus to Rudi, as the *primum mobile*, this book is dedicated.

A driving philosophy behind this project has always been that good policy analysis can be made only on the basis of good data and rigorous methodology. While alternative methodologies can always be considered, accurate and comprehensive data is a universal prerequisite. However, at the end of the 1980s when Eustáquio and Sérgio were working on their paper, the statistical evidence on the extent of Amazonian deforestation was practically non-existent. This lack of reliable data gave rise to wild speculation on the extent of deforestation and the probable fate of the remaining forest. Simple extrapolations based upon two or three points in time led to dire predictions of the complete disappearance of the Brazilian Amazonian rainforest within a few decades. These types of analyses were clearly unsatisfactory, but the lack of hard data hampered any fruitful discussion on the matter.

A key insight at that time was that if you can assume that geography mimics history, it could be possible to compensate for the lack of time series data with the (albeit scanty) estimates of deforestation at the municipal level that were available for the Brazilian Amazon. In other words, the difference between heavily deforested versus pristine municipalities in one year could proxy for the change over time within a single municipality as land cover evolve from virgin forest to developed land uses.

Eustáquio got to work, and the resulting municipality-level data set, complemented by socio-economic information from the Census, proved to be a research gold mine. It opened up new possibilities for spatial analysis of geo-ecological factors in the process of Amazonian deforestation. Indeed, based upon the new data set, econometric estimation and simulation of simple panel data models predicted that Amazonian deforestation processes would converge to levels that were indeed worrisome, but not catastrophic. These estimation exercises contributed greatly to ongoing debates about the economic determinants, costs, and benefits, of Amazonian deforestation.

Since 1989, then, a large part of the research effort at IPEA has been dedicated to extending both the time span as well as the geo-ecological dimensions of the data base on Amazonian deforestation at the municipal level. Concurrent with this effort was a need for new and specialized analytical tools to deal with the particular properties of this spatially rich and dynamic, but relatively short, panel data set. In 1992, the same year that the United Nations Conference on Environmental Development (UNCED) in Rio de Janeiro focused the international spotlight on the problem of deforestation in the Brazilian Amazon, a Brazilian doctoral student at UCSD, João Issler (now a Professor at the Fundação Getulio Vargas in Rio de Janeiro), approached Professor Clive Granger and a fellow graduate student, Diana Weinhold (now at the London School of Economics), about the possibility of working with Eustáquio and his colleages at IPEA to analyze this extensive data set. Thus a UCSD group was formed including Professor Granger, Diana Weinhold, and Ling-Ling Huang and together with Eustáquio they applied for research funding from the National Science Foundation. Although this was a period when global warming projects were getting plenty of funding, the proposal faced some skepticism about the quality of the economic data for such a large and diverse region. Nevertheless a year of funding was granted (NSF grant SBR-930081) to evaluate the data, develop and assess some models, produce forecasts and policy scenarios, and consider the policy implications.

The original UCSD group was soon joined by Lykke Andersen who was a visiting graduate student from the Centre for Nonlinear Modeling in Economics of the University of Aarhus, Denmark. She quickly decided to write her doctoral thesis on the topic of the project and provided a great deal enthusiasm and ability. By the end of the year the initial report was available and presentations were made at conferences in New Orleans, Louisiana, Washington, DC, Rio de Janeiro, and Oslo, Norway. The first report was issued in November 1996 as a working paper of the

Department of Economics, UCSD (number 96-40) and the empirical work was largely conducted by the now Dr. Lykke Andersen.

Once Cambridge University Press showed interest in publishing an updated version of this work, the study was extended to include more recent data, discuss other literature on deforestation and ecological economics, and to discuss institutional fact, particularly about the Brazilian economy, as well as the implication of the results. Dr. Andersen updated and revised the cost–benefit model (chapter 8) while the model estimation for this new version (chapter 6) was done by Dr. Weinhold updating the methodology but broadly basing the modelling on the simultaneous equations approach utilized earlier by Dr. Andersen. Dr. Sven Wunder provided additional analyses of the alternatives to deforestation (chapter 5). The remaining chapters are updated and expanded sections based on both the original UCSD working paper and Dr. Anderson's Ph.D. dissertation with various contributions from all the co-authors. The completion of the task illustrates the benefits of teamwork, with a diverse group of participants from different backgrounds and specializations, but with a common interest and objective.

As should be clear from the proceeding discussion, while this immediate book may have five co-authors, in fact throughout the years the project of data collection at IPEA, which forms the basis for the research, has involved funding from many different organizations and hard work from many diligent research assistants, and to all of them we are truly indebted. In particular we would like to especially acknowledge the meticulous, rigorous and ever dependable computer work of IPEA's Márcia Pimentel who has labored all these years building, cleaning, and expanding the data base, and without whose contribution this book could never have been written. In addition we would like to thank Flávia Barbosa, Arilda Campos, Alexandrew Brandão, Maria José Pessoa, Andrew Brinn, Elenora Santos, Andréa Amancio, Márcia Rapini, Joana Pires, Ramon Ortiz, Breno Pietracci, and Rodrigo Gandra for their research assistance at IPEA. Many other young scholars were pioneer explorers of the data base while working on their Ph.D. dissertations, and in particular Carlos Eduardo Young, Alexandre Rivas, Ling-Ling Huang, Alex Pfaff, and Tsuneo Otsuki made significant contributions in terms of data analysis and methodological development.

Research life at IPEA has always been lively and interactive, with the result that many colleagues and visitors have made their mark on the project over the years and have had significant influence on our work. Particular thanks are extended to Rolando Garcia, Fernando Blanco, Marina Paez and Kátia Queiroz. Cláudio Bohrer from the Universidade Federal

Fluminense (UFF) and Ricardo Braga from IBGE provided invaluable guidance through the mysteries of the geo-ecological data of the Brazilian Amazon. At IPEA, the econometric expertise of Ajax Moreira and the knowledge of environmental economics of Ronaldo Seroa were both always at hand. As research associates of the Network on Spatial Models (NEMESIS), Steven Helfand, Gervásio Resende, Denisard Alves, Newton Rabello de Castro, Carlos Roberto Azzoni, and Honório Kume contributed methods, data, and ideas and provided invaluable feedback in the regular workshops.

Several institutions and corresponding individuals have provided key support for the project in different ways. The Brazilian Institute of Geography and Statistics (IBGE) was the crucial source of socio-economic and geo-ecological data. At IBGE, the staff of the Department of Natural Resources (DERNA) and Lidia Valles deserve special gratitude for their generosity and patience. Sérgio Margulis at the World Bank and Matti Palo at the Finnish Forest Research Institute (FFRI) have been enthusiastic supporters of the project with both ideas and funds. Maria de Lourdes Davies de Freitas from the National Fund for the Environment (FNMA/IBAMA) was an earlier supporter of the project, providing funds for the acquisition of satellite images of the Brazilian Space Research Agency (INPE) where Diógenes Alves and Telma Krugger kindly tabulated them at municipal level. David Skole made available the NASA-University of New Hampshire data on Amazon deforestation. Thanks are also due to João Victor Issler at Fundação Getúlio Vargas for first bridging IPEA-UCSD.

The ongoing costs of data collection, maintenance, and analyses at IPEA have been enormous, and at various stages funding has come from a number of additional institutions including the Instituto Bancario San Paolo de Torino, Fundo Nacional do Meio Ambiente do Instituto Brasileiro do Meio Ambiente (FNMA/IBAMA), Conselho Nacional de Desenvolvimento Cientifico (CNPq), the Rockefeller Foundation, the National Science Foundation (NSF), the World Bank, the World Institute on Development Research of the United Nations University (UNU/WIDER), Nucleo de Estudos e Modelos Espaciais Sistemicos (NEMESIS/CNPq/FINEMPE/MCT). Lastly we would like to acknowledge the financial support of the authors' home institutions including IPEA, UCSD, the Institute for Socio-Economic Research at the Catholic University in La Paz, Bolivia, The London School of Economics, and CIFOR.

This book has also benefited enormously from insightful critiques and comments from colleagues and referees who have generously lent their time and intellectual energy to reading earlier versions of the manuscript.

In particular we would like to thank David Kaimowitz and two anonymous referees whose contributions have been instrumental. In addition we would like to thank the Economics Editors of Cambridge University Press, and particularly Ashwin Rattan and Chris Harrison, for considerable help in getting this book ready for publication, and also Barbara Docherty for the copy-editorial work. Naturally all errors and omissions are our own.

Our hope is that the results presented here will not only present to a wider audience the problems facing the future of the awesome Amazon forest, but also quantify the changes that are occurring to it now, and what can be expected in the future. The emphasis throughout is on the dynamics of the deforestation process as revealed by the available data and viewed taking into account the relevant economics, institutional constraints, and current Brazilian policies. Needless to say, given the available data there are multiple approaches one could justifiably take for this endeavor, and with five co-authors from different backgrounds and institutional environments this has also meant that we have not necessarily come to agree on all the results and policy implications presented in this book. The lack of full consensus is not viewed by the authors as a disadvantage, however. Rather, the richness of the discussion reflects the complexity of the problems and the fact that significant challenges remain for further research. Consequently we have been especially conscious of the need to explain the implications of particular methodological choices in such a way that any major inherent ambiguities are apparent, without being unduly confusing to casual readers. In sum, this is an important and interesting topic and we hope that readers feel that we have made a worthwhile contribution to it.

Lykke E. Andersen
Clive W. J. Granger
Eustáquio J. Reis
Diana Weinhold
Sven Wunder

Acronyms and abbreviations

AIC	Akaike Information Criterion
ARCH	Auto-Regressive Conditional Heteroskedasticity
BIC	Bayesian Information Criterion
CBA	Cost-Benefit Analysis
CBO	Congressional Budget Office, United States
CCZEE	Comissão de Coordinação do Zoneamento Ecológico-Econômico (Commission for Coordination of Ecological–Economic Zoning in the National Territory)
CFC	Chlorofluorocarbon
CGE	Computable General Equilibrium
CO_2	Carbon dioxide
CT	Carbon Tax
CU	Conservation Unit
CVRD	Companhia Vale do Rio Doce
DESMAT	Dados Ecológicos e Sociais para Municípios da Amazônia Tropical (Ecological and Social Data for Municipalities in Legal Amazonia)
DICE	Dynamic Integrated Climate–Economy model
DIPES	Diretória de Pesquisa (Brazilian Ministry of Research)
DNPM	Departamento Nacional de Producão Mineral (Brazilian Ministry of Mineral Production)
EC	European Community
ELECTROBRAS	Brazilian state power-utility holding company
ELECTRONORTE	Brazilian state power-utility holding company's subsidiary for northern Brazil
EMBRAPA	Empresa Brasileiro de Pesquisa Agropecuária (Brazilian Agricultural Research System)
EMF	Energy Modeling Forum

ERL	Environmental Resources Limited
FAO	Food and Agriculture Organization of the United Nations
FINAM	Fundo de Investimento da Amazônia (Investment Fund for Amazonia)
FOB	Free on Board
FUNAI	Fundação Nacional do Índio (National Indian Foundation)
FUNATURA	Fundação Pró Natureza (Pro-Nature Foundation)
FZM	Free Zone Manaus
GCM	General Circulation Model
GDP	Gross Domestic Product
GEIPOT	Empresa Brasileira de Planejamento dos Transportes (Brazilian Transportation Planning Agency under the Ministry of Transport)
GIS	Geographical Information System
GLS	Generalized Least Squares
GVABP	Gross Value Added at Basic Prices
HAC	Heteroskedasticity and Autocorrelation Consistent
IBAMA	Instituto Brasileiro do Meio-Ambiente e dos Recusos Naturais Renováveis (Brazilian Institute for the Environment and Renewable Resources)
IBGE	Instituto Brasileiro de Geográfia e Estatística (Brazilian Institute of Geography and Statistics)
IMAZON	Instituto do Homem e Meio Ambiante da Amazônia (Institute for Amazonian People and Environment)
INCRA	Instituto Nacional de Colonização e Reforma Agrária (National Institute for Colonization and Agrarian Reform)
INPA	Instituto Nacional de Pesquisa da Amazônia (National Institute for Research in the Amazon)
INPE	Instituto Nacional de Pesquisas Especiais (Brazilian National Space Agency)
IPAM	Instituto de Pesquisa Ambiental da Amazônia (Institute for Environmental Research in the Amazon)

IPCC	Intergovernmental Panel on Climate Change
IPEA	Instituto de Pesquisa Econômica Aplicada (Institute for Applied Economics Research)
IR	Indigenous Reserve
ISPN	Instituto Sociedade, População e Natureza (Institute for Society, Population and Nature)
MCA	Minimum Comparable Area
MFZ	Manaus Free Zone
NASA	Laboratory for Terrestrial Physics at NASA and Goddard Space Flight Center
NEMESIS	Núcleo de Estudose Modelos Espaciais Sistêmicos (Research Project on the Modeling of Spatial Processes)
NPK	Nitrogen–Phosphorus–Potassium (Fertilizer)
NPV	Net Present Value
NSF	National Science Foundation (of the United States)
OECD	Organization for Economic Co-operation and Development
OLS	Ordinary Least Squares
PAM	Produção Agrícola Municipal (Municipal Agricultural Production)
PEV	Produção Extrativa Vegetal (Extractive Vegetal Production)
PEVS	Producão da Extração Vegetal e da Silvicultura (Extractive Vegetal and Plantation Forestry Production)
PGC	Programa Grande Carajás (Greater Carajás Program)
PIFI	Projeto Integrado Floresta Indústria (Industrial Forest Management Plans)
PIN	Plano de Integração Nacional (National Integration Program)
PLANAFLORO	Plano Agropecuário e Florestal de Rondônia (National Plan for Forests in Rondônia State)
PNAD	Pesquisa Nacional por Amostra de Domicílios(Annual Survey of Households)
POLOAMAZONIA	Programa de Pólos Agripecuários e Agrominerais da Amazônia (Program for Agricultural, Livestock, and Mineral Poles in Amazônia)
POLOCENTRO	Program for the Development of the Cerrado

POLONOROESTE	Programa Integrado de Desenvolvimento do Noroeste do Brasil (Northwest Brazil Integrated Development Program)
ppm	Parts per million
PROTERRA	Land Development Program in Amazonia
R&D	Research and Development
RRSS	Restricted Residual Sum of Squares
RSS	Residual Sum of Squares
SAE	Secretária de Assuntos Estratégicos (Secretariat of Strategic Affairs)
SEMA	Secretária do Meio-Ambiente (Secretariat of the Environment)
SIPAM	Sistema de Proteção da Amazônia (System for Amazonian Protection)
SIVAM	Sistema de Vigilância Ambiental (System for Environmental Monitoring)
SNA	System of National Accounts
SPVEA	Superintendência do Plano de Valorização Econômica da Amazônia (Superintendency for Economic Valorization of Amazonia)
SUCAM	Superintendência de Campanhas de Saúde Pública (Superintendency for Public Health Campaigns)
SUDAM	Superintendência de Desenvolvimento da Amazônia (Superintendency for the Development of Amazonia)
SUR	Seemingly Unrelated Regressions
tC	Ton Carbon
TEV	Total Economic Value
UN	United Nations
UNCED	UN Conference on Environment and Development
UNEP	UN Environmental Programme
UNH	Institute of Earth, Oceans, and Space at University of New Hampshire
URSS	Unrestricted Residual Sum of Squares
VAR	Vector Auto Regressive
WIAGEM	World Integrated Assessment General Equilibrium Models
WTP	Willingness to Pay

1 Introduction

> I used to worry that all the trees in the jungle would be cut down to make paper for their reports on how to save the rainforest!
>
> Nick Birch, Forester in Rondonia (Breton 1993, p. 26)

It could be argued that there is no one single region in the tropics that has received so much attention from naturalists, scientists, and explorers the world over than the Amazon. It represents about 40 percent of the world's remaining rainforests and holds by far the largest intact section of diverse tropical wildlife. To many people the Amazon has become *the* quintessential symbolic last stand of a major wild, natural environment against the encroachment of civilization. Undoubtedly the Amazon has captured the imaginations of millions; but the future of this region should not be left to imagination, but rather to studied analyses based on the facts as we can best ascertain them. There has been remarkable progress over the past decades in conducting hard, scientific studies of the ecology, biology, and economics of the Amazon rainforest. Nevertheless the region is still the subject of many popular myths.

Indeed, the ongoing public and governmental struggle over the Amazon's future mirrors broader current discourses on "the environment." While opinions among experts and laypersons alike vary widely along a continuum of perspectives, the two poles between which most of the discourse lies can broadly be thought of as (1) the school of defenders of global ecological services ("conservationists") and (2) the school of development interests in the countries hosting these forests ("developmentalists"). Both conservationists and developmentalists make a number of valid points and sport very good arguments. Developmentalists note that countries in the North cut down their own forests centuries ago and benefitted greatly from the land uses that replaced those forests. They find it hypocritical that these developed countries now try to deny developing countries the same opportunities, and they fail to see justice in the insistence that the poor bear the costs of preserving forests whose benefits primarily accrue to wealthy foreigners and future generations.

Conservationists, on the other hand, argue that we have a very incomplete understanding of the tropical forests' functions in the global eco-system, and that we may cause catastrophic damages to the global life support systems if we clear too much forest. They point out that at the current rate of deforestation of approximately 11.3 million hectares of forest worldwide each year (FAO/UN 1997), the forests may be irreparably depleted long before a full scientific understanding of the implications of that loss is achieved. Furthermore, they generally find that the long-run value of an intact forest is much higher than the value of alternative land uses. The following quote from Anderson (1990) typifies this position:

> The tragedy of deforestation in Amazonia as well as elsewhere in the tropics is that its costs, in . . . economic, social, cultural, and aesthetic terms, far outweigh its benefits. In many cases, destruction of the region's rainforests is motivated by short-term gains rather than the long-term productive capacity of the land. And, as a result, deforestation usually leaves behind landscapes that are economically as well as ecologically impoverished. (Anderson 1990, p. xi)

Developmentalists argue quite the opposite: that the tangible benefits of current deforestation and the land uses that replace the forest outweigh the potential future benefits of standing forests. They note that the total amount of forested area in the world has been reduced from a maximum of about 6 billion hectares to about 3.5 billion hectares without yet causing catastrophic damage to global life support systems, and they question the proposition that such a change, were it to occur, would prove insurmountable. They contend that a more likely scenario is that global climate change could be dealt with by adaptation and the development of new technologies, leaving their populations better off (on net) in the long run.

Successive Brazilian governments have been clear proponents of the developmentalist view and very skeptical of the environmentalists. Indeed, as Barbosa (2000) notes:

> [Many Brazilians found] the call for preservation ironic because it was coming from governments with a long history of environmental destruction and, in the case of the United States, a long history of violation of Indian rights. Brazilian officials claimed that the rich countries had used their natural resources to achieve very high levels of economic development. Now, it was the turn of third-world countries. (Barbosa 2000, p. 85)

The Brazilian president José Sarney (1985–1989) argued that it was unrealistic to expect Brazil to restrict its economic development to accommodate the environmental concerns of the North, especially in light of staggering foreign debts. Furthermore, he contended that industrialized countries such as the United States had no right to lecture Brazil on environmental responsibility when they were, after all, the biggest global polluters of all (*Time*, September 18, 1989).

In theory, much of the practical, if not philosophical, discrepancy between environmentalists and developmentalists could be minimized if it were possible for the people who value forests' environmental services to pay owners to conserve the forest. In that manner the global benefits of the standing forest would be internalized, and the owners of the forests could more easily decide whether preservation or conversion would be the most beneficial use for a given plot of land. Although theoretically sound, in practice the task of creating well-functioning markets for forest services and monitoring their maintenance over time is daunting. It will require extraordinary international cooperation to set up the necessary institutions and mechanisms to create markets that could facilitate the sales and purchases of environmental services in an efficient manner.

Even if we do accept the idea that some sort of payment should be made by those who benefit from forests' environmental services to those who must bear the costs (mainly opportunity costs) of providing these services, several key questions remain. In particular, how much forest is "enough" for current and future generations? What would be an equitable payment to ensure that such an amount is preserved? These are very difficult questions, which require us to put a value on tropical forests as well as values on alternative land uses. However, the practice of valuing public goods is still in its infancy; for example Graves (2001) argues that by not taking into account the behavioral effects that the actual creation of heretofore hypothetical markets could have on peoples' choices, economists have tended to underestimate the value of most public goods.

Furthermore, quite aside from the technical difficulties, some conservationists argue that it is ethically wrong to try to attach a monetary value to tropical forests. From their point of view, the forests and all the species they house have an inherent right to exist independent of any services or benefits they provide to mankind, and thus we have a moral obligation to preserve them. Our response to these claims is that, whether or not they are true, in the world in which we exist today it is extremely unlikely that the remaining forests will be preserved to the levels deemed necessary or socially optimal unless their value and the true trade-offs to the actors involved are better understood. Such an understanding is a necessary prerequisite for any international effort to compensate poor countries for preserving their forests.

This book attempts to move in this direction, by improving our understanding of the services that tropical forests generate as well as the benefits that derive from alternative land uses in the Brazilian Amazon.

Both issues have already been the focus of intense debate and numerous studies, but we hope to contribute to the knowledge base by thoroughly analyzing new deforestation and development data covering the entire Brazilian Amazon at the municipal level at several points in time during the period 1970–1996. By making explicit some of the major trade-offs involved, we wish to enrich the current debate, raise new questions, and stimulate additional research. We believe this kind of analysis is all the more important given the current ongoing discussions about major infrastructure developments, as well as huge donor-led conservation initiatives in the Amazon.

We acknowledge that the results of such an exercise will always come with their own set of methodological caveats and disclaimers, ranging from limitations in the available data and estimation methods to large uncertainties in the underlying biophysical processes. For this reason we emphasize that the underlying research that has culminated in this book represents but a starting point. There is a severe need for much more scientific, agricultural, economic, and statistical research in this area even as hard policy decisions need to be taken today.

Deforestation and development

As the title of the book suggests, along with much of the more recent academic work on tropical ecology, we recognize the dynamic nature of deforestation and development. Indeed, over the course of history, many misunderstandings and misconceptions have arisen from viewing the Amazon rainforest as a static, virgin forest and considering deforestation a once-and-for-all conversion that will either civilize the place and bring great prosperity to its conquerors, or result in ecological disaster and desertification. These rather simplistic views have ignored the fact that everything about the Amazon forest, its use and development, is more dynamic and much less homogeneous than has perhaps been commonly perceived.

In fact recent research has shown that the Amazon forest is a dynamic entity that has been affected by both natural and man-made disturbances for thousands of years. The geological record suggests considerable ebb and flow of the forest cover in response to climatic conditions (e.g. Colinvaux 1989; Turcq *et al.* 1998). Historically there have also been relatively dense populations of indigenous people practicing slash-and-burn farming, hunting, and gathering in the region. Before European arrival there were probably between 1 and 6 million people living in Amazonia (Smith 1980). Over the years, these people have had a large influence on the current structure of the Amazon forest through clearing and promotion of the more useful species (Smith *et al.* 1995).

While historical Amerindian settlement in the Amazon occurred without government support, more recent migration to the region was instigated by aggressively expansionary official development policies beginning in the 1960s. Since that time the non-indigenous population of the region has increased almost tenfold, from 2 to 18 million people. Along with other factors, this has resulted in an historically unprecedented rate of change of land-use.

In fact, nowhere in the world has so much forest disappeared so rapidly as in the Brazilian Amazon. According to FAO's statistics, Brazil deforested annually 25,540 km^2 between 1990 and 1995, the bulk of which occurred in the Amazon. This national figure is between double and triple the amount of forest lost by any other single country (Indonesia is second on the list, with 10,840 km^2). In spite of this large absolute loss, FAO estimates that the Brazilian deforestation rate is a modest 0.5 percent per year. The sheer size of the forest means that accumulated deforestation over the last forty years of aggressive development policies has thus far affected less than 15 percent of the Amazon forest. Much of the Amazon thus remains a relatively undisturbed environment, and the land-use decisions made by many local actors often reflect this perception of drawing on a seemingly endless pool of forest resources.

Before any meaningful statements can be made about the current state of the Amazon, some agreement on what constitutes "forested" and "deforested" land must be made. Traditionally, deforestation in the Amazon has often been defined as "the complete and permanent destruction of forest" (e.g. Myers 1993) for the purpose of allowing for alternative land uses (agriculture, pasture, infrastructure, etc.). This reflects a choice by many observers to focus on land-use change, recognizing the tendency of deforestation in the Amazon to be driven by demand for new crop land and pastures rather than predominantly by demand for timber, as in much of Asia, or firewood, as in parts of Africa (e.g. Geist and Lambin 2001).

At first glance it appears that areas of "complete and permanent destruction of forest" would be easy to detect and measure. In fact, this is far from the case. Natural vegetation patterns are generally not uniform and forests of different types and densities are mixed with savannah, lakes, rivers, and natural clearings, creating a mosaic of vegetation covers. Along most of the border of the Amazon basin, natural savannah gradually blends into transitional forest, which gradually blends into open or seasonal forest. This makes it difficult to define what is naturally forested and what is not. Hence, there are few countries in the world where estimates on forest stocks differ so dramatically as do those for Brazil: FAO's national forest estimate for 1995 was 5.51 million km^2 (65 percent of Brazil's land area). The same figure is used by the World Bank, implying that about 90 percent of the national forest stock (around 5 million km^2) was in the Amazon (Lele *et al.* 2000). These "inclusive" estimates contain large transition zones to the *cerrado* savannah areas. However, the World Conservation Monitoring Centre, which applies a more "purist" forest definition, yields a Brazilian forest estimate of just 3.42 million km^2 – corresponding to less than two-thirds of the "inclusive" figures (Harcourt and Sayer 1996, table 25.2).

The choice between "purist" and "inclusive" forest definitions thus has a large impact on forest stock estimates. Furthermore, since most of the land clearing in the Amazon since 1960 has taken place in areas with relatively open vegetation, especially in the border areas to Southern Brazil where a so-called "arch of deforestation" has developed, the choice of definition has an even larger impact on estimates of forest *change*.

In this book we distinguish between "clearing" and "deforestation." Both refer to the complete removal of natural vegetation cover for alternative land uses. "Clearing" is the more inclusive term of the two, since it can take place on land with all kinds of vegetation ranging from dense forest to open savannah to wetlands. "Deforestation," on the other hand, takes place only in areas with natural forest vegetation ranging in tree density from transitional forest to dense forest. We have chosen to focus on clearing for three different reasons. First, clearing is much more accurately measured than deforestation in our data set. Second, as mentioned above, it has been noted that much of the change in forest cover in the Amazon has been driven by the need for new agricultural land and thus an understanding of the dynamics of land clearing is of primary importance. Finally, from an ecological perspective the non-forested areas of our study area are remarkably rich in biodiversity and store surprisingly large amounts of carbon (mostly below ground); in fact many naturalists argue that the naturally non-forested areas are just as important as the forested areas. Mares (1992), for example, points out that the drylands in South America are habitat to 53 percent more endemic mammalian species, and 440 percent more endemic genera, than the Amazonian lowlands. Thus, while we do use a more narrow deforestation measure in order to facilitate comparisons with other estimates of deforestation, for our analysis of the causes and consequences of replacing the natural vegetation in Legal Amazonia we have chosen the more inclusive concept of "clearing." The focus on conversion of natural areas to alternative land uses means that we ignore some important intermediate processes that are not directly intended to create agricultural land, e.g. logging and wildfires, although these may often be intimately linked to a subsequent complete removal.

Both purist and inclusive definitions of deforestation face an additional complication in the issue of how to treat forest fallow and secondary re-growth. How tall and how dense does vegetation cover have to be to merit the label "forest?" Forest re-growth is not accounted for in the definition of "permanent" land-use change, but the fact is that large amounts of cleared forest have been abandoned and are now growing into secondary forest, part of which will become indistinguishable from primary forest over time. Studies by Browder (1989a) and Uhl (1987) suggest that 20–40 percent of deforested land in Amazonia was beginning to feature secondary growth by the late 1980s, a figure which has probably increased since then owing to the nationwide slowdown in agriculture.

Not only is the forest a dynamic and heterogeneous entity with the concept of "deforestation" difficult to precisely define, but perceptions about land-use potentials are also undergoing continuous change. In the middle of the eighteenth century the lush greenery caused Europeans to view the Amazon as a potential "world granary" (see Faminow 1998). Eventually, after several failed efforts at colonization, the conventional wisdom switched to the view that the rainforest covered very poor soils which could not sustain agriculture for more than a few years before being left barren. More recently a different view of the Amazon has emerged, owing primarily to a number of careful site-specific studies carried out in areas that were settled relatively early, and where farmers thus have had time to experiment with and adapt alternative agricultural strategies (e.g. Mattos and Uhl 1994; Almeida and Uhl 1995; Toniolo and Uhl 1995; Arima and Uhl 1997). At the center of this new thinking is the recognition that the region is really a mosaic of micro-environments, each with its own unique characteristics and potential. Some areas in fact have excellent soils, but even the highly leached oxisols and ultisols widely found in the Amazon may have potential for sustainable agriculture if adequately managed (Smith *et al.* 1995).

The international debate surrounding deforestation in Brazil has also evolved dramatically over time. In the 1970s and 1980s there was a considerable literature questioning the economic rationale of the deforestation process and subsequent land uses, especially cattle ranching (Bunker 1985; Hecht 1986; Mattos and Uhl 1994). Non-destructive uses of the standing forest, such as sustainable non-timber forest product extraction, were believed to have both a socially and economically superior potential (Anderson and Jardim 1989; Peters *et al.* 1989; Anderson *et al.* 1991). The fact that forest clearing continued despite these economically preferable alternatives was largely blamed on policy failures. These included infrastructure projects and land-conversion incentives, such as tax exemptions and credit subsidies (Browder 1985; Mahar 1989) that were deemed socially "irrational" and economically perverse. In addition, these policies were seen as favoring the vested interests of land speculators and large cattle ranchers to the detriment of both the environment and the Brazilian society as a whole (Hecht and Cockburn 1989).

However, in the 1990s an increasing number of case studies and economic analyses began to question this mainstream view of Amazon deforestation as a "lose–lose" scenario, and pointed to a more differentiated outlook. It was observed that much deforestation, especially in the Western Amazon, had actually been carried out *without* government subsidies (Almeida and Campari 1995; Schneider 1995; Lele *et al.* 2000). In particular, cattle ranching appeared to be a profitable land-use option, even in the long run and without subsidies (Faminow 1998). It also became increasingly clear that the anti-inflationary policies of fiscal restraint and subsidy reduction had reduced the rate of deforestation only during the recessionary period of 1987–1991. As investment rates and economic growth recovered in the 1990s, the rate of deforestation gradually increased again (Young 1995). Finally, non-destructive alternatives such as non-timber forest product extraction, bio-prospecting, eco-tourism, and sustainable timber management were found to have much less economic potential than had been previously claimed (Southgate 1998). The recent literature thus paints a very different picture of Amazonia, one in which deforested land has economically profitable and sustainable alternative uses. The recent debate also points to a sharper conflict of interest between economic development and forest conservation (Kaimowitz 2001), and emphasizes the importance of gaining a better understanding of the trade-offs.

This book belongs to and complements this "new generation" of deforestation studies. We focus on the economics of land clearing, recognizing that at some levels and under some conditions the benefits of deforestation may outweigh the costs. However, the "old" theories have not been proven to be wrong across the board. As Moran (1989) points out in his stages hypothesis, frontier settlement is a gradual learning-by-doing adjustment process. Many earlier studies of Amazon deforestation prematurely judged the profitability of different land uses exclusively on the basis of the first settlement stages. In parts of the Amazon, we are now able to observe the agricultural intensification and consolidation taking place in later stages. The long-term profitability of deforestation can only be judged using an extended time horizon, and if the land turns into permanent and sustainable agriculture supporting local urban areas, indirect benefits could be large, as they have been for most of the developed world.

Our main objective here is not to promote more or less deforestation *per se*, but to analyze how changes in land-use affect the lives of the people living in the Amazon and what the implications are for the rest of the world in terms of reduced environmental services. Recognizing that deforestation has both costs and benefits, and beginning to measure the magnitude of these, is the first step towards developing meaningful international and domestic policies that will deliver both the environmental services so desired in the North as well as the economic development so needed in the South.

Structure of the book

This book presents an empirical analysis of the development processes in the Brazilian Amazon using municipality-level data for the entire region at several points in time between 1970 and 1996. We present summary statistics and analyze trends for a number of important variables as well as developing econometric models with which we can analyze policies and compare outcomes under different scenarios. In contrast to site studies, which by definition focus on a specific bit of land, our data covers the whole of the Brazilian Amazon. Throughout the book the models and analyses pay due respect to the dramatic spatial differences in vegetation, soil, rainfall, market access, population density, and many other important factors. However, we are still operating at the municipal level, which means that we cannot take into account differences at the plot level, which site studies and very detailed GIS studies can and do.

The remainder of the book is structured as follows. Chapter 2 highlights central features of the study area, and discusses the changing governmental policies that have been applied in Brazil over time. Chapter 3 describes the data set we are using to analyze deforestation processes and compares our measure of deforested and cleared areas with estimates derived from satelite imagery. Chapter 4 discusses the different agents and drivers of deforestation, i.e. cattle ranching, agriculture, logging, mining, etc. Chapter 5 discusses extractivism as a possible alternative to deforestation.

In chapter 6 we present an econometric model that takes into account both the dynamics of development in the Amazon and the spatial features of frontier development. The model is estimated using municipality-level data from the agricultural surveys covering Legal Amazonia in 1975, 1980, 1991, and 1996. This chapter estimates the trade-off between land clearing and economic growth, i.e. the economic benefits that result from land clearing. The estimated model is used to simulate the effects of two currently proposed, and controversial, development policies: the *Avança Brasil* government plan to expand and improve infrastructure and promote other development investments in the Amazon and a revised ceiling limit on the percentage of privately held land plots that can be cleared by law. We then compare our estimates to those of other recent studies.

In chapter 7 we use another dynamic model of land-use changes to estimate carbon emissions arising from land-use changes in the Brazilian Amazon. Our estimates are lower than the estimates provided by many previous studies because we take into account the heterogeneity of the natural vegetation and we allow for secondary forest re-growth.

Chapter 8 attempts to estimate the opportunity costs of land clearing. For this purpose we gather estimates from the literature of the value of the economic and environmental services that an intact forest provides and present them in a consistent framework.

Conclusions and policy recommendations are provided in chapter 9.

2 Development of the Brazilian Amazon

> "Brazil almost overnight became an environmental villain when the ecopolitics of the world-system changed in the mid-1980's."
>
> (Barbosa 2000)

The geographic focus: the Brazilian Legal Amazonia

The Amazon tropical rainforest covers approximately 5.5 million km^2, of which 60 percent is located in Brazil, where it occupies 3.55 million km^2, or nearly 40 percent of the national territory. This area of Brazil is called the North region, and consists of seven states: Acre, Amapá, Amazonas, Rondônia, Roraima, Pará, and Goiás/Tocantins.[1]

Legal Amazonia refers to a slightly larger area, including Mato Grosso and parts of Maranhão[2] (see figure 2.1). Legal Amazonia was defined for regional planning purposes, and this region is also the basis of our data set.[3] It covers an area of approximately 5 million km^2, or 58 percent of the national territory of Brazil.

Legal Amazonia is by no means a uniform forest biome. Though predominantly a tropical forest region, it comprises a complex mosaic of forests, savannahs, inundated lowlands, and steppes. In terms of major vegetation types, Legal Amazonia is composed of 68.2 percent closed and open dense forest, 3.0 percent seasonal forests, 15 percent savannahs or *cerrados*, 6.4 percent *campinaranas*, 2 percent wetlands, and 5.1 percent ecological transition vegetation (May and Reis 1993).

The term "Legal Amazonia" can occasionally cause confusion as it is a politically, rather than ecologically, demarcated region. In fact only about

[1] The state of Tocantins was created in 1989, when it was separated from the state of Goiás. Since some of our data are from before the separation, we will use the term Goiás/Tocantins to refer to this part of Legal Amazonia.

[2] The part west of meridian 44°W.

[3] Some municipalities in Maranhão and Tocantins are only partly located within the official borders of Legal Amazonia. In our data set, however, we include whole municipalities, owing to the difficulty in splitting up many of our measures, such as federal transfers and infant mortality rates. This means that our data set actually covers a slightly larger area than what is officially known as Legal Amazonia.

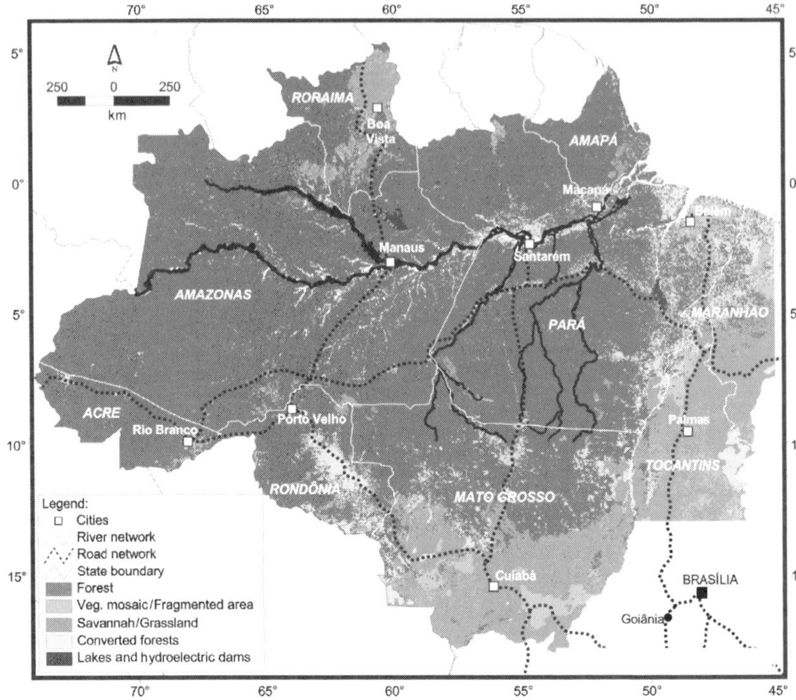

Figure 2.1 Legal Amazonia, Brazil
Source: GVM-TREES Project (1999).

79 percent of Legal Amazonia would be naturally forested in the absence of human intervention. The cause of this confusion, the expansion of the legal borders of Amazonia into areas not technically dominated by rainforest, resulted from a political compromise designed to allow the *cerrado* areas in Mato Grosso and Maranhão to benefit from regional development incentives aimed at Legal Amazonia.

In this book we include all of Legal Amazonia rather than just the North Region, for an important reason. Our study focuses on the decisions of farmers to clear land of its natural vegetation to create new agricultural land. Since most of this conversion is taking place in border areas between forest and *cerrado*, we get much more variation in our sample if we include these areas. Such variation is important for estimation purposes and it is by no means irrelevant in environmental terms. As pointed out earlier, the boundary between forest and non-forest is not well defined; dense forest blends into open or seasonal forest which blends into transitional forest which blends into *cerrado* or savannah. Furthermore, according to many ecologists these transitional areas are just as valuable as the dense forest in terms of both biodiversity and biomass stored. The Brazilian *cerrado* areas are similar in vegetation and climate to the African savannah with two clearly defined seasons: a rainy season, from October to March, and a dry season, from April to September. The vegetation is composed of open natural pastures with sparse twisted trees. Natural fertility of the soils is low and until recent advances in soybean cultivation, the *cerrado* areas have been considered marginal in terms of agricultural potential.

Historical perspectives

The building of the Forte do Presépio on the delta of the Amazon river in 1616 was the first landmark of Portuguese colonization in the North region of Brazil. From then until 1950 open access to forestry resources was the *primum mobile* of settlements, which were mainly based upon extraction of rubber and Brazil nuts for exports.[4] During this era deforestation was minimal and restricted to the riparian areas along main rivers and to the Bragantina region, located south of the Amazon delta, where agricultural settlements dates back to the seventeenth century.

The discovery of the vulcanization process by Goodyear in the 1840s brought on the rubber boom and an outstanding period of prosperity that lasted for almost seventy years. Regional income *per capita* increased sixfold and population growth was 3.3 percent per year (see table 2.1). The exceptional economic opportunities attracted substantial migratory flows, especially from the Northeast region where a lethargic economy was ravaged by frequent droughts. However in 1912 rubber prices collapsed owing to the excess supply brought by emergent Asian competitors, and the expansion came to an end.

The fall in rubber prices was the start of a secular downturn. With the exception of a short revival of the rubber industry in the 1940s owing to the second World War, the economy lacked a sustainable basis for growth and frontier expansion. As Mahar (1989) points out, the "story of the turn-of-the-century rubber boom illustrates how an activity that is environmentally suited to the rainforest can at the same time be economically unsustainable."

From 1912–1950, the North region economy remained practically stagnant, despite a small recovery in income *per capita*, and population growth suffered as migration flows diverted towards other regions. The existing frontier settlements were still based on the extraction of rubber,

[4] Other minor exports were drugs, timber, cocoa, vanilla, cinnamon, cloves, and aromatic resins.

Table 2.1. *Historical information on key variables for the North region of Brazil, 1840–1980*

Year	*Per capita* income (1985-US$)	*Per capita* income growth rate (% p.a.)	Population size (thousand)	Migration rate (% p.a.)	Farm area (% of area)	Cattle herd (million)
1840	63	—	139	—	—	—
1910	416	2.7	1,217	—	—	—
1920	95	−13.7	1,091	—	6.0	—
1940	147	2.3	1,462	−1.00	7.1	1.0
1950	155	0.5	1,845	−0.01	6.5	0.2
1960	193	2.2	2,562	0.05	6.5	1.9
1970	273	3.5	3,603	0.06	6.5	3.3
1980	906	12.5	5,880	2.15	11.6	8.8

Source: Santos (1980, p. 338); IBGE (1990); Martine (1989, p. 143).

Brazil nuts, and other minor forest products. The numbers available for area under farms and cattle herd size clearly indicate the weakness of the pace of settlement before 1970 (see table 2.1).

Within the region, the demographic consequence of the lack of a sustainable basis for frontier expansion was a "premature" process of rural–urban migration, which accelerated the take-off of regional industrialization in cities like Belém and Manaus during the 1950s. Thus, the share of the population living in cities larger than 20,000 inhabitants went up from 19 percent in 1940 to 25 percent in 1960, 32 percent in 1970, and 40 percent in 1980.

"Operation Amazonia" and SUDAM

In the 1960s the patterns of settlement began changing and deforestation rates started increasing significantly. Government policies played a decisive role. Credit and fiscal subsidies to agriculture coupled with the expansion of the road network pushed the agricultural frontier in a northwestern direction, while colonization programs and regional incentives fostered settlements inside the Amazon region. Cattle ranching became a main source of deforestation. Other activities – like timber extraction, charcoal production, mining, and hydroelectric dams – had minor and indirect roles through their stimuli to agricultural settlements inside the region.

With the change of the federal capital from Rio de Janeiro to Brasília in 1960, the expansion of the frontier toward the Amazon region became *de facto* an objective of Brazilian development policy. A fundamental step was the massive road building program starting with the Belém–Brasília road in the early 1960s, and followed by major axial roads like the Transamazônica, the Cuiabá–Santarem road, and the Cuiabá–Porto Velho road in the 1970s. The Belém–Brasília road provided an overland connection with the rest of the country and thus, for the first time in history, economic settlements in the Amazon were freed from a dependence on rivers.

The series of legislative acts and decrees enacted in 1966 and 1967 with the aim of developing and occupying the Amazon region and integrating it with the rest of Brazil was collectively known as "Operation Amazonia." The plan was based on the creation of development "growth poles" which would enjoy cheap credit, tax breaks, land concessions, and other government perks. It was then hoped that "trickle-down" effects would ensure that supporting industries, services, and commerce would flourish around the favored target sectors. Furthermore, the growth poles were to be connected with major highways, along which small farmers were encouraged to settle. The Superintendency for the Development of Amazonia (SUDAM) was created to administer a generous system of fiscal and credit incentives purported to attract private business investment to the region.

Further phases of regional economic policies for Legal Amazonia can be distinguished according to presidential terms (Santos 1989). Although the institutional framework was similar throughout, guidelines and emphases concerning targets, actors, and policy instruments tended to shift from administration to administration.

From 1971–1975, during the Medici administration, emphasis shifted toward social integration, although national security remained the *leitmotif*. At least for ideological purposes, the frontier agent became the landless rural worker from the Northeast. Major instruments of economic policy were the construction of the Transamazônica road and the small-scale colonization programs directly implemented by the federal government. In particular, regional incentives for agriculture and livestock projects flourished during this period (Yokomizo 1989).

From 1975–1979, under the Giesel administration, the emphasis of Amazonian policy shifted back to the idea of growth poles. Fifteen of them were defined in a program called "Poloamazonia." There was also a shift back in emphasis toward large-scale private entrepreneurs. According to Reis Velloso, then Minister of Planning, "up to here the Transamazon gave emphasis to colonization, but the necessity to prevent a predatory occupation, with a consequent process of deforestation, and to promote the ecological equilibrium force us to invite large entrepreneurs to command the task of developing the region." However, although official rhetoric supported cattle ranching as a mainstay of economic integration, the number of approved projects slowed down considerably during this phase.

In the 1970s, the region emerged once again as a booming frontier. Regional income *per capita* more than tripled and population grew at the astonishing rate of 5 percent per year, almost half of which was owing to migration. This explosive pace of frontier settlement was of an entirely different nature than had ever been experienced before in the Amazon. Unlike historical booms, the economic basis of this expansion was not extractivism, rather, the *primum mobile* was government policies.

Regional policies to open up the frontier coupled with the favorable economic context of the 1970s resulted in an astonishing spurt of economic growth during this period. From 1970–1980, GDP growth rates averaged 18 percent per year in real terms. The industrial sector was the clear leader, with average growth rates of 30 percent per year. As a consequence, the composition of regional output experienced dramatic changes, with the share of industry rising from 15 percent in 1970 to 37 percent in 1980.

Regional incentives were decisive factors for the industrial boom, and geographically these incentives, and thus industrial growth, were concentrated in the Belém and Manaus areas. For example, at least 70 percent of the 420 industrial projects approved by SUDAM from 1966 to 1989 were located in those two areas (Yokomizo 1989).

Figures for agriculture were also impressive, and give, perhaps, a better picture of the pace of land clearing and frontier settlement. Average annual growth rates were 6 percent for farm areas, 11 percent for crop areas, and 8.9 percent for the cattle stock.

The fourth phase of regional policies was in the early 1980s. It was characterized by a strong presence of state-owned enterprises in a few big projects in mining and hydroelectric power generation, some of the biggest being the Carajás mining complex led by Companhia Vale do Rio Doce (CVRD) and the associated Tucuruí hydroelectric power plant built by ELECTROBRAS. Another major initiative of this phase was the POLONOROESTE Development Program, where the government provided infrastructure for agricultural settlements in the southwestern region of Legal Amazonia, where spontaneous settlement had been taking place since the early 1970s.

Despite the big projects and the rise in the numbers of approved projects in the agricultural and livestock sectors, in the early 1980s a national recession slowed the rates of frontier expansion and economic growth. Nevertheless, despite the recession, the Northern economy sustained an average GDP growth rate of 7.7 percent per year (3.3 percent in *per capita* terms). However, these seemingly robust figures belie the very real impact the recession had on the region; behind the aggregate data a dramatic sectoral shift took place, with a slowdown of industrial activity compensated for by the higher growth experienced in agriculture, cattle raising, and the service sector.

Finally in the mid-1980s, against a background of hyperinflation, fiscal crisis, and the rise of international concern for a perceived environmental crisis, deforestation in Amazonia began to rise to become one of the central issues of concern for regional policy makers. Thus began the fifth and present phase of regional policies that, in combination with macroeconomic recession, has been associated with a slowdown in the rate of frontier expansion. With the "Nossa Natureza" program inaugurated in 1988, government policies, for the first time, directly addressed the deforestation issue.

The rise of environmental concern

In the late 1980s, against a backdrop of a national economic recession squeezing the government's development budget coupled with increasing global environmental concerns over the Amazon, the Brazilian government began to scale back the scope of its development aims and formally incorporate ecological considerations into its treatment of the region. The government's "Nossa Natureza" program, inaugurated in 1988, was the first example of this. Bureaucratic re-shuffling also contributed to a more environmentally friendly attitude towards the region. Brazil's leading ecologist, José Lutzemberger was appointed head of the newly created Secretariat of the Environment (SEMA) which in 1994, together with the Secretariat of Strategic Affairs (SAE) (Reis and Blanco 1996a), became formally responsible for Legal Amazonian affairs. Environmental departments were established in all the major government departments; a Research Centre for Tropical Forests was created to study the problems of sustainable development in the Amazon; IBAMA (the Brazilian environmental protection agency) got a new director and more financial resources; and a working group was appointed to review environmental zoning in the Amazon.

These institutional changes were coupled with important revisions of regional policy priorities, and as a consequence major development projects in the region were downsized, indefinitely postponed, or totally abandoned. In 1991 President Collor signed a decree removing fiscal incentives for cattle ranching in any forested portion of the Amazon, including transitional forest (Smith *et al.* 1995, p. 55). The Carajás pig iron Program also fell victim to both the growing ecological concerns over the deforestation impact of charcoal production, as well as the downturn in the international markets for steel. Production targets for 2010 were reduced from 2100 to 1500 ton/year and, consequently, only four of the thirteen pig iron mills originally approved were operating as of 1994 (Reis and Blanco 1996a). An ambitious investment program in the hydroelectricity generation in the Amazon basin was also considerably scaled back, and most of the investment in infrastructure projects contemplated in the Calha Norte development program (which consisted of several projects along an axial road planned to run parallel to the 6,500 km of northern Brazilian frontier) was downsized or postponed indefinitely (Allen 1990). Moreover, the new *Avança Brasil* plan shows no indication that the Calha Norte project is to be resurrected any time soon.

In addition to the scaling back of existing projects, several corrective programs were initiated to address the existing environmental damage left over from previous megaprojects. For example, the National Plan for

Forests in Rondônia State (PLANAFLORO) was created in 1990 with financing from the World Bank in order to mitigate the deforestation consequences of previous development programs in Rondônia. The Forestry Poles of Eastern Amazonas program, proposed by CVRD in 1989, was intended to reforest a degraded area of 1 million hectares affected by the Carajás Mining Project. This reforestation was expected not only to meet the charcoal demand for the existing pig iron mills, but also to support ten pulp and paper plants. Total investments were expected to amount to 6.5 billion dollars over ten years and generate annual revenues of 2.2 billion dollars. Indeed, apart from generating 40,000–80,000 jobs, this program would also be expected to help to absorb carbon from the atmosphere. While well intentioned, however, the implementation of this initiative has suffered from a lack of financial resources (Serôa da Motta 1993).

Further efforts to contain the ecological costs of development were initiated in 1990 by the creation of the Commission for Coordination of Ecological–Economic Zoning in the National Territory (CCZEE). The first priority of CCZEE was to develop a zoning system in the Amazon region that discriminated between areas where preservation was critical and areas where economic activities, under specific sustainable practices, could be undertaken (Serôa da Motta 1993). Today, these ecological zoning laws also regulate the use of privately owned natural resources. Thus, specific areas inside private properties (river springs and margins, vegetation on steep hills, etc.) are considered by law as ecological reserves, or areas of permanent preservation. In addition, a certain share of all private property is required to be publicly registered as areas of permanent forest cover preservation. For the Amazon region this share increased from 50 percent to 80 percent in 1996 (Reis and Blanco 1996a). It is not clear, however, how land holders who had already cleared more than 20 percent of their land are supposed to comply with this regulation, as reforestation does not count towards the 80 percent supposed to be in original vegetation. Thus, the government is under pressure to restore the 50 percent limit to the proportion of private land that can be developed. We discuss this law further in our policy simulations in chapter 6.

In addition to new initiatives, since the 1930s the federal, state, and municipal governments have had the power to regulate the use of natural resources on both private and public land by creating Conservation Units (CU) and Indigenous Reserves (IR). These are integral areas where natural resources are preserved by strict regulations on the kind of economic activities allowed (Reis and Blanco 1996a). The first CU in Legal Amazonia was a National Park in Tocantins created by decree on the last day of 1959 covering 562,312 hectares. The creation of new CUs was slow until the boom in 1989–1990, where 60 new CUs were created adding 22.8 million hectares of theoretically protected area. More than half of all existing CU area was created in those two years.

Decrees alone, however, do not protect these areas. FUNATURA estimates that the total implementation costs needed to establish the 37 million hectares of CUs will amount to US$523 million, or about US$14 per hectare. Total annual operating costs are expected to amount to US$26.8 million, or 72 cents/hectare.

There are many types of conservation units and their operating costs vary greatly. The biggest unit is a 2.7 million hectare National Forest in Roraima which cost only 34 cents/hectare to implement, mainly because none of the area was privately owned and because there was little encroachment pressure in that region. Then there is a small Federal Ecological Reserve near Manaus that only covers 109 hectares, but with implantation costs of US$1,550 per hectare: a hundred times more than the average implantation costs and almost 5,000 times more expensive per hectare than the National Forest in Roraima.

Licensing from IBAMA is another major policy instrument for natural resource regulation. Licenses are now required for forest clearing as well as for the economic exploitation of forest areas in private properties. In addition, large industrial consumers are required to implement industrial forest management plans (PIFI) to guarantee self-sufficiency in their consumption of forestry raw material within a timetable.

Improvements in monitoring capacity and enforcement

While the zoning and licensing laws should theoretically improve the ability of the government to limit the environmental impact of economic activity in the Amazon, in practice the enforcement of these policies has suffered from a lack of governmental administrative capacity for monitoring and enforcing the regulations, as well as for prosecuting violators.

Since the late 1990s the Brazilian government has been attempting to improve the situation by investing and committing billions of dollars to systems of environmental monitoring (SIVAM – Sistema de Vigilância Ambiental) and systems of protection (SIPAM – Sistema de Proteção da Amazônia).[5] The systems are ambitious and involve many types of remote sensing devices such as satellites (RADARSAT, LANDSAT, SPOT), aircrafts equipped with Multi-Spectral Scanners (MSS), Forward Looking

[5] The total cost of implementing the SIVAM project alone is approximately US$1.4 billion. Financing has been secured from Banco do Brazil/Eximbank (USA) = US$1,022,800,000; Raytheon Credit Facility (USA) = US$239,200,000; SIVAM Vendor's Trust (USA) = US$48,000,000; and SEK/EKN (Sweden) = US$85,000,000.

Infra-Red (FLIR) and Aperture Radar (AR), manually operated surveillance planes, weather stations on land and in the air, and communications monitors (CCSIVAM 1997). In addition, the project involves several regional and national centers of information processing which are meant to serve a wide range of clients, from the state governments to the ministry of health, even the ministry of foreign affairs.

The principal goals of such expensive monitoring include not only the protection of indigenous reserves and the detection of illegal logging, but also the monitoring of international borders, the detection of drug trafficking, the detection and control of disease, and pollution control (CCSIVAM 1997).

Enforcement has also improved both at the federal and at local levels. In 1998, an "environmental crimes" bill was passed by the Brazilian Congress, which empowers IBAMA to levy fines and issue jail sentences for illegal deforestation, logging, and burning activities (Nepstad *et al.* 2002). IBAMA has used this legislation, for example, to suspend previously approved timber management plans in Pará requiring them instead to use reduced-impact forest management methods (Barreto *et al.* 1998). The G-7 Pilot Program for Preservation of Brazilian Rainforests is working together with state and municipal governments to strengthen the local capacity for planning and regulation, while also involving local stakeholders in the process (Nepstad *et al.* 2002).

These recent developments imply that the capacity of the governments for planning, monitoring, and enforcing regulations in the Amazon is increasing rapidly, and this is likely to reduce the degree of lawlessness and illegal exploitation of natural resources in the long run. In the short run, however, there is still ample room for illegal private exploitation of the riches of the Amazon.

The distributional impact of Amazon development

The economic consequences of the regional development policies have been dramatic. Generous amounts of government investment, complemented by private investment encouraged by fiscal incentives as well as international finance, led to a boom in the Legal Amazonian economy until the mid-1980s. Real *per capita* GDP growth rates averaged 6.9 percent in 1970–1975, 10.5 percent in 1975–1980, and 3.5 percent in 1980–1985. Between 1985 and 1995, the average annual growth rate of *per capita* GDP slowed to 1.2 percent.

Figures 2.2 and 2.3 shows how growth was distributed across the region during the period of rapid growth (1970–1985) and during the period of slow growth (1985–1995).

Figure 2.2 Average annual *per capita* GDP growth in the municipalities of Legal Amazonia, 1970–1985
Source: IBGE, NEMESIS/PRONEX.

During the boom period 1970–1985, growth of real *per capita* GDP was high almost everywhere in Legal Amazonia. Only a few scattered municipalities experienced low or falling income *per capita*. During the 1985–1995 period, however, negative or very small growth rates were widespread. The areas that maintained high growth rates were most of Mato Grosso owing to highly successful soybean and cattle production, some of Acre, and several municipalities traversed by the Belém–Brasília highway.

The low growth rates in 1985–1995 are mainly due to a strong contraction in urban GDP *per capita*. Rural GDP *per capita* kept growing at impressive rates in many parts of Legal Amazonia (see figure 2.4). Virtually all of Mato Grosso and Rondônia experienced real rural *per capita* GDP growth in excess of 4 percent per year, and so did many municipalities in Tocantins and Pará. Negative rural growth in the 1985–1995 period was primarily experienced in the most remote part of Amazonas state, in Roraima, in the southeastern part of Pará, and in many municipalities in Maranhão.

By 1995 GDP *per capita* averaged US$2,477. Unsurprisingly, the regions with high levels of income by 1995 correspond quite closely to the

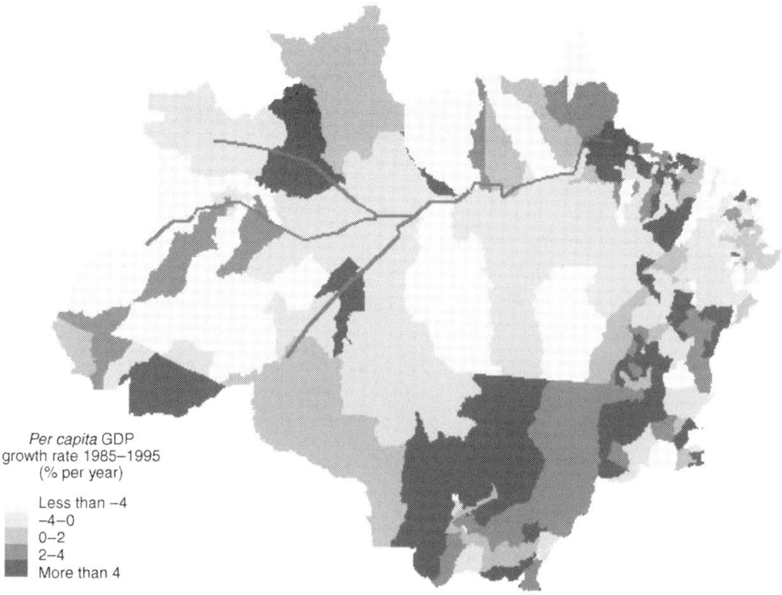

Figure 2.3 Average annual *per capita* GDP growth rates in the municipalities of Legal Amazonia, 1985–1995
Source: IBGE, NEMESIS/PRONEX.

regions that experienced rapid economic growth in the preceding twenty-five year period: Rondônia, Mato Grosso, and most parts of Pará (see figure 2.5). The regions with the lowest levels of *per capita* GDP are found both in the regions with the lowest levels of clearing (Amazonas state) and in the regions with highest levels of clearing (Maranhão state). This *could* be taken as evidence of the boom–bust cycle of frontier expansion: beyond the agricultural frontier, clearing as well as income levels are low; on the frontier clearing rates are high and income grows rapidly; behind the frontier incomes drop and the area is left with high levels of clearing.

There is also another possible explanation, however. The migrants who arrived to the Maranhão part of Legal Amazonia mainly came from the neighboring very poor Northeast region of Brazil (see table 2.2). They were more or less pushed into the Amazon region by the extremely poor conditions in the Northeast, and they arrived virtually without economic resources. Very few of the migrants[6] into Maranhão came from the North region, and they were thus unlikely to be familiar with the forest environment and the agricultural techniques suitable for their new environment.

[6] "Migrants" are here defined as people who arrived in the municipality within the last ten years. Data are from 1991.

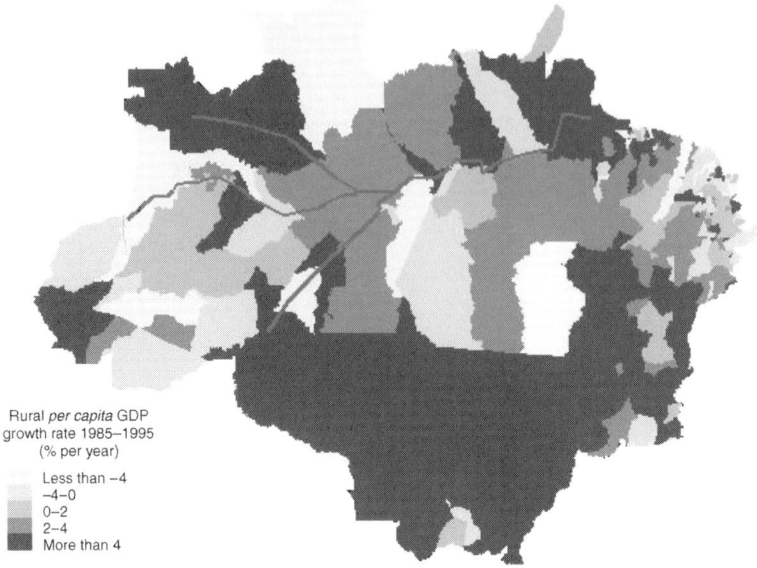

Figure 2.4 Average annual growth rate of rural *per capita* GDP in the municipalities of Legal Amazonia, 1985–1995
Source: IBGE, NEMESIS/PRONEX.

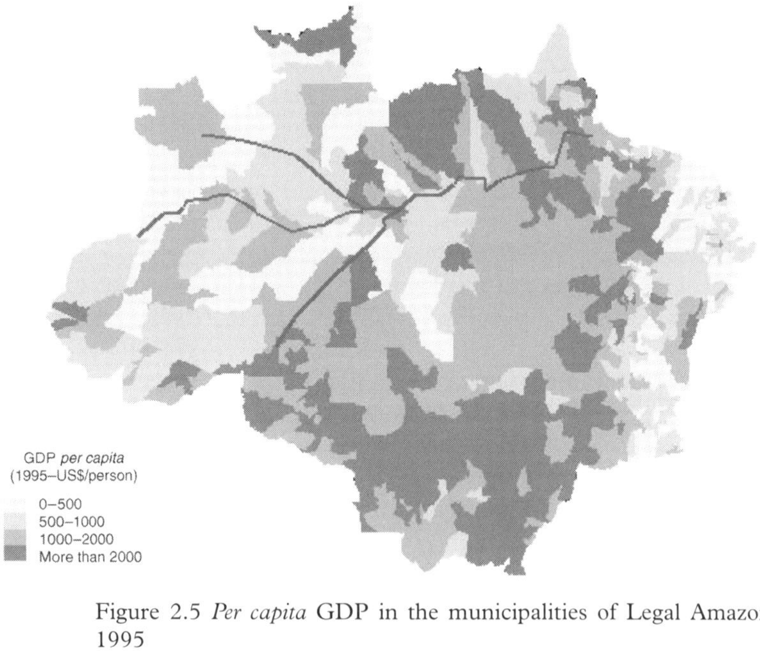

Figure 2.5 *Per capita* GDP in the municipalities of Legal Amazonia, 1995
Source: IBGE, NEMESIS/PRONEX.

Table 2.2. *Migrants into Legal Amazonian states, by source region*

	Source region in % of all migrants[a] to the state				
Destination state	North	North-East	South-East, South or Center-West	Others[b]	Total
Acre	73	5	13	9	100
Amapá	70	10	4	16	100
Amazonas	67	11	8	14	100
Goiás/Tocantins	49	17	24	10	100
Maranhão	7	81	5	6	100
Mato Grosso	5	5	83	7	100
Pará	62	21	8	8	100
Rondônia	38	8	45	9	100
Roraima	38	40	9	13	100

Notes: [a]"Migrants" are defined as those who have arrived within the previous ten years.
[b]"Others" include foreigners and migrants with unknown origin.
Source: Authors' calculations based on municipality-level migration data from 1991, from IBGE.

The migrants who came to Mato Grosso and Rondônia, on the other hand, came primarily from the South, South-East, or Center-West regions of Brazil. They were attracted into the Amazon region by cheap land and fiscal incentives, and they most likely arrived with greater initial resources.

The latter groups experienced much higher income growth than the former, which is exactly what economic theory would predict in a land-abundant but labor- and capital-scarce environment. Those who arrive with capital will tend to get a very high return on that capital because of its scarcity. Those who arrive with nothing tend to get little out of their land, because they lack the resources to buy the necessary complementary inputs such as seed, fertilizer, labor, tools, and vehicles.

We don't have direct data on the level of wealth of migrants arriving to Legal Amazonia, but we do know which municipality they came from and what the average level of income in that municipality was. If we are willing to assume that migrants are reasonable representatives for the municipality they come from (or at least that their relative income is correlated with the relative average income of their home municipality), we can get some idea about the level of income that migrants into each of the Amazonian municipalities had before they moved. The results are summarized in table 2.3. They clearly show that the average pre-move

Table 2.3. *Average level of income in migrants' municipality of origin, 1991*

State	Weighted level of income in source municipality[a]
Acre	0.86
Amapá	0.91
Amazonas	0.93
Goiás/Tocantins	0.86
Maranhão	0.56
Mato Grosso	1.16
Pará	0.78
Rondônia	1.00
Roraima	0.94

Note: [a]Incomes in source municipalities are weighted by the distribution of migrants across source municipalities.
Source: Authors' calculations based on municipality-level migration data from 1991, from IBGE.

income levels of the people migrating into Maranhão were much smaller than the average income levels of the people who moved into Mato Grosso and Rondônia.

Another way to show the importance of the "quality" of migrants is to correlate the average pre-move income level of migrants with some indicator of municipality performance. For example, the correlation between pre-move income levels and poverty rates in 1991 is −0.61, and the correlation between pre-move income levels in 1991 and rural *per capita* GDP in 1995 is 0.32. Both of these correlations indicate that municipalities with migrants from richer regions tend to perform better than municipalities with migrants coming from poorer parts of Brazil. Figure 2.6 shows the average pre-move income level of migrants in each muncipality of Legal Amazonia plotted against the poverty rate in the municipality in 1991. It is clear that most of the migrants into the municipalities of Maranhão had very low average pre-move income levels and they contribute to very high poverty rates at their destination. Conversely, the migrants into Mato Grosso had relatively high average pre-move income levels and they contribute to relatively low poverty levels at their destinations in Legal Amazonia.

The variation of *per capita* income levels indicated in figure 2.5 is thus consistent with the theory that the "quality" of migrants is important for the performance of agriculture in Legal Amazonia. Migrants who arrive with more initial resources are more likely to establish successful agriculture and contribute to rapid growth and poverty reduction than migrants who arrive with fewer initial resources. The data are much less consistent

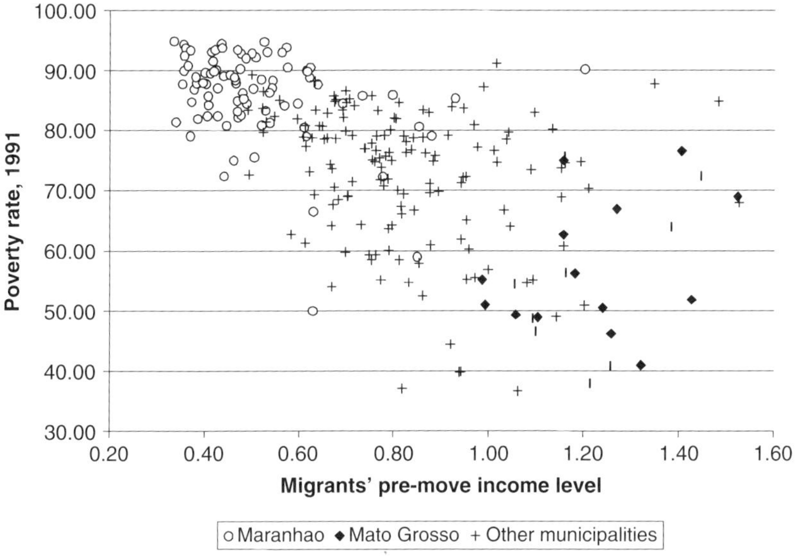

Figure 2.6 Relationship between average pre-move income level of migrants and poverty rates in the municipalities of Legal Amazonia, 1991

with the boom–bust story of natural resource mining, since most of the municipalities in Maranhão have never experienced rapid growth rates, while most of the municipalities in Mato Grosso seem to sustain their very high growth rates despite the dramatic economic slowdown in both Legal Amazonia and in the rest of Brazil.

Although the dispossessed, landless poor migrants from the Northeast did not fare as well in their new home as their more prosperous brethren, nevertheless the perception remained that such a move would give them a chance, unavailable in their home region, to improve their lives. Thus, clearly the perception persisted that the Amazon offered a higher degree of social mobility than other regions of the country. However, since wealthier migrants had a higher probability of success in the Amazon than poorer migrants, migration to the Amazon may have actually tended to increase regional inequality as well.

While we don't have the data to test the net impact on inequality directly, we can examine some indicators of poverty across municipalities and compare them with national trends to see if the Amazon region has kept up, exceeded, or fallen behind poverty reduction efforts in the rest of the country.

Figure 2.7 shows how poverty rates in the municipalities of Legal Amazonia have changed over time. The poverty line is defined as one

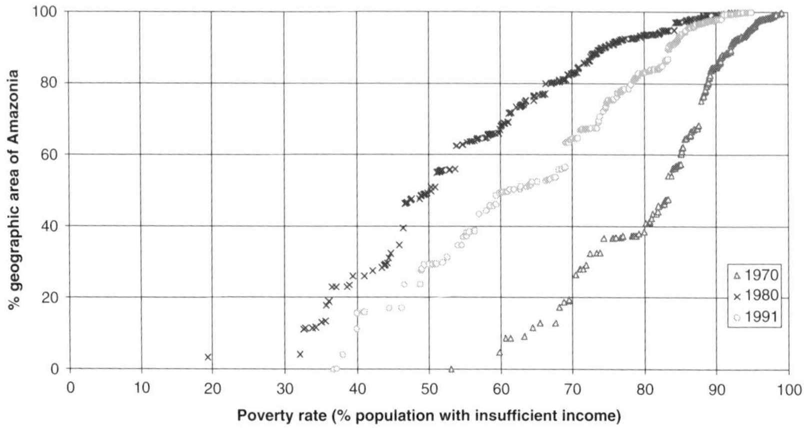

Figure 2.7 Poverty rates in the municipalities of Legal Amazonia, 1970, 1980, and 1991

minimum wage per household and is fixed across all of Brazil. Since one minimum wage would tend to stretch much further for a family with land in the Amazon than for a landless family in the slums of São Paulo, poverty rates are not comparable across the country, and especially not between rural and urban areas. According to this definition, however, poverty rates are very high in Legal Amazonia, averaging 83 percent in 1970, 57 in 1980, and 62 in 1991. During the booming 1970s, poverty rates fell dramatically in Legal Amazonia. In 1970, 60 percent of the geographical area of Legal Amazonia had poverty rates in excess of 80 percent. By 1980, only 7 percent of the area had such high poverty rates. During the 1980s, poverty rates increased again, and by 1991, 18 percent of the area had poverty rates in excess of 80 percent.

Since the official poverty rates depend on a centrally determined national minimum wage, it is difficult to meaningfully compare poverty rates across regions. However, life expectancy, infant mortality, and illiteracy rates are three possible alternative indicators of poverty which all are more comparable over time and space. Furthermore, by comparing the levels and rates of change of these indicators in the Amazon with the levels and changes of the Brazilian national average we can get some idea of whether the general trends have been more, or less, poverty-reducing in the Amazon compared to the country as a whole.

Figure 2.8 shows that life expectancy has increased dramatically across all the municipalities of Legal Amazonia. Average life expectancy in the Amazon increased from 50 years in 1970, to 57 years in 1980, reaching 62 years in 1991. The comparable figures for Brazil as a whole are 59, 63 and

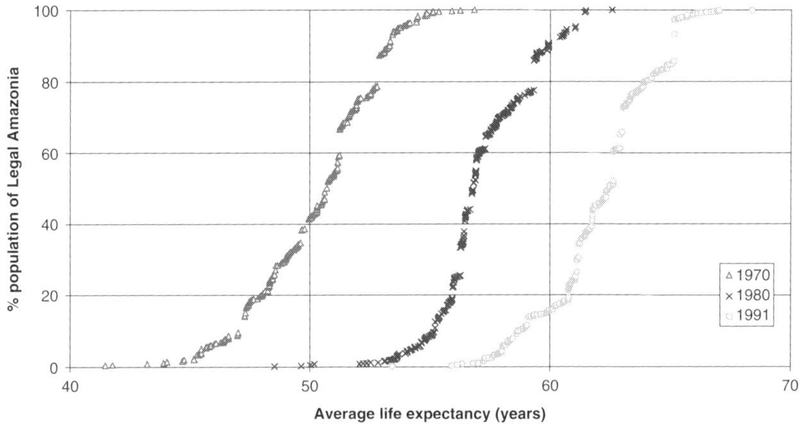

Figure 2.8 Life expectancy in the municipalities of Legal Amazonia, 1970, 1980, and 1991

65.6 years, respectively. Thus, although life expectancy is somewhat lower in the Amazon compared to the rest of the country, the rate of increase has been significantly higher for the Amazon, with the difference between regional and national life expectancy narrowing from nine years in 1970 to less than three years in 1991. Within the Amazon itself the trends can be further analyzed. In particular, during the booming 1970s the increase in life expectancy was greatest among the municipalities with lowest life expectancies, indicating that the poorer municipalities benefitted most from growth. In the less spectacular 1980s life expectancy kept increasing, but not as much in the municipalities with initially low life expectancy. This indicates that the slower growth in the 1980s was less beneficial for the poor municipalities than for the richer ones.

Infant mortality and illiteracy rates tell a similar story. During the booming 1970s adult illiteracy rates fell from an average of 44 percent in 1970 to 37 percent in 1980, with the biggest gains experienced in the municipalities with relatively high illiteracy rates. During the 1980s illiteracy rates kept falling to an average of 28 percent in 1991, but during this period the municipalities with initially relatively low illiteracy rates improved the most (see figure 2.9). Again, the national figures for 1970, 1980, and 1991 are 33, 25.5, and 18.9 percent, respectively, indicating that trends in the Amazon have kept up with, and in the latter period exceeded, the improvements in the rest of the country.

Infant mortality rates also decreased substantially from an average of 124 deaths per 1,000 live births in 1970, to 82 in 1980, and 57 in 1991, compared to the national averages of 94.6, 66.6, and 48.2, respectively.

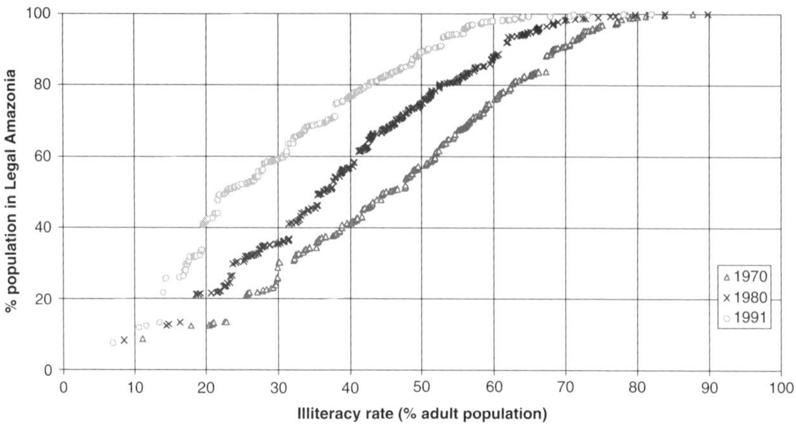

Figure 2.9 Illiteracy rates in the municipalities of Legal Amazonia, 1970, 1980, and 1991

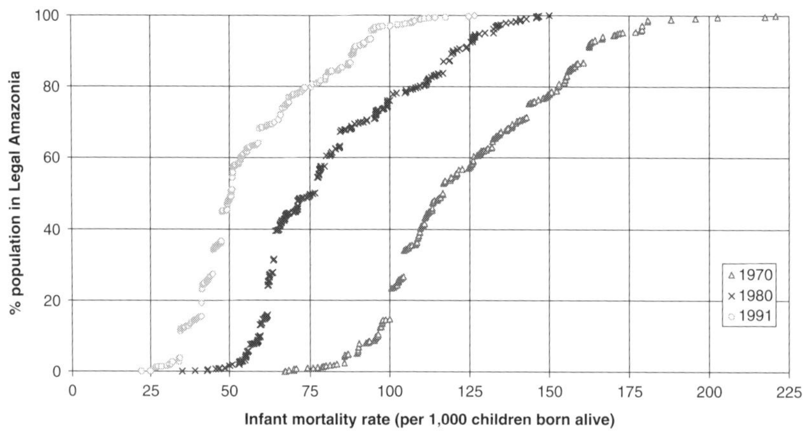

Figure 2.10 Infant mortality rates in the municipalities of Legal Amazonia, 1970, 1980, and 1991

Infant mortality in the Amazon was thus reduced by 55 percent over those two decades, compared to a 49 percent reduction throughout all Brazil. In 1970, 84 percent of the population had to live with infant mortality rates in excess of 100. By 1991, less than 3 percent of the population experienced such high infant mortality rates (see figure 2.10).

While poverty indicators show that the level of poverty in Legal Amazonia is still higher than the national average, the trends in these variables have been improving at a faster rate in the Amazon. Thus, while

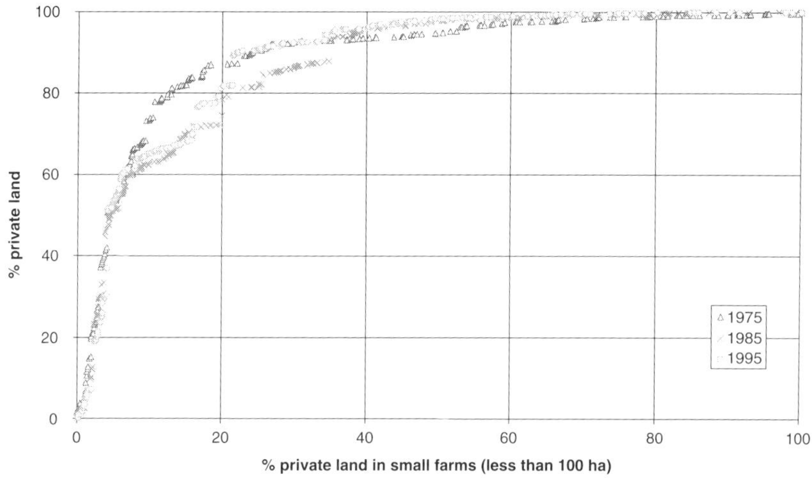

Figure 2.11 Percentage of private area in small farms in Legal Amazonian municipalities, 1975, 1985, and 1995

the wealthy did benefit hugely from government support, the effects of economic development have not bypassed the poor entirely and in fact they seem to be improving their lot at a faster rate than the rest of the country. Furthermore, farm-level studies complement the municipality-level figures in indicating successful settlement of the Amazon. Based on evidence from studies by FAO/UNDP/MARA (1992), Jones *et al.* (1992), Mattos *et al.* (1992), and Almeida (1992b), Schneider (1995) concludes that settlers in the Amazon *do* appear to be improving their standard of living compared to people with the same education and skills outside the Amazon, and that yields tend to be increasing at farm level.

Schneider (1995) also concludes that land distribution in the Amazon is substantially more equal than for Brazil as a whole and trending toward greater equality. Our municipality-level data show mixed evidence on the trend of land distribution. On average the share of private land occupied by small farms increased from 10.7 percent in 1975 to 12.6 percent in 1985. But then it fell to 11.1 percent in 1995. Figure 2.11 shows that among the municipalities with many small farms (more than 40 percent of the area in small farms) there was some consolidation between 1975 and 1995. However, municipalities with a more normal number of small farms (10–20 percent of the area in small farms) experienced considerable fragmentation of farms between 1975 and 1985. This trend was reversed between 1985 and 1995, however. Among the municipalities with few small farms, there has been no visible change. Rondônia is an example

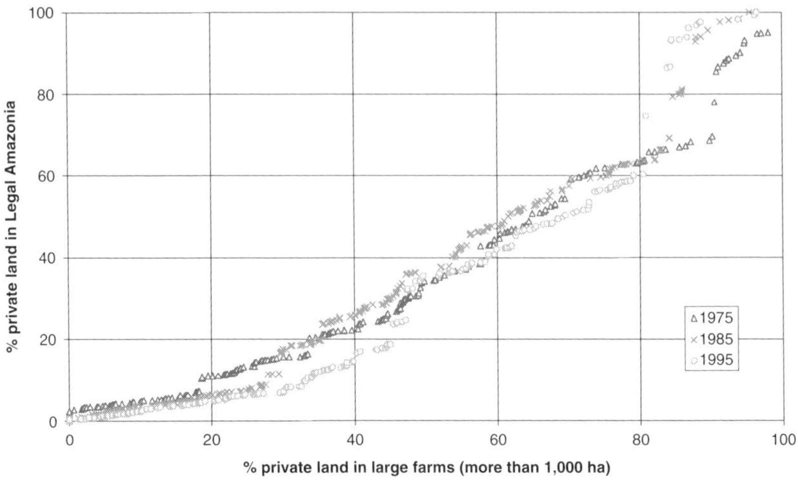

Figure 2.12 Share of private area occupied by large farms in the municipalities of Legal Amazonia, 1975, 1985, and 1995

of a state that first experienced fragmentation and later consolidation. In 1975, only 10.7 percent of private area was occupied by small farms (less than 100 hectare). By 1985, that share had increased to 34.9 percent, only to drop to 21.4 percent in 1995.

Figure 2.12 shows the changes in the share of private area occupied by large farms (more than 1,000 hectares). It shows no clear trend. There was fragmentation among the municipalities with many large farms, but consolidation among the municipalities with few large farms. Overall, the share of private land occupied by large farms decreased from 63.2 percent in 1975 to 60.3 percent in 1985 and then increased again to 63.1 percent in 1995.

The data thus show no clear trend of increasing or decreasing inequality between 1975 and 1995. Rather they show that there tends to be a redistribution of land within each municipality towards the average for the region: municipalities which initially had relatively many big farms tend to experience fragmentation into more manageable units, while municipalities which initially had relatively many small farms tend to experience consolidation.

In the 1960s and 1970s people with the right political connections could acquire titles to huge estates in the Amazon at very little cost. Those who did not have political connections could acquire land titles by developing the land, living on it, and cultivating it. Since this required a great deal of commitment and work, the farm areas claimed by the latter method were generally relatively small. These two methods of acquiring land thus led to a large number of small farms, accounting for about 11 percent of total farm area, and a smaller number of large farms, accounting for about 63 percent of total farm area. That leaves only 26 percent for medium-sized farms (between 100 and 1,000 hectares).

While obtaining titles to vast stretches of land in the Amazon was cheap and thus involved little risk, the process of demarcating, defending, and developing the land was costly. Many of the big land-owners therefore left the land in forest, adopting a wait-and-see attitude. Many of them did not find it worthwhile to fight squatters on their land. Indeed some land-owners encouraged a number of squatters to settle on their land to look after it. By Brazilian law a squatter can obtain the rights to land that he has been occupying and cultivating for at least ten years, so these huge estates would tend to be broken up into smaller units over time unless the land-owners could effectively deter squatters. Squatting is thus likely to be the explanation for the observed fragmentation in municipalities which initially had many large land holdings. On the other hand, the consolidation that has taken place in municipalities which initially had many small farms is likely to be a reflection of small slash-and-burn farmers selling off to cattle ranchers or more modern farmers after having benefitted from the first few years of high crop yields.

In conclusion, while we cannot discern from this analysis whether the poor now living in the Amazon could have been better served by some alternative set of policies which did not include development of the region, the living standards of the poor in the Amazon do appear to have been improving faster than in other parts of Brazil. Policies have not been particularly pro-poor, however, and relatively wealthy migrants from the South and Central regions of Brazil are more likely to prosper in the Amazon than the very poor migrants from the Northeast.

Avança Brasil

The late 1990s witnessed a resurgence of interest in development and integration plans in Brazil. This is clear from the governments' pluriannual plan for 2000–2003, which has been named "*Avança Brasil.*" This plan stresses equality enhancing growth both socially and regionally with the purpose of creating a more united and homogeneous country. This implies a lot of investment in the Amazon region.

The *Avança Brasil* plan calls for investments during the 2000–2007 period of R$24.1 billion in the western and northern parts of Legal Amazonia (Acre, Amapá, Amazonas, Roraima, and most of Pará) and of R$49.8 billion in the border areas to the east and south of the heart of the

Amazon (Rondônia, Mato Grosso, Maranhão, Tocantins, the most eastern part of Pará, and areas bordering Legal Amazonia). These amounts cover mostly infrastructure projects (road improvements, bridges, airports, ports, channels, floodgates, railways, terminals, powerplants, natural gas pipelines, telephone lines, etc.) but about a third cover social development projects (education, health, housing, water and sanitation) and 5–8 percent are intended for environmental projects and information collection.

Environmentalists are very concerned with the consequences of such investments in the Amazon. In a much-noticed article published in *Science*, Laurance *et al.* (2001a) have made a provocative prognosis of the expected deforestation impact of *Avança Brasil*, combined with two other plans (*Programa Brasil em Açao* and ELECTROBRAS' Ten-Year Expansion Plan B 1998–2007). Extrapolating the observed impact of such infrastructure from the 1980s, two scenarios derived by the authors from map overlays show that between 28 percent and 42 percent of the area will be deforested or heavily degraded by the year 2020. Another 24–28 percent of the remaining forest will be lightly degraded; only between 5 percent and 28 percent will remain pristine forests.

In chapter 6 we will try to analyze the impact of *Avança Brasil*'s road improvement projects in Legal Amazonia using a dynamic and spatial econometric model estimated at municipality level.

Conclusions

This chapter has discussed the distinctive characteristics of the Amazon region and the development policies that have been pursued to develop and integrate the region into the Brazilian economy. The period from the late 1960s to the mid-1980s, were characterized by very aggressive development policies with little regard for the environmental consequences. This changed in the late 1980s, for several reasons. First, Brazil went into an economic recession and could not afford to continue subsidizing Amazonian development on the same scale as it had previously. In addition, growing international environmental concerns significantly increased the pressure on Brazil to reduce the rate of deforestation.

The late 1990s saw a resurgence of interest in development and integration plans, but coupled with increased concern for the environment. The *Avança Brasil* program does not contain plans for major new road building, but focuses on the improvement of already existing roads. This may be a sign that the Brazilian government wishes to stimulate agricultural intensification in old frontier areas while, at least for the moment, they do not want to actively encourage the opening of new frontiers.

The capacity to monitor activities in the Amazon has also been increasing through the implementation of ambitious environmental monitoring and protection systems. These systems should facilitate both better planning in the region and better enforcement of regulations. In the long run we would expect these developments to lead to increases in land productivity through reductions in privately beneficial but socially wasteful activities.

3 The municipal database

> Deforestation is not an event, that just happens and then is over forever. Deforestation is actually an ongoing process of continuous human interference, preventing the forest from growing back, which it would if it was simply left alone.
>
> (Patrick Moore 2000)

This chapter presents and discusses the unique panel data set, DESMAT, that provides the empirical base for this book. The data set is constructed and maintained, under the oversight of Eustáquio Reis, at the Institute of Applied Economic Research (Instituto de Pesquisa Econômica Aplicada – IPEA) in Rio de Janeiro. The original motivation for the creation of this database was to develop econometric models for forecasting and policy analysis of Amazon deforestation and its environmental consequences – in particular the contribution to CO_2 emissions. However, the scope of analytical possibilities is much broader. Data on several hundred economic, demographic, agricultural and ecological variables have been collected for the years 1970, 1975, 1980, 1985, 1991, and 1996 for 257 consistently defined geographic areas in Legal Amazonia.

The significance of the time and effort that has been put into developing and maintaining this huge database cannot be emphasized enough. The data set is an enormous contribution to our knowledge about, and ability to analyze, change and growth in the Amazon. It was the existence of the data set which originally inspired the ongoing research collaboration which has resulted in this book. Over the years along with the Amazon itself, the data set has changed and evolved. In 1970 there were 316 municipalities in Legal Amazonia. However, as they developed economically and their populations increased, they tended to split and/or regroup, so that by 1996 the number of individual municipalities had grown to 628. In order to produce data that could be analyzed consistently through time and across space it was necessary to define geographic areas that are consistent throughout the sample period. Made up of municipalities or groups of municipalities, these are called Minimum Comparable Areas (MCA). Table 3.1 shows the actual number of municipalities in 1996 for

Table 3.1. *Municipalities and Minimum Comparable Areas (MCAs) in Legal Amazonia, 1996*

State	Number of municipalities, 1996	Number of MCAs in data set
Acre	22	4
Amapá	15	4
Amazonas	62	27
Goiás/Tocantins	127	37
Maranhão	109	88
Mato Grosso	117	23
Pará	128	72
Rondônia	40	1
Roraima	8	1
Total	628	257

each of the nine states in Legal Amazonia together with the number of MCAs in our data set. In total we have 257 MCAs.

Rondônia has experienced especially rapid development since 1970 and the two original municipalities have now evolved into forty. However, as some of the new municipalities contain parts of both of the two original municipalities it is impossible to construct more than one MCA for Rondônia. This means that the whole state of Rondônia counts as one single observation in our regressions in chapter 6. This is unfortunate given that Rondônia has experienced some of the most dramatic developments in Amazonia during our study period; we discuss the implications of this in more detail in chapter 6 and in the Technical appendix.

The remainder of this chapter defines and discusses all the variables that we use in this book, and discusses the quality of the data and potential measurement errors and biases that might arise.

Deforestation: concepts and measures

Cleared land

The main source of land use data are the agricultural census conducted every five years by the Brazilian Institute of Geography and Statistics (IBGE). These censuses provide detailed information on private land uses and, at least in principle, include all agricultural establishments in Legal Amazonia. The unit of analysis in the census is the "agricultural establishment," producing any plant or animal output during the time span under analysis, be it a household or a firm, a farm owner or a tenant, a profit or deficit making unit, of rural or urban residence. The individual(s) interviewed refer to the one(s) that actually manage production, which may or may not be identical to the owner of capital and land – a tenant, sharecropper or farm administrator are some of the alternatives. Census participation is mandatory so that, in principle, a total coverage is aimed at.

The richness of the information in terms of socio-economic and land-use variables obtained simultaneously by the censuses is a clear advantage compared to the binary forested/non-forested information obtained through satellite pictures. There are, nevertheless, several potential problems with the data. These will be discussed in a section on data reliability below.

The agricultural censuses group all land into private land and public land. Private land is stratified into eight categories according to agricultural use. Areas used for (i) annual crops, (ii) perennial crops, (iii) planted forest, (iv) planted pasture, (v) short fallow, and (vi) long fallow are classified as cleared land, while areas maintained as (vii) natural forest and (viii) natural pasture are considered non-cleared. A small category of private non-usable land (rivers, mountains, etc.) is not considered cleared either.

All land that is not claimed by anyone is considered public land and by definition non-cleared. This is a drastic assumption, but it can be at least partly justified by the fact that land clearing has been an important method of obtaining property rights in the Amazon, so most cleared land automatically becomes private land. In some municipalities, the amount of privately claimed land actually exceeds the total area of the municipality. The assumption must, nevertheless, contribute to making the land survey measure of deforestation rather conservative. Areas flooded by hydroelectric facilities, areas cleared for mining and logging, areas cleared for public roads, railways, and other kinds of infrastructure, and areas cleared by illegal squatting are ignored, as are areas cleared by wild fires and floods.

Natural vegetation

As mentioned, not all land in Legal Amazonia is naturally forested. Especially in the southern and eastern parts of Legal Amazonia, the land is naturally covered with savannah-like vegetation and conversion to agriculture in these open areas cannot be considered deforestation. We are mainly interested in cleared area for modeling purposes, but most other researchers and data sources focus on deforested area, so in order to compare our data with other sources we also use our data to provide an estimate of deforested area in Legal Amazonia. The difference between

Table 3.2. *Natural vegetation types in Legal Amazonia*

Type of vegetation	Share of area (%)
Prairie (biomass < 5 ton/ha)	3.15
Bush vegetation (5 < biomass < 50)	15.82
Low-density forest (50 < biomass < 150)	8.88
River bank, mangrove and swamp forest	8.90
Seasonal forest	4.98
Dense forest (biomass > 150)	56.39
Other or missing	1.88
Total	100.00

Source: IBGE.

cleared land and deforested land is the land that has been converted to agricultural land uses but was not forested originally. In order to estimate deforested area we thus need to know the natural land cover at any given point in Legal Amazonia. The data from IBGE provides the following classifications:

- Savannah (*Campos: Vegetação Savana + Formação Pioneira Gramineo (Lenhosa + Herbacea)*)
- Bush vegetation (*Vegetação Arborea-Arbustiva: Savanna Estepica + Campinarana*)
- Low density forest (*Floresta Baixa*)
- River bank, mangrove and swamp forest (*Florest Aluvial*)
- Seasonal forest (*Floresta Semidecidual*)
- Dense Forest (*Floresta Densa*)
- Reforestation.

Table 3.2 shows the share of each type of vegetation in Legal Amazonia, i.e. the vegetation that would naturally be present in the absence of human intervention. For the purpose of calculating deforestation rates we classify savannah and bush vegetation as naturally non-forested and the rest as naturally forested. This leads to an overall natural forest share of 79.2 percent, which is similar to other estimates of forest share from the literature (e.g. Downton 1994).

Forest is very unevenly distributed across municipalities. Some municipalities have no natural forest at all, while others would have been completely covered by forest in the absence of human intervention. Table 3.3 shows that the proportion of naturally forested land varies from less than 20 percent in the state of Tocantins on the eastern border of the basin, to 98.5 percent in the western state of Acre. In addition, more than 40 percent of Mato Grosso state is natural savannah, which explains why cattle ranching is mainly concentrated in this state.

Table 3.3. *Natural forest shares, by state*

State	Natural forest share (%)
Acre	98.5
Amapá	77.5
Amazonas	93.1
Goiás/Tocantins	19.3
Maranhão	58.9
Mato Grosso	58.9
Pará	90.1
Rondônia	88.9
Roraima	78.8
Total	79.2

Source: IBGE.

Our estimates of deforestation in each municipality are constructed by multiplying the amount of cleared land by the share of naturally forested land in each municipality under the assumption that clearing is randomly distributed across the municipality. This assumption is likely to lead to an overestimation of deforestation since people would tend to clear the most open areas first. An alternative assumption could have been that people convert all non-forested area to agriculture before they start attacking the dense forest, but this assumption leads to a clear underestimation of deforestation and is thus not adopted.

Another source of overestimation of deforested area is that our estimate includes planted forest, which counts as forest by most other definitions in the literature. We count planted forest as cleared land (and thus as deforested land) as these are areas that have indeed been cleared at some point and support less biodiversity than virgin forest. The implication of this assumption will vary with the objective of a given analysis. For example, for studies concerned mainly with biodiversity our measure would be perfectly appropriate. However for studies that focus on the carbon sequestration services of the Amazon our measure would overestimate deforestation; instead such a study would want to include both planted forest in the forested area together with secondary forest re-growth in their measure.

Comparing deforestation estimates based on land surveys and satellite data

The Brazilian National Institute of Space Research (INPE – *Instituto Nacional de Pesquisas Especiais*) has provided annual deforestation data

Table 3.4. *Gross deforestation based on INPE satellite data, 1978–1995*

State	State area (km^2)	Gross deforestation (% of state area)		
		1978	1988	1995
Acre	152,589	1.64	4.83	8.72
Amapá	140,276	0.14	0.57	1.27
Amazonas	1,567,125	0.11	1.26	1.70
Goiás/Tocantins	285,793	1.12	7.56	8.80
Maranhão	257,451	24.82	35.27	37.97
Mato Grosso	881,001	2.27	8.12	12.73
Pará	1,248,042	4.52	10.54	13.54
Rondônia	243,044	1.73	12.34	18.99
Roraima	230,104	0.04	1.17	2.23
Total	5,005,425	3.04	7.54	9.93

Source: INPE, http://www.grid.inpe.br/amz/prodes2000/ for deforested area and Mahar (1989) for state area.

for Legal Amazonia since 1988, but previous to that there are data only for 1978. Table 3.4 presents INPE's latest estimates of accumulated deforestation by 1978, 1988, and 1995.

By appropriate interpolation and extrapolation it is possible to calculate the approximate level of deforestation according to satellite data for 1975, 1980, 1985, and 1995 for each state and compare with our estimates based on land surveys. Table 3.5 shows the results of such a comparison.

In general, the satellite measures start at a lower level of deforestation in 1975 than our land survey measure, but end at a higher level in 1995. We speculate that a primary reason for this discrepancy is that the land survey measure does not count abandoned land as cleared or deforested, while the satellite measure counts all areas that have once been cleared as deforested even if they show advanced forest re-growth. This means that the satellite data will reflect gross deforestation (i.e. once deforested always deforested), while the land survey data will reflect net deforestation (i.e. gross deforestation minus secondary forest). This difference is particularly pronounced in the state of Maranhão, where the satellite measures includes large areas (57,800 km^2) of old secondary vegetation (deforested prior to 1960), which the land survey measure counts as not cleared. "Old" deforestation, however, can explain only the large initial difference in 1975. By 1995 the difference observed in Maranhão has grown so large that it is difficult to come up with convincing explanations. In order to account for this discrepancy, the poor

Table 3.5. *Comparing deforestation estimates from satellite and land surveys, 1975–1995*

State	1975	1980	1985	1995
	(% of state area[a])			
Land survey				
Acre	1.13	2.61	3.06	4.76
Amapá	0.70	1.02	1.37	0.91
Amazonas	0.50	0.67	0.64	0.45
Goiás/Tocantins	2.60	3.83	4.70	5.38
Maranhão	11.33	15.40	16.94	12.80
Mato Grosso	3.50	5.91	7.46	13.14
Pará	3.08	4.92	6.27	6.24
Rondônia	1.58	3.71	5.93	12.51
Roraima	0.39	0.68	0.95	2.01
Total	2.47	3.87	4.75	5.90
Satellite data				
Acre	0.42	2.44	4.60	8.69
Amapá	0.01	0.22	0.43	1.24
Amazonas	0.00	0.30	0.96	1.69
Goiás/Tocantins	0.00	2.22	5.68	8.58
Maranhão	19.89	24.20	29.35	34.38
Mato Grosso	0.51	3.34	6.18	12.37
Pará	3.07	5.46	9.06	13.49
Rondônia	0.00	3.72	9.63	19.35
Roraima	0.00	0.30	0.81	2.28
Total	1.97	3.79	6.25	9.79
Difference				
Acre	−0.71	−0.17	1.54	3.93
Amapá	−0.69	−0.80	−0.94	0.33
Amazonas	−0.50	−0.37	0.32	1.24
Goiás/Tocantins	−2.60	−1.61	0.98	3.20
Maranhão	8.56	8.80	12.41	21.58
Mato Grosso	−2.99	−2.57	−1.28	−0.77
Pará	−0.01	0.54	2.79	7.25
Rondônia	−1.58	0.01	3.70	6.84
Roraima	−0.39	−0.38	−0.14	0.27
Total	−0.50	−0.08	1.50	3.89

Notes: [a]Only the part of state area that is inside Legal Amazonia is counted, since only deforestation that takes place inside Legal Amazonia is counted. The state areas used are from IBGE data, which differ slightly from the state areas Mahar (1989) used. INPE does not explicitly indicate what measure of state areas they use, but according to their maps, they use only the part within Legal Amazonia.

Source: IBGE Agricultural Censuses and INPE (2000).

farmers in Maranhão would have to be much more likely to abandon their land than other farmers in the Amazon, and they would have to be much more sensitive to a temporary recession in agriculture than other Amazonian farmers. Given that the farmers in Maranhão are the poorest in the Amazon, they may be so close to the minimum existence income that a temporary bad year like 1995 would indeed prompt them to abandon their lands. It is not clear, however, where they could go to improve their situation.

In Mato Grosso, the land survey measure of deforestation is higher than the satellite measure, even by 1995. This is likely to be owing to the assumption of random clearing across vegetation types in the land survey measure mentioned above. Mato Grosso is dominated by cattle ranches owing to the presence of large areas of natural pastures and savannahs, and cattle ranchers are likely to have preferred these open areas first as the cost of clearing is much lower than for dense forest. To the extent that both forest and non-forest is mixed within the same municipality, our assumption of random clearing within the municipality will tend to lead to an overestimation of the extent of deforestation. The satellite method, on the other hand, can keep the non-forested areas completely out of the calculation.

The year 1995 was unusual both for the Census and the satellite data. Annual economic indicators show that 1995 was an unusually bad year for agriculture all over Brazil, and this is likely to be reflected in the 1995/1996 agricultural census, which provides the data for the land survey measure of deforestation. The satellite data, on the other hand, show an unexpected large upward blip in deforestation in 1995. While annual deforestation in every year in the early 1990s were below 15,000 km^2, the deforestation rate suddenly jumped inexplicably to 29,059 km^2 in 1995, only to return to more normal levels (below 18,000 km^2/year) in the following years. These annual variations in opposite directions in 1995 are thus likely to explain at least some of the large difference between the satellite measure and the land survey measure of deforestation in 1995.

Apart from the obvious differences mentioned above, there are more subtle possibilities of errors for both measures. In the collection stage the satellite data are less prone to error than the land survey, which may suffer from biases owing to mis-reporting on the part of interviewed farmers and undercounting as discussed below. However, in the processing stage there is more room for discrepancies in the interpretation of the satellite photos, potentially leading to very different estimates, depending on the method used. Just how large this variation can be is illustrated by how much the deforestation estimates based on satellite data differ from interpretation to

Table 3.6. *Satellite deforestation estimates, 1978 and 1988*

	Gross deforestation (in % of state area)	
State	1978	1988
Acre	1.6	12.8
Amapá	0.1	0.4
Amazonas	0.1	6.8
Goiás/Tocantins	3.6	11.6
Maranhão	2.8	19.7
Mato Grosso	3.2	23.6
Pará	0.8	9.6
Rondônia	1.7	23.7
Roraima	0.1	1.4
Total	1.5	12.0

Source: Mahar (1989).

interpretation. Table 3.6 shows satellite deforestation estimates for 1978 and 1988 as presented in Mahar (1989, p. 6) and widely quoted[1] to this day.

Despite the fact that the estimates in table 3.6 are derived from the same primary data as the estimates in table 3.4 there are enormous discrepancies. The deforestation levels in the states of Pará and Maranhão have been adjusted substantially upwards in table 3.4, in an attempt to include "old deforestation" (prior to 1960). Apart from that, estimates for 1978 have generally been adjusted upwards while deforestation estimates for 1988 generally have been adjusted downwards. While the early interpretations of the satellite data suggested that 10.5 percent of the entire Legal Amazonia had been deforested in the decade between 1978 and 1988, this estimate has now been reduced to 3.5 percent. This difference of a factor of 3 is owing to different interpretations of the same satellite pictures. Fearnside (1990) and Downton (1994) both provide very interesting discussions on the sources of these discrepancies.

Interpretation of satellite data can either be done manually by visual interpretation of paper images or it can be done by a computer program, thus eliminating inconsistencies of judgment about what is counted as "deforestation." Digital methods are particularly useful for analyzing

[1] For example, Hecht and Cockburn (1989, p. 52); Pearce *et al.* (1990, p. 193); Cummings (1990, p. 3); Anderson (1990, p. 6); Downton (1994, p. 233); and Faminow (1998; p. 96).

changes over time as the previous status of a pixel can be included in the information set. Manual methods often give better results, however, as common sense can be applied (Rasch 1994).

In addition to the different interpretations of the same raw data, several different types of remote sensing data are available. Although they tend to provide conflicting estimates of the extent of deforestation, the process of comparing and criticizing the different measures has narrowed the range of estimates over time (Downton 1994). The Mahar (1989) estimates of deforestation are now generally regarded as seriously overestimated, while INPE's present annual estimates of deforestation are considered much better and at least reasonably consistent over time. Their classification algorithms are by no means perfect, however, and as these algorithms are improved over time this will inevitably lead to adjustments in past deforestation estimates.

The complete set of satellite data over time theoretically allows for quite accurate estimation of secondary forest growth and its age. With all the reported land abandonment in the Amazon, this is an important issue in terms of both carbon sequestration and economic policy oriented towards sustainability. However, instead of using this information, INPE's current computer algorithms just block out all pixels that have once been declared deforested, and calls them forever deforested. This seems to be a waste of very valuable information.

For both satellite methods and land survey methods, the biggest problem for estimating deforestation comes from the problem of deciding what is naturally forested land and what is not. The problem is particularly severe because clearing tends to take place in the most open types of vegetation (these areas happen to be closer to southern markets and are cheaper to clear), which is exactly the types of vegetation which is most difficult to classify in the binary forest/non-forest classification. This is one of the reasons why the rest of this book will deal with "cleared area" instead of deforested area. In that way we avoid the difficult problem of classifying cleared areas as either naturally forested or naturally non-forested.

The Agricultural Censuses

Our principal data on changes in land use come from the Brazilian Agricultural Censuses, which are usually conducted every five years. The 1990 census was canceled, however, owing to the economic crisis, and by 1995 IBGE had decided to change the reference period from the calendar year to the agricultural year (August 1, 1995 to July 31, 1996). There were good reasons for such a change, one of which was that previous Agricultural Censuses provided information about planting and harvesting that were not from the same agricultural cycle. For economic analysis of the sector, this lack of correspondence presents substantial obstacles (Helfand and Brunstein 1999). However, the change in reference period also implied a change in the period in which the data were gathered. Rather than collect the data starting in January the following year, as had been done for the 1970, 1975, 1980, and 1985 Censuses, the gathering of data for the 1995/1996 Census began in August 1996. IBGE therefore warns that the results of the 1995/1996 Census are not strictly comparable to those of the previous Agricultural Censuses. Some researchers have suggested that at least part of the apparent drop in agricultural establishments and agricultural workers in Brazil between 1985 and 1995 is spurious and caused by the change in reference period. The argument is that "many establishments are of a precarious nature, and are easily identifiable only in the period between planting and harvest. In the off-season, many times there are few vestiges of the agricultural activity that took place on the land during the previous harvest, and frequently the person in charge of production cannot be found" (Helfand and Brunstein 1999).

While it seems plausible that the change in reference period may have caused an undercount of the most transient agricultural establishments, there have been plenty of macroeconomic changes during the period in question that could have produced similar results. For example, credit subsidies for agriculture were eliminated in the late 1980s, trade was liberalized, and the state's involvement in agriculture was generally reduced. The loss of protection and subsidies in the agricultural sector likely caused the least efficient farmers to abandon the sector in search of employment elsewhere. At the same time, the farms that remained are likely to have sought out new technologies to enhance their competitiveness. The resulting modernization process is likely to have been labor saving. These changes in the economic environment are therefore likely to have contributed substantially to both the drop in the number of agricultural establishments and the drop in the number of agricultural workers all over Brazil.

Helfand and Brunstein (1999) try to assess the importance of the change in reference period by comparing agricultural area estimates from the agricultural census with information from the IBGE Municipal Agricultural Production (PAM) report. The PAM did not change its methodology during the period and is the official annual source of information on agricultural area and production. However, the PAM data are intended to provide timely information so they are not estimated from a random sample of producers, but are rather based on a "subjective

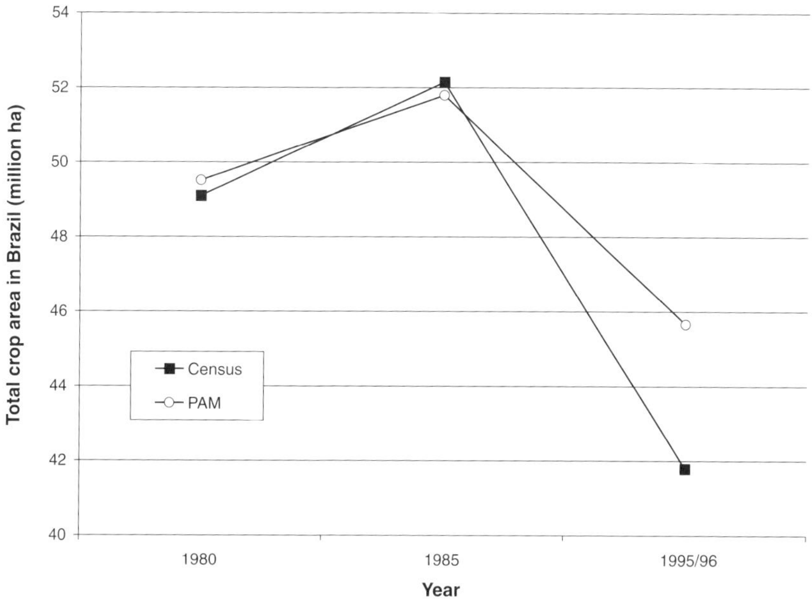

Figure 3.1 Total crop area in Brazil according to Agricultural Census and PAM data, by year, 1980–1996

survey" of experts' opinions. We do not know which of the two sources is most accurate, but for the purposes of investigating changes in discrepancies over time a comparison makes sense. Figure 3.1 shows the development of temporary and permanent crop area according to the Census data and the PAM data. Both data sources show a sharp decrease in crop areas between 1985 and 1995/1996, so the change in reference period seems not likely to be the only explanation for the large drop in crop area observed in the Agricultural Census data. However, the decrease for the census data is larger than the decrease for the PAM data, so the change in reference period may exaggerate the actual decrease somewhat.

If the problem of undercounting is spread randomly across the municipalities of Legal Amazonia, it should not affect our econometric results in chapter 6, as the coefficient estimates are based on the variation across municipalities, not variations over time.[2] However, in analyses where the aggregate level of clearing is important, such as in the estimation of carbon emissions in chapter 7, undercounting in 1995/1996 could seriously bias the estimates downwards. For that reason, we use data until 1985

[2] Only the constant terms would be affected, and we are not trying to interpret that. In our simulations the constant terms will cancel out, as we always compare different scenarios rather than attempt to make forecasts.

only in chapter 7, while in our econometric model we also use data from 1995/1996.

Socio-economic dimensions

Apart from land clearing we have eight other important variables that we try to model endogenously. These are the growth of rural and urban populations, the growth of rural and urban GDP, the growth of the cattle herd, the growth of land prices, and the growth of the network of paved and unpaved roads. We will discuss these in turn.

Demographic variables

Rural and urban populations are derived from the Brazilian Demographic Census for 1970, 1980, and 1991. The population values for 1975 and 1985 are estimated by interpolation. For 1996 the data come from a small mid-decade Demographic Census that IBGE conducted, together with the Agricultural Census.

Owing to massive inmigration, the total population of Legal Amazonia has increased dramatically over time from about 7.3 million in 1970 to 17.8 million in 1996. The average population density remains very low, however, at only 3.6 persons per km^2. Since most of the population (61 percent) is concentrated in urban conglomerations, vast areas of Legal Amazonia are still extremely thinly populated. Figure 3.2 shows that as late as 1996, 70 percent of the Legal Amazon territory had a rural

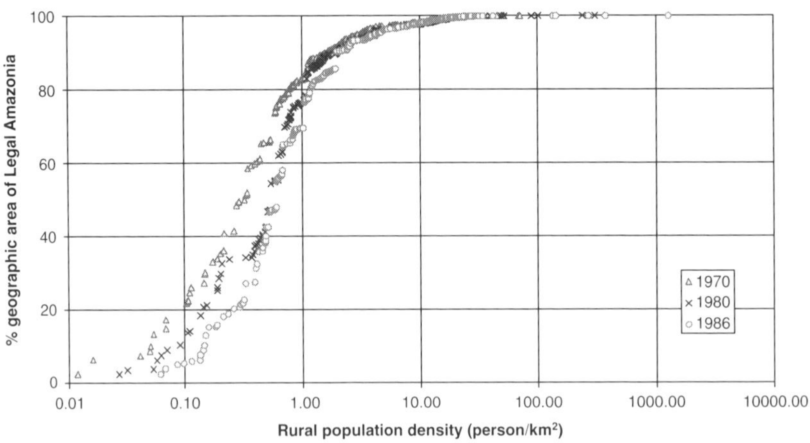

Figure 3.2 Rural population densities in the municipalities of Legal Amazonia, 1970, 1980, and 1996

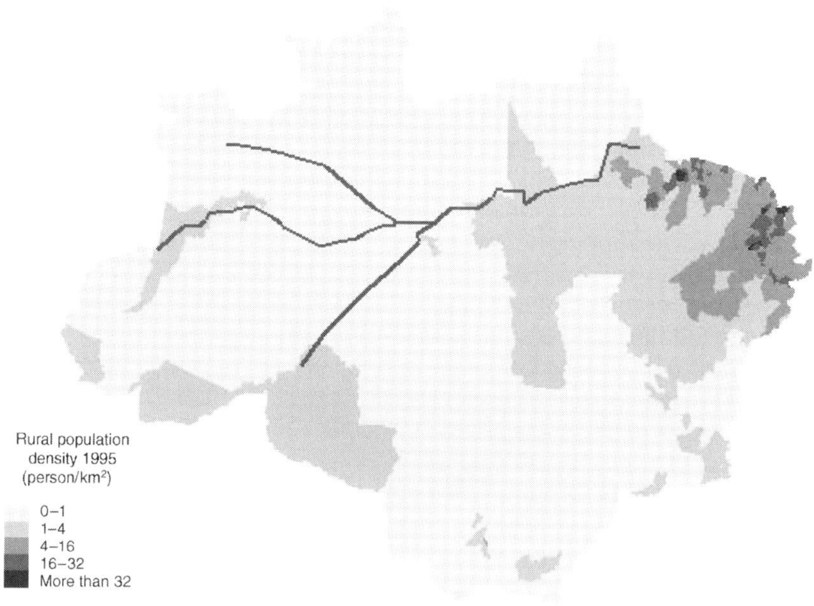

Figure 3.3 Rural population densities in the municipalities of Legal Amazonia, 1995
Source: BCE.

population density of less than 1 person per km^2. Only a few percent of the area has a rural population density of more than 10 persons per km^2, which was the average rural population density in the neighboring Northeast region of Brazil in 2000. The rural population is mainly concentrated in the old frontier areas of northern Pará and Maranhão (see figure 3.3). The rest of the region still has extremely low rural population densities.

While the average growth rate of the rural population only was a modest 1.7 percent per year between 1970 and 1995, some municipalities have experienced explosive growth. Figure 3.4 shows that Rondônia, the northern part of Mato Grosso and the southern part of Pará experienced average annual rural population growth rates in excess of 5 percent over the twenty-five-year period from 1970 to 1995. Many municipalities in Maranhão and Tocantins actually experienced negative rural population growth rates during that period. Presumably, many of the farmers who were at the border of the region in 1970 have moved further into the forest, contributing to the high rural population growth rates observed at the more recent agricultural frontier going through Rondônia, northern Mato Grosso, and southern Pará. Many of them, however, have

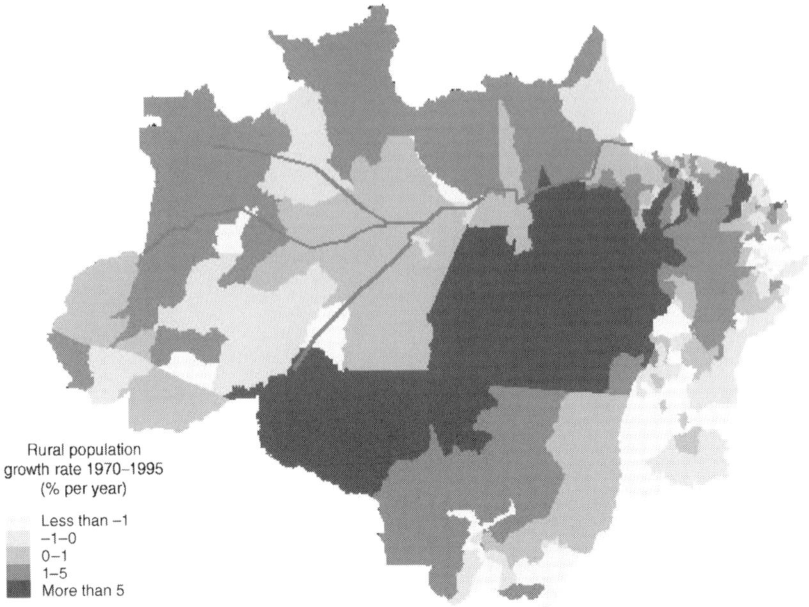

Figure 3.4 Average annual growth rates of rural population in Legal Amazonia, 1970–1995
Source: BCE.

also contributed to the rapid growth of the urban population in the region.

The urban population increased much more rapidly than the rural population, from 2.7 million in 1970 to 10.8 million in 1996, corresponding to an average annual growth rate of 5.7 percent. The big urban centers in Legal Amazonia are Belém with a current population of 1.9 million in the state of Pará at the mouth of the Amazon river, Manaus with 1.5 million inhabitants in the state of Amazonas, and São Luís with 1.1 million inhabitants in the state of Maranhão.[3] Cuiabá, the capital of Mato Grosso state, has around 800,000 inhabitants, while all remaining cities in the region have fewer than half a million inhabitants.

GDP

IPEA/NEMESIS has estimated valued added at the municipal level for main economic activities: Industry, Agriculture, Trade, Transportation, Communication, and Energy in 1970, 1975, 1980, 1985, and 1996 using data mainly from the Economic Censuses of IBGE, but complemented

[3] *The World Gazetteer, 2001* (http://www.gazetteer.de/st/statn.htm).

by data from the Demographic Census of 1970, 1980, and 1996 and the Annual Survey of Households – PNAD. "Value added" is defined as the value of output minus the value paid for intermediate consumption. For some municipalities this can actually be negative, potential reasons being crop failure, prices below expectations, industrial units that sell at non-market (transfer) prices to other establishments, etc. The problem of negative values is not restricted to the municipal level though it is more likely the lower the level of geographic disaggregation (or temporal disaggregation, for that matter; for instance, in 1999. Q1 value added in Brazilian agriculture as a whole was negative owing to the large exchange rate devaluation).

For each main economic activity and each state, municipal estimates of value added are added up to calculate the share of each municipality in the state. The System of National Accounts (SNA) presents estimates of Gross Value Added at Basic Prices (GVABP; before 1985 this was known as GDP at factor cost) at state level for the Census years 1970, 1975, 1980, and 1985–1999. Multiplying the share by the SNA estimates of GVABP we then calculate the value of GVABP for the municipalities for the years 1970, 1975, 1980, 1985, and 1996. Figures are therefore consistent with figures for Brazilian GVABP at state and national level. We define rural GDP as agricultural GDP, while urban GDP consists of GDP from industry, commerce, the service sector, and the government sector.

All values have been converted into 1995-Reais using the Implicit GDP Deflator used in the SNA, together with information about all the currency changes during the period. Since the exchange rate in 1995 was US$1 = 1 Real, all numbers can be interpreted as fixed 1995-US$.

Table 3.7 shows that average rural GDP *per capita* grew steadily between 1970 and 1995. By 1995 it had reached US$1,417 per person, but with substantial variation across states. Mato Grosso, which is the foremost cattle ranching state in Legal Amazonia, was blessed with a substantially higher average of US$4,311 per person.

Urban GDP *per capita* has generally been substantially higher than rural GDP *per capita*, but during the 1985–1995 period most states saw their urban *per capita* GDP drop substantially (see table 3.8). Manaus enjoyed unusually high *per capita* income in the 1980s owing to the Manaus Free Zone (MFZ, see below), but with the reduction of import barriers owing to general structural reforms, Manaus lost its relative advantage within Brazil, and *per capita* incomes decreased by almost 50 percent between 1985 and 1995.

Between 1970 and 1985, rural GDP increased from US$1.61 billion to US$5.22 billion (expressed in fixed 1995-US$). This represents an average annual growth rate of 8.2 percent in real terms. Owing to the

Table 3.7. *Rural GDP* per capita, *by year and state, 1970–1995 (in 1995-US$)*

State	1970	1975	1980	1985	1995
Acre	547	492	760	894	1,089
Amapá	294	404	673	817	2,467
Amazonas	488	554	726	1,145	1,280
Goiás	298	483	763	973	1,846
Maranhão	270	376	434	404	509
Mato Grosso	424	629	1,307	1,202	4,311
Pará	356	473	784	909	1,436
Rondônia	712	755	832	1,139	2,304
Roraima	785	1,126	1,121	1,102	202
Total	350	467	688	786	1,417

Source: IBGE Agricultural Censuses.

Table 3.8. *Urban GDP* per capita, *by year and state, 1970–1995 (in 1995-US$)*

State	1970	1975	1980	1985	1995
Acre	2,385	1,695	2,900	3,020	4,089
Amapá	2,936	1,922	2,985	3,264	3,232
Amazonas	2,342	3,277	5,219	5,221	3,864
Goiás	811	1,180	1,478	933	864
Maranhão	1,211	1,464	2,112	2,714	2,135
Mato Grosso	1,354	2,719	3,100	3,685	3,157
Pará	1,506	1,902	3,277	3,662	3,684
Rondônia	2,474	2,284	4,234	5,470	4,170
Roraima	2,283	2,275	3,049	3,348	4,267
Total	1,587	2,075	3,239	3,629	3,151

Source: IBGE.

corresponding rapid population growth, the real annual growth rate of rural *per capita* incomes was somewhat lower, but still an impressive 5.4 percent. Urban GDP grew even more dramatically, from US$4.24 billion in 1970 to US$23.71 billion in 1985, corresponding to an average annual growth rate of 12.1 percent in real terms, or 5.7 percent in real *per capita* terms. After 1985 both rural and urban GDP growth slowed considerably. Between 1985 and 1995 the growth rate of rural GDP averaged 6.6 percent per year, while urban GDP growth had decreased to 3.6 percent and was falling in *per capita* terms. Industry was by far the leading sector in the boom of the Legal Amazonian economy. The share of industry in the economy increased from 15 percent in 1970 to more than 40 percent in 1980. With the exception of the MFZ, which temporarily encouraged a flourishing electronics industry in the heart of the Amazon, the industrial activities in the Amazon are closely linked to local agriculture and extractivism.

Pará, with its many mineral and timber processing companies, is the state that contributes most to industrial output in Legal Amazonia. Pará accounted for almost 90 percent of international exports from Legal Amazonia in 1995 (Maia Gomes and Vergolino 1997). Examples of industrial activities in Pará include the aluminium processing complex Albrás-Alunorte in the municipality Barcarena, the bauxite mining complex run by Companhia Mineração Rio do Norte in the municipality Oriximiná, a Mineral Water plant run by Indaiá, as well as iron, copper and gold mining and processing plants run by CVRD (Maia Gomes and Vergolino 1997). In addition to mineral processing plants, there are hundreds of timber processing facilities spread across the state and numerous food processing plants near the urban centers.

Manaus, the capital of the state of Amazonas, is another industrial center in Legal Amazonia. This status is mainly owing to the implementation of the MFZ, which was set up to promote the production of durable goods (electronics, motorcycles, etc.) as a substitute for imports. Because of the favorable tax conditions, many large companies moved their plants to Manaus, where the price level for appliances and food quickly dropped to 30–40 percent below those charged in Rio de Janeiro and São Paolo. The MFZ thus generated considerable employment opportunities for the local population and spurred rural–urban migration (Rivas 1998). The MFZ has suffered severely from the general reduction in import protection in Brazil, however, and the industry in Manaus contracted substantially during the 1990s. Urban GDP in the Amazonas state fell by 16 percent between 1985 and 1995, while it kept increasing in most other states.

The industry in the remaining Amazonian states are mainly oriented towards servicing local urban markets and markets in central and southern Brazil. The paving of highways connecting Maranhão, Tocantins, Mato Grosso, Rondônia, and Acre to the heart of Brazil has facilitated a dramatic increase in inter-regional exports. Exports from the North region to the rest of Brazil increased at an impressive annual rate of 20 percent in real terms between 1961 and 1991. In 1991 the value of inter-regional exports from the North region amounted to US$6.2 billion, while international exports amounted to only 1.3 billion (Maia Gomes and Vergolino 1997).

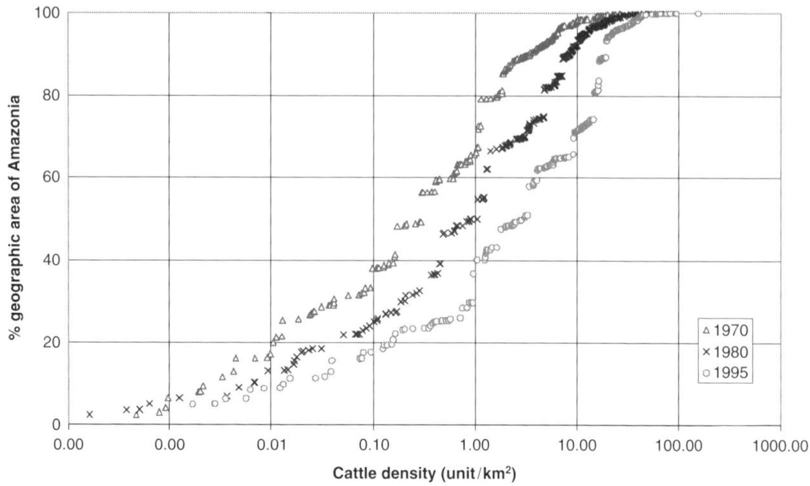

Figure 3.5 Cattle densities in the municipalities of Legal Amazonia, 1970, 1980, and 1995

Industrial activities thus include food processing and timber processing which mainly serve local and regional markets, and mineral processing, the output of which mainly goes to Europe. All of these activities contribute to urban GDP growth, but depend on inputs from the rural sector. There is thus a strong link between rural development and urban development in the Amazon, and the impressive growth of industry in the Amazon would not have been possible without simultaneous developments in the rural sector and without the improvements in infrastructure. The expansion of the rural sector, on the other hand, has also been highly dependent on the expansion of urban demand, which implies that the links between the rural and the urban sector go both ways.

Cattle herd

Information on the size of the cattle herd in each of the Amazonian municipalities is also derived from the IBGE Agricultural Censuses. The total herd grew from 6.5 million in 1970 to 36 million in 1995, at an average annual rate of 7.1 percent (figure 3.5). In terms of density, however, cattle still remain very scattered. Only one tiny municipality in Tocantins has an average of more than 1 piece of cattle per hectare. More than 70 percent of the Legal Amazonian territory has less than 10 cattle per km^2. Mato Grosso, with its extensive natural savannahs, is home to 40 percent of all the cattle in Legal Amazonia.

Land prices

The price of land is a very important variable, because land price influences land use. If land is relatively inexpensive, farmers will tend to use land-extensive agricultural methods such as slash-and-burn cycles with long fallow periods. If land is relatively more expensive, on the other hand, land-intensive farming, such as perennial cropping, becomes more attractive. We have obtained land price data at municipality level for the years 1970, 1975, 1980, 1985, and 1995 from both IBGE Agricultural Censuses of 1970–1985 and from Fundação Getulio Vargas for the years 1985 and 1995.

Road building

Prior to the early 1960s access to the Amazon was severely restricted by the lack of roads and infrastructure, leaving the rainforest essentially undisturbed. From the government's perspective, therefore, the first step for successful occupation and development of the region was to construct a road network, preferably one that was passable throughout the year. The proposed road network was based on a few major axial roads: (1) the 1,900 km Belém–Brasília highway running north–south through Pará, Maranhão, and Goiás; (2) the 1,500 km Cuiabá–Pôrto Velho highway running north-east through southern Mato Grosso and Rôndonia; (3) the 2,300 km Transamazônica highway running east–west through the whole region from the North-eastern part of Brazil to Peru; (4) the 1,000 km Pôrto Velho–Manaus highway running north–south through Roraima, Amazonas, and Rondônia, and (5) the 1,800 km Cuiabá–Santarem highway running south–north through Mato Grosso and Pará (see figure 2.1, p. 12).

Alves (1999, 2002) shows that 33 percent of deforestation between 1991 and 1995 took place within 50 km of the eastern road network linking central Brazil to Pará and Maranhão; 24 percent took place within 50 km of the central road network including the Cuiabá–Santarém and Transamazon highways and roads northern-central Mato Grosso; and 17 percent occurred within 50 km of the western road network including the Cuiabá–Porto Velho–Rio Branco road link. Thus, 74 percent of all deforestation between 1991 and 1995 took place within 50 km of a main road.

To model the effects of roads, we obtained municipality-level data on paved and unpaved state and federal roads from 1976, 1985, and 1995[4] road maps from the Ministry of Transportation.

[4] The 1995 data were estimated at municipality level by Newton Rabello de Castro.

Table 3.9. *Road building in Legal Amazonia, by type and state, 1960–1995*

State	Federal share (%)	State share (%)	Municipal share (%)	Total roads (km)
Acre	51	14	34	2,053
Amapá	28	30	42	1,603
Amazonas	42	14	45	5,728
Goiás/Tocantins	7	28	65	24,270
Maranhão	4	9	88	50,568
Mato Grosso	0	20	81	74,356
Pará	10	16	74	32,056
Rondônia	6	19	75	21,849
Roraima	24	35	41	4,788
Total	6	18	76	217,271

Sources: Anuário Estatístico dos Transportes; GEIPOT.

For farmers and travellers in the Amazon it makes a big difference whether roads are paved or unpaved. Paved roads provide reliable and relatively rapid access to markets all year around, while unpaved roads provide a quite unpredictable throughfare, with long delays to be expected owing to trucks being stuck in the mud and blocking the road.

From an econometric modeling point of view it also makes a big difference whether the roads are constructed by federal or state governments or whether they are constructed by the local municipalities. The roads constructed by federal and state authorities are more likely to be exogenous, in the sense that their location has little relation to the location of previous clearing. Roads built by local municipalities, on the other hand, are more likely to be endogenous since their construction is a result of demand from local farmers. Municipalities do not construct roads in the same grand way that federal and state governments do. Federal roads are typically meant to create new opportunities in previously underdeveloped areas, whereas municipal roads are meant to satisfy local demand for infrastructure. This is seen from table 3.9, which shows that the share of municipal roads is much larger in old frontier states like Pará and Maranhão and in very dynamic states like Mato Grosso and Rondônia. In the more remote and unsettled states, like Acre, Amazonas, Amapá, and Roraima, on the other hand, federal and state roads account for the majority of all roads.

Since the major axial roads mentioned above were centrally planned without much regard for topography, soil quality, or local demand for

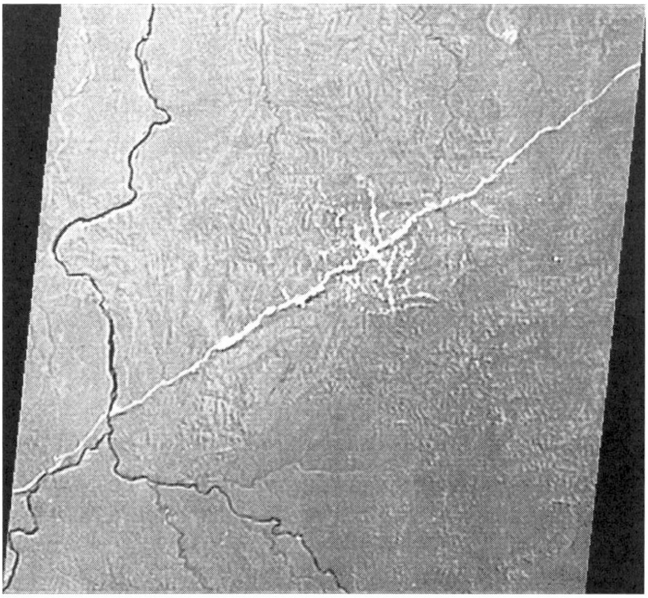

Figure 3.6 LANDSAT satellite image from 1991 of a piece of the Transamazônica highway
Source: INPE.

infrastructure, the impacts were quite mixed. Some of these roads (e.g. the Transamazônica) had a relatively small effect on development. Figure 3.6 shows a 1991 satellite image[5] of a stretch of the Transamazônica highway in the state of Amazonia. As can be seen, very little settlement or land clearing had occurred around the highway, despite the ambitious settlement programs that accompanied it.

However, other roads such as the Cuiabá–Pôrto Velho highway attracted and channeled large numbers of migrants through the region and thus had a much larger impact on population dynamics and land clearing. In 1960 there were only about 70,000 people living in Rondônia, mostly itinerant rubber tappers and prospectors, and the rainforest remained virtually intact (Mahar 1989). When the 1,500 km-long highway connecting Rondônia with the South was completed in 1968, however, a veritable explosion of inward migration occurred. Along the highway route INCRA had established seven colonization projects covering 2.7 million hectares; settlers were entitled to 100 hectare plots at little or

[5] *Source*: INPE at http://www.inpe.br/grid/quick-looks (22 August 1996).

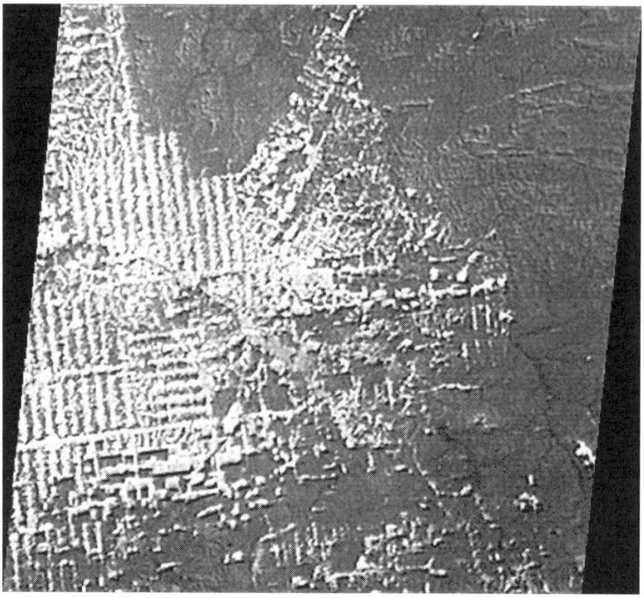

Figure 3.7 LANDSAT satellite image from 1991 of deforestation in Rondônia along the Cuiabá–Pôrto Velho highway
Source: INPE.

no cost (Mahar 1989). Demand for the plots quickly exceeded supply, and many migrants grabbed land outside the official projects, encroaching into indigenous reserves, forest reserves, or stealing from each other. As a result by 1996 the population had exceeded 1.2 million. This uncontrolled settlement had devastating effects on the rainforest, as illustrated in figure 3.7.

Despite the initial boldness of construction in Legal Amazonia, even state and federal road building have over time become a more endogenous process responding to local demand. This means that it becomes increasingly difficult to say whether roads cause deforestation or deforestation causes roads. To address this problem we model both paved and unpaved roads[6] endogenously in chapter 6.

In order to assess the quality of our road data we aggregate paved and unpaved roads to the state level and compare with GEIPOT data on federal and state roads at the state level. The result is shown in tables 3.10 and 3.11.

[6] Federal and state roads only, as we do not have municipal road information at the municipality level.

Table 3.10. *Comparing estimates of paved federal and state roads, 1975–1995*

State	1975	1980 (km)	1985	1995
DESMAT				
Acre	92	142	203	484
Amapá	0	58	131	182
Amazonas	1,076	1,422	1,855	1,125
Goiás/Tocantins	1,098	1,067	1,028	1,313
Maranhão	1,488	2,016	2,675	3,053
Mato Grosso	597	1,537	2,711	3,804
Pará	908	1,558	2,372	2,878
Rondônia	15	430	948	1,340
Roraima	0	18	40	58
Total	5,274	8,248	11,963	14,237
GEIPOT				
Acre	14	151	224	315
Amapá	0	20	111	201
Amazonas	1,021	1,187	1,241	634
Goiás/Tocantins	—	—	—	1,274
Maranhão	1,602	2,385	2,833	4,004
Mato Grosso	1,662	838	2,667	3,904
Pará	1,923	2,122	2,379	3,098
Rondônia	29	119	735	1,392
Roraima	0	26	40	350
Total	6,251	6,848	10,230	15,172

Sources: DESMAT data set and *Anuário Estatístico dos Transportes*; GEIPOT.

While the correlation at state level is 0.95 for paved roads and 0.83 for unpaved roads, there are quite big discrepancies between the two data sets. Both paved and unpaved roads (state and federal) in Mato Grosso, for example, increase dramatically between 1975 and 1980 according to the DESMAT data set, whereas they fall dramatically according to GEIPOT data. This is at least partly because the 1975 data from GEIPOT includes roads outside the present Mato Grosso, since Mato Grosso do Sul split away from Mato Grosso in 1978. As a result the roads in our data set are more comparable over time. In addition, our data set includes fewer roads in Maranhão than the GEIPOT data set, since only part of Maranhão belongs to Legal Amazonia, and we are only interested in that part.

Data on the municipal network of rivers (with more than 2.1 m of depth at least 90 percent of the time) were estimated from maps available in the *1985 Portobrás Statistical Yearbook*.

Table 3.11. *Comparing estimates of unpaved federal and state roads, 1975–1995*

State	1975	1980 (km)	1985	1995
DESMAT				
Acre	500	881	1,357	1,172
Amapá	1,515	1,345	1,132	1,065
Amazonas	1,812	1,801	1,787	1,833
Goiás/Tocantins	3,435	5,066	7,106	8,200
Maranhão	3,408	4,167	5,115	3,953
Mato Grosso	6,293	11,333	17,633	16,460
Pará	4,012	5,574	7,526	7,332
Rondônia	1,606	1,798	2,037	2,078
Roraima	1,569	2,131	2,835	2,754
Total	24,150	34,096	46,528	44,847
GEIPOT				
Acre	1,100	1,174	1,150	1,178
Amapá	907	1,124	1,507	1,116
Amazonas	1,779	1,722	1,706	2,716
Goiás/Tocantins	—	—	—	7,197
Maranhão	4,695	4,308	2,716	4,010
Mato Grosso	20,229	12,709	12,780	18,188
Pará	6,031	7,632	7,120	6,928
Rondônia	1,240	2,176	1,555	4,624
Roraima	1,088	2,225	3,161	2,519
Total	37,069	33,070	31,695	48,476

Sources: DESMAT data set and *Anuário Estatístico dos Transportes*; GEIPOT.

In addition to the extent of roads and rivers, we also use the distance between the administrative center of each municipality and the state and federal capitals as proxies for access conditions to local and national markets.

Subsidized credit

Since the initiation of the National System of Rural Credit in 1964, Brazilian agriculture has enjoyed exceptionally favorable credit conditions compared to the non-agricultural sector. In fact, before the economic crisis of the early 1980s subsidized rural credit was the main instrument used to promote agricultural modernization. From the early to mid-1980s onwards, however, the rural credit supply declined dramatically, falling from US$26.8 billion in 1979 to US$6.1 billion in 1991 (FAO 1994).

Rural credit in the Amazon has always been controversial, especially with regard to both the quantity and distribution of the credit supplied.

Early in the program credit lines were extended at fixed rates, and thus the subsidy element of each loan varied with the rate of inflation. As inflation accelerated in the 1970s, the subsidy element of the credit became very large. From 1970 to 1986 real interest rates on these loans were actually negative (see figure 4.1, p. 76) and as demand (understandably) increased the volume of credit supplied ballooned upwards to unsustainable levels. In the mid-1980s efforts were made to rein in these subsidies and interest rates became indexed to inflation, and since 1987 real interest rates have been positive.

To model the effect of credit on deforestation and development in the Amazon, we obtained financial data on the projects approved by SUDAM in the period 1967–1985. For each MCA we have the area in SUDAM-approved establishments in 1985 as well as the accumulated credit obtained through SUDAM until 1985. In addition, we have the total amount of credit extended to each municipality in 1995.

Logging

Data on logs and firewood collected also come from the Agricultural Censuses. However, given the nomadic and transient character of vegetal extractivist activities, a significant proportion of wood extraction is not counted. The Agricultural Censuses include only agricultural establishments that can be identified through the land they occupy, and thus many "wild cat" loggers will therefore necessarily be excluded. This is clear when comparing Agricultural Census data with that from the Annual Survey of Vegetal Extraction Production (PEV), also conducted by IBGE. The PEV data show an increase in production of logs from 7 million m^3 in 1975 to 52 million m^3 in 1995, which is a much sharper increase than the Agricultural Census data indicate. Unfortunately the PEV data are not available at municipality level and thus cannot be incorporated into our analysis. The PEV data have the further disadvantage that they are not based on a primary survey, but rather on "best guesses" from local experts.

Given the weakness of our logging data, we should therefore be very cautious in interpreting any results.

Geo-ecological dimensions

Soil quality, rainfall, and temperature

Studies by Chomitz and Thomas (2000) and Schneider *et al.* (2000) indicate that too much rainfall is a serious limitation to agricultural activities in most parts of the Amazon. Areas where annual rainfall exceeds 2,200 mm typically have more pests, diseases, and weeds, lower annual

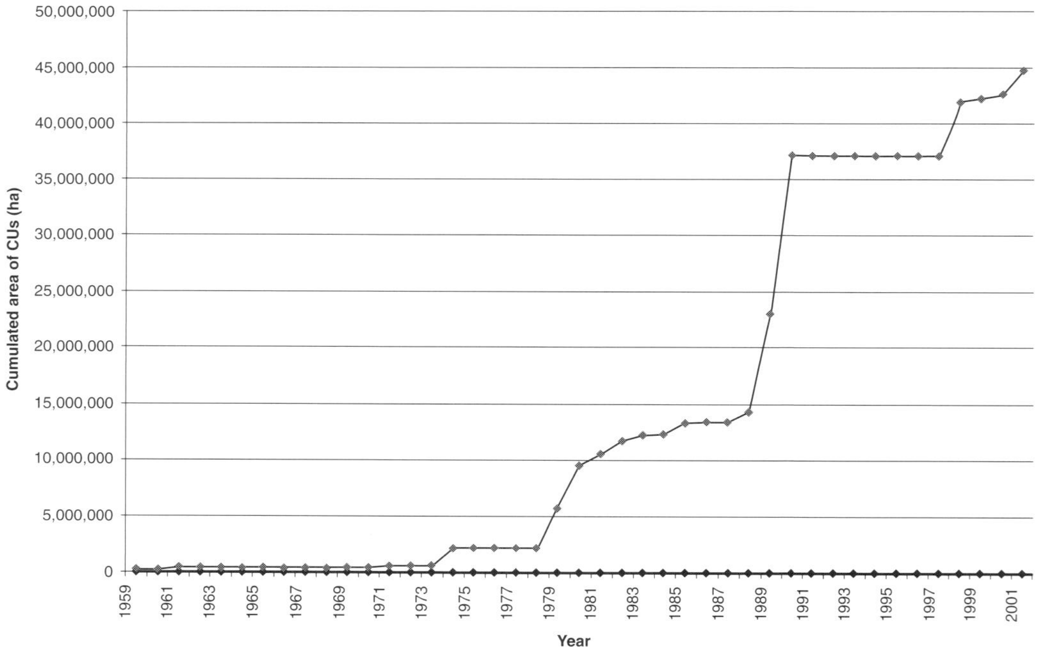

Figure 3.8 Cumulated Area of CUs created in Legal Amazonia, 1959–2001
Sources: FUNATURA (1992) and IBAMA's homepage: http://www2.ibama.gov.br/unidades/geralucs/tabl.htm.

crop yields, and higher transportation costs. That is one reason why farmers have cleared only 3 percent of the humid Amazon for crops or livestock, compared to 38 percent of the drier areas. It also helps explain why land-owners have already abandoned one-fifth of their agricultural land in the regions with higher rainfall, but only one-twelfth of such land in the drier regions.

To capture the effect of rainfall on clearing and agricultural output we use a dummy for the municipalities that receive more than average rainfall annually. This dummy was generated based on detailed seasonal rainfall data from IBGE.

Allowing for the possibility that high temperatures may have a similarly negative effect on agriculture in the Amazon, we include average temperatures in March, June, September, and December, obtained from IBGE.

Detailed data on soil quality was also obtained from the Agricultural Censuses. The first level of stratification divides the soils into high, average, and low yields. Each of these strata is then divided according to the drainage conditions. This report uses the share of high-yield soil as a proxy for soil quality in each municipality.

Conservation Units and Indigenous Reserves

The extension of Conservation Units (CUs – parks, ecological reserves, biological reserves, forest reserves, and extractive reserves) and indigenous reserves (IRs) were estimated for each municipality in 1991, based on information from the Brazilian Institute for the Environment and Renewable Resources (IBAMA) and the National Indian Institute for Research in the Amazon (FUNAI).

The first National Park in Legal Amazonia was created in 1959 in Goiás. Figure 3.8 shows that the creation of CUs has been very uneven since then. The big booms in CU creation took place in 1979–1980 (7.5 million hectares) and 1989–1990 (22.8 million hectares).

The CUs come in fourteen different types. By 1991 there were twelve National Parks, eight Federal Biological Reserves, twelve Federal Ecological Stations, twenty-four National Forests, four Federal Extractivist Reserves, one Environmental Protection Area, three Federal Ecological Reserves, nine State Parks, three State Biological Reserves, three State Ecological Stations, eleven State Forests, three State Extractivist Forests, six State Environmental Protection Areas, and one State Ecological Reserve.

Indigenous Reserves (IRs) covered more than twice the area of CUs by 1991, but the restrictions on land use are less severe. In fact, the residents

Table 3.12. *CUs and IRs in Legal Amazonia, 1992*

State	CUs (km^2)	IRs (km^2)
Acre	23,327	16,796
Amapá	19,707	10,136
Amazonas	169,514	311,755
Goiás/Tocantins	5,623	20,262
Maranhão	10,447	18,510
Mato Grosso	4,160	123,844
Pará	31,570	211,782
Rondônia	62,576	27,752
Roraima	32,492	28,486
Total	359,416	769,323

Source: FUNATURA (1992, table 15).

of IRs are exempted from the laws that govern other Brazilian residents and they can therefore do as they please with their land.

Table 3.12 presents evidence on the distribution of CUs and IRs in the Amazon region.

Neighbor/spatial variables

Deforestation maps based on satellite pictures clearly show that clearing is not randomly distributed across the region but rather that deforestation appear to grow inertially around areas of pioneer deforestation. Alves (1999, 2002) shows that 86 percent of observed deforestation between 1991 and 1995 was found within 25 km of areas that were already deforested by 1978. This phenomenon arises because most new clearing takes place on a moving agricultural frontier. Ahead of the frontier there is little economic activity and thus little clearing. On the frontier, there is rapid clearing and a quickly emerging economy, while the area behind the frontier is characterized by a high level of clearing, a more mature economy, but less new clearing.

To capture this "frontier effect" in our econometric models, we introduce neighbor variables describing conditions in neighboring municipalities. If a particular municipality is surrounded by municipalities experiencing high rates of clearing, we would expect this municipality to show clearing rates over and above the rates that would be indicated just from population, market access, and other relevant indicators for that municipality.

The variable measuring the level of clearing in neighboring municipalities is constructed as a weighted average of the proportion of cleared land in the closest five municipalities. The weights are inversely proportional to the distance between municipality centers and scaled to sum to one. Similar neighbor variables are created to indicate the population situation, the income situation, the land price situation, and the road conditions in neighboring municipalities.

4 The sources and agents of deforestation

> Suzuki (1990) has condensed these many causes into three emotive words: ignorance, injustice and greed.
>
> (Brown and Brown 1992)

> Deforestation is not an evil plot, it is something we do on purpose in order to feed and house the 6 billion and growing human population.
>
> (Patrick Moore 2000)

In the 1970s 97 percent of Legal Amazonia was undisturbed and another 2 percent were fallow lands in the process of forest regeneration. Only about 1 percent of the area was being used actively for crops and planted pastures (see table 4.1). This has changed, but not as dramatically as many people have been led to believe. By 1995, less than 15 percent of the total area had been transformed from its original natural state.

Land-use in the Amazon is far from static. There are several different possible cycles depending on the remoteness of the plot, the quality of soils, the skills and resources of the farmer, and many other factors. In order to get a very general sense of the land-use transition patterns in Legal Amazonia, we categorize the land-use types into three main uses: crop land, fallow land, and planted pasture, and examine the probability that land allocated to one of these three uses will transition into a different use in the next five-year period. As we do not have data on the specific fate of any particular plot within each municipality, this is accomplished by estimating a land-use transition model. We define "uncleared" land as public land, private planted forest, private virgin forest, and private natural pasture. "Cleared" land is divided between crop land, planted pasture, and fallow land. Since this is a closed system, crop land in each period must come from one of four sources: newly cleared land, crop land from the previous period, fallow land from the previous period, or pasture land from the previous period. The same is true for fallow and pasture land.

Table 4.1. *Changes in agricultural land-use, 1970–1995 (km^2)*

	1970	1975	1980	1985	1995
Uncleared area	**4,924,208**	**4,869,378**	**4,756,939**	**4,686,285**	**4,589,645**
Public area	4,458,682	4,289,836	4,036,615	3,921,855	3,869,618
Reserves	—	—	—	924,927	1,128,739[a]
Private natural forest[b]	260,243	352,958	463,347	523,222	538,731
Private natural pasture	205,283	226,584	256,976	241,207	181,296
Cleared area	**151,246**	**206,076**	**318,515**	**389,169**	**485,809**
Annual crops area	15,095	25,994	43,544	50,153	46,659
Perennial crops area	1,970	3,447	7,810	9,344	9,419
Planted forest	643	1,159	2,529	2,060	3,459
Planted pasture	32,967	71,544	133,466	191,255	335,785
Short fallow	9,177	2,748	28,630	36,979	24,442
Long fallow	91,395	101,184	102,536	99,377	66,045
Total area	5,075,454	5,075,454	5,075,454	5,075,454	5,075,454

Notes: [a]Reserve areas are from 1991 based on information in FUNATURA (1992).
[b]Private non-usable land is counted together with private natural forest.
Source: IBGE Agricultural Censuses.

We define cleared land and the change in cleared land, *Dclear* as:

$$clear_{it} = crop_{it} + pasture_{it} + fallow_{it} \tag{4.1}$$

$$Dclear_{it} = clear_{it} - clear_{i,t-1} \tag{4.2}$$

We then write the land-use transition system as:

$$crop_{it} = \beta_1 Dclear_{it} + \beta_2 crop_{it} + \beta_3 pasture_{it} + \beta_4\, fallow_{it} \tag{4.3}$$

$$pasture_{it} = \psi_1 Dclear_{it} + \psi_2 crop_{it} + \psi_3 pasture_{it} + \psi_4\, fallow_{it} \tag{4.4}$$

$$fallow_{it} = \nu_1 Dclear_{it} + \nu_2 crop_{it} + \nu_3 pasture_{it} + \nu_4\, fallow_{it} \tag{4.5}$$

The closed nature of this system implies that $\beta_j + \psi_j + \nu_j = 1$ for $j = 1, 2, 3, 4$. The intuitive explanation for this property is that all cleared land in period $t-1$ must turn either into crop land, pasture land, or fallow land in the following period. Land cannot disappear, and it is assumed that land cannot grow back into virgin forest in such a short time period. Andersen *et al.* (1997) show that the coefficients will always sum exactly to one when the system is estimated by OLS and no restrictions are imposed on the model.

The system was estimated for the period 1970 through 1985.[1] Data from 1995 was not included as the transition period is ten, rather than

[1] See Andersen *et al.* (1997) for a detailed discussion of the estimation strategy.

Table 4.2. *Land-Use Transition Matrix, 1975–1985*

	Crop land	Pasture	Fallow land
Dclear	0.12	0.29	0.59
	(0.0061)	(0.0121)	(0.0126)
Crop (−1)	0.50	−0.05	0.55
	(0.0285)	(0.0570)	(0.0592)
Pasture (−1)	0.01	1.13	−0.14
	(−2.35)	(0.0154)	(0.0160)
Fallow (−1)	0.11	0.12	0.77
	(5.88)	(0.0144)	(0.0150)

Note: Standard errors are given in parentheses.
Source: Authors' estimations based on IBGE Agricultural Censuses.

five, years and since methodological changes in the Agricultural Census in that year could introduce too many uncertainties about consistent land-use measurement, possibly biasing the results (see the discussion in chapter 3). Since 1995 is omitted, we can use a less aggregated data set with 316 consistently defined municipalities and thus have a total of 948 observations.

To help interpretation of table 4.2, it is important to note that it should be read horizontally – that is, across rows, rather than vertically. Each row has to add to one and shows how land in one category in one period is transformed into other categories in the next period. Each type of land-use (crop, pasture, or fallow) in one year had to belong to one of these categories in the previous year, or come from cleared land (*Dclear*). Looking at the first row, it shows how newly cleared land ends up within a five-year period. Approximately 12 percent of newly cleared land ends up in crop land, 29 percent in pasture, and almost 60 percent in either short or long fallow. Crop land, on the other hand, has about 50 percent chance of remaining in crops five years later and 50 percent chance of being turned into fallow. Pasture tends to remain pasture. The numbers in the body of the table are easiest to interpret when they are positive. However, the values shown are estimated and so need not all turn out to be positive, either because of sampling variation or because of misrecording problems.

These transition probabilities are consistent with the well documented pattern of crop land often being left fallow after a few seasons owing to rapidly declining soil fertility.[2] Pasture land primarily remains as pasture, while about a quarter of fallow land undergoes transition to other uses;

[2] See Weinhold (1999) for more discussion of land degradation using this data set.

in particular to crop land (11 percent) and to pasture (12 percent). The results thus indicate that pasture is the "absorbing" land-use category.

Some care must be exercised before extrapolating these results into the future. During the sample period of this exercise both the design of property laws (see below) and government incentives created strong incentives to clear land for pasture, or to officially claim that land was in use as pasture even where it was actually left idle. Most of those government incentives have now been repealed and property rights laws have evolved over time. Furthermore, the incentives for more intensive use of land close to settled areas and within easy reach of urban markets have increased substantially since the mid-1980s. With luck the Brazilian government will resume regular Agricultural Censuses and future analyses can document any changes in these land-use transition patterns.

While the land-use transition exercise is informative as a descriptive (and, at this point, primarily historical) device, it cannot tell us about the rate of clearing, nor does it provide any explanation of why particular patterns are observed. In the remainder of this chapter we explore how deforestation in the Brazilian Amazon since the 1970s has resulted from a multiplicity of factors and actors, including road and railway construction, directed and spontaneous colonization, subsidized agropastoral projects, timber extraction, charcoal production, hydroelectric facilities, mining (both placer and corporate), and uncontrolled forest fires associated with human activities.

Owing to the intricate relationships among the various stages of the settlement process, it is very difficult to separate specific causes of deforestation. The complex dynamics of the process makes a rigorous identification of causes and consequences impossible. Slash-and-burn agriculture, because it precedes other activities, is usually identified as the "cause" of deforestation, even though, on many occasions, the *primum mobile* is the subsequent profitability of cattle raising. Analogously, in many regions, logging is a by-product of deforestation "caused" by agriculture, while quite often agricultural settlements become feasible owing to roads built for logging purposes. Finally, in a long-run perspective, even roads (and to an extent other government policies) are frequently induced by economic activity and population growth instead of "causing" it. Thus, it is safer to talk about sources rather than causes of deforestation.

The segregation of prime agents of deforestation in the Brazilian Amazon, as well as of their economic motivations and environmental consequences, are issues pervaded by controversy (Mahar 1979; Myers 1989; Binswanger 1991; Almeida 1992a; and Fearnside 1993, among others). Apart from insurmountable ideological and theoretical divergences, the settlement of disputes is impaired by the lack of empirical evidence on both deforestation and the related socio-economic processes and agents.

The main characters on the stage are the squatters and shifting cultivators raising subsistence crops in small farms with limited access to credit and fiscal subsidies, and opposed to them the large farms, specialized in commercial crops and cattle ranching, with plenty of official subsidies. Logging plays a small supporting role with growing importance in recent times. The appraisal of the contribution of each of them to deforestation is a crucial issue both to evaluate the social benefits and costs of this process and to find effective ways to control it.

This chapter presents empirical evidence on the main sources of deforestation, as well as on the major actors of this process. For this purpose, the Brazilian Agricultural Censuses from 1970 to 1995/1996 are used to identify the main sources of deforestation/clearing. The amount of cleared land is defined as the sum of the following land-use: crops (both annual and perennial), planted pasture, planted forest, and fallow lands (both short and long fallow). We assume that natural pastures, natural forests in farms, as well as areas under public domain are not cleared.

Cattle ranching

The dramatic growth of cattle herds in the Amazon has consistently been cited as one of the primary factors behind land clearing in the region. At the same time there is considerable controversy about the underlying causes of this growth, and correspondingly what the best policy response should be. One influential school of thought holds that cattle ranching is not economically profitable by itself *per se*, but that its growth is primarily owing to external forces such as government subsidies and land price patterns (e.g. Browder 1988; Hecht *et al.* 1988). More recently, however, a competing perspective has emerged arguing that, given the regional economic patterns in the Amazon, cattle ranching may very well be an economically rational activity (see, in particular, Faminow 1998). The implied policy prescriptions that arise from these two opposing viewpoints are obviously dramatically different, and thus this debate has become of paramount importance in the field.

There is no debate about the fact that cattle ranching, traditionally a socially prestigious activity in Latin America, has in the past received substantial government support. It is also true that despite the widespread condemnation of cattle ranching and sharp reductions in subsidies, the number of cattle in the Brazilian Amazon has continued to increase rapidly. In fact, the total herd in Legal Amazonia almost doubled from 19 million heads in 1985 to 36 million in 1995, as illustrated in table 4.3.

Table 4.3. *Cattle herd, by state and year, 1970–1995*

	Cattle herd (1,000)				
State	1970	1975	1980	1985	1995
Acre	72	120	292	334	847
Amapá	65	63	46	47	60
Amazonas	263	203	356	425	734
Goiás/Tocantins	1,545	2,579	3,440	4,118	5,929
Maranhão	1,252	1,571	2,548	2,973	3,619
Mato Grosso	1,958	3,110	5,243	6,546	14,438
Pará	1,044	1,442	2,730	3,479	6,080
Rondônia	23	55	251	771	3,937
Roraima	239	246	314	306	400
Total	6,461	9,390	15,220	18,999	36,045

Source: IBGE Agricultural Censuses.

With more than 40 percent of the total cattle herd, Mato Grosso is by far the most important cattle state in Legal Amazonia. This is, of course, owing to the vast areas of natural savannah and *cerrado* areas present in the southern part of this state. These *cerrado* areas have traditionally been considered marginal from an agricultural viewpoint and have thus principally been used for extensive cattle ranching. Recent advances in tropical soybean research and *cerrado* soil management, however, have introduced profitable alternatives, and cattle ranchers are increasingly seen to intensify by investing in better and more productive pastures for their cattle. While cattle grazed extensively on natural pastures typically take four–five years to reach slaughter size as they gain and lose weight through the annual weather cycle, cattle raised on improved pastures are taken to market in just eighteen months (Schuh 2001).

Over the sample period the number of cattle has grown at an average annual rate of 7.1 percent, much faster than the growth rate of private pasture. As a result the stocking intensity has increased steadily from an average of 27 cattle per km^2 in 1970 to 70 in 1995 (see table 4.4). This is still a relatively low intensity by national and international standards, which reflects the fact that land is generally not the scarce factor for farmers in the Amazon.

In the remainder of this section we will take a closer look at the claims that cattle ranching is primarily due to government subsidies and land speculation. In addition we go beyond these primary culprits to discuss a range of other reasons that Amazonian farmers might invest in cattle.

Table 4.4. *Cattle stocking intensity, 1970–1995*

	Number of cattle per km^2 of private pasture[a]				
State	1970	1975	1980	1985	1995
Acre	114	97	111	103	138
Amapá	21	18	24	10	24
Amazonas	109	106	90	89	139
Goiás/Tocantins	22	26	28	36	49
Maranhão	44	46	59	59	73
Mato Grosso	20	28	35	40	67
Pará	41	47	60	53	82
Rondônia	19	25	33	70	135
Roraima	21	18	20	25	26
Total	27	31	39	44	70

Note: [a]Private pasture includes both natural and planted pasture.
Source: IBGE Agricultural Censuses.

Government subsidies

The Superintendency for the Development of Amazonia (SUDAM) was the primary agency in charge of managing development incentives in the Amazon and they had a preference for cattle ranching projects, especially very large ones. Until March 1989, cattle ranches accounted for 58 percent of the total number of approved projects, mostly in Mato Grosso and Pará (Faminow 1998). Fiscal incentives came in the form of a tax credit of the amount of investment firms were willing to make in SUDAM-approved projects in the Amazon region. Subsidized credit was available from FINAM (Investment Fund for Amazonia) to ranchers and farmers who held titles or other land documents recognized by the credit institution, and the subsidy element in the credit was large. The real interest rate averaged ± 20 percent during the 1971–1986 period (Schneider 1992, p. 30). Tax incentives and other subsidies accounted for 72 percent of the funds invested in Amazonian cattle ranches in 1977 (Kohlhepp 1980, p. 71).

Not only the level of subsidized credit, but also the distribution of that credit drew criticism. Complex bureaucratic rules made it effectively impossible for less sophisticated rural farmers to even apply for many government loans. As a result, the major beneficiaries of subsidized credit were large scale and well-connected farmers (Reis and Blanco 1996b). These subsidies to the relatively wealthier sectors exacerbated the existing rural income inequality, and while a direct line of causality from these policies cannot be inferred, Hoffman (1988) shows that between 1970

Table 4.5. *Subsidies to cattle ranching until 1985*

State	Herd in SUDAM-approved ranches	Accumulated FINAM credit (1,000 1985-US$)
Acre	0	2,896
Amapá	1,618	7,890
Amazonas	15,416	6,759
Goiás/Tocantins	94,971	33,957
Maranhão	282,687	3,507
Mato Grosso	747,698	85,870
Pará	895,966	59,053
Rondônia	0	497
Roraima	5,008	2,724
Total	2,043,364	203,152

Source: SUDAM.

and 1980 the Gini index of rural income distribution for the nation went up from 0.415 to 0.543. In the early 1990s an attempt was made to address some of the distributional problems by offering lower real rates of interest to smaller producers: 9 percent versus 12 percent for large producers (FAO 1994).

The characteristics of the rural credit policy, including both the levels of credit offered and their distribution, have been cited as causing economically irrational deforestation in the Amazon (e.g. Browder 1985; Mahar 1989). However, when both the amount and the beneficial terms of rural credit decreased significantly after the early 1980s, deforestation did not slow down accordingly, raising some doubt about the importance of the credit policies in the first place. In addition, credit had been concentrated in only a few regions. During the 1970s, for example, only 20–25 percent of farmers had access to subsidized credit and less than 5 percent of the farmers received half of the total credit (World Bank 1989, quoted in Goldin and Rezende 1993, p. 25).

Rondônia was the state which experienced the most dramatic increase in the number of cattle (annual growth of 23 percent in Rondônia compared to 7 percent in all of Legal Amazonia), but it was at the same time the state which received the least amount of subsidies from FINAM and SUDAM. In 1985, none of Rondônia's 771,000 cattle were in SUDAM-approved ranches and Rondônia enjoyed less than 1 percent of the total FINAM credit extended to Legal Amazonia in 1985. Among all the states in Legal Amazonia in 1985 only about 2 million cattle were in SUDAM-approved ranches, while about 17 million were not (see table 4.5).

Moreover, the unsubsidized herd continued to grow, a trend which continues to this day.

In 1991 all fiscal incentives for cattle ranching in the Amazon forest were removed by presidential decree (Smith *et al.* 1995, p. 55). Thus, by 1995 there were 36 million cattle in Legal Amazonia enjoying little or no direct government subsidies. These facts make it difficult to blame fiscal incentives alone for the popularity of cattle ranching in the Amazon.

Land speculation

A second explanation for the growth of the herd posits that while cattle ranching itself is not economically productive, agriculturalists lay claim and clear land in order to accrue windfall profits down the road when the land is later resold for much higher prices. Cattle ranching is seen as a relatively inexpensive way to occupy the land in the meantime. As Faminow (1998, p. 137) remarks: "This viewpoint has been extremely influencial in focusing attention on the idea that cattle ranching is unprofitable and that gains from land speculation are a primary source of returns to cattle ranching." However, Wunder (2000) points out that the combination of falling productivity and increasing land prices is not possible in the long run. Financial land values must maintain a relation to the incomes that can be derived from their possession – they cannot be continuously delinked from the real economy.

Faminow (1998) traces the evidence behind the speculation story and finds that the only real underlying evidence is essentially anecdotal, with one data set from Mahar (1979) comparing land prices and inflation between 1966 and 1975. Later land price information indicates that land prices have generally remained stable or even fallen since the mid-1970s. Most importantly, returns to land in the Amazon were significantly lower than returns to land purchased elsewhere in Brazil. Faminow (1998, p. 139) concludes: "These data indicate that between 1970 and 1985 land speculation in the Amazon was a poor investment in general, but especially relative to land in the rest of Brazil."

The fact that we observe *ex post* lower systematic and predictable gains from land speculation in the Amazon than in the rest of Brazil does not necessarily preclude land speculation as a motive, however. Land price movements have varied greatly from place to place within the Amazon, the time span involved was relatively short, and information flows were far from complete. Some farmers did realize dramatic gains and speculators could have expected increasing land prices for some period, even if they never actually materialized.

Table 4.6 shows the land price developments by state in Legal Amazonia from 1970 to 1995. The table shows the tremendous variation

Table 4.6. *Land prices, by state and year, 1970–1995*

State	1970	1975	1980	1985	1995
Acre	21	63	46	72	48
Amapá	47	49	74	137	108
Amazonas	118	170	112	218	242
Goiás/Tocantins	33	162	239	309	—
Maranhão	55	130	363	454	382
Mato Grosso	55	271	302	598	290
Pará	109	216	253	295	109
Rondônia	19	222	209	679	340
Roraima	8	23	47	97	105
Average	73	173	271	365	294

Note: 1995 figures are derived from a limited sample of eighty-six municipalities.
Sources: IBGE and FGV.

in land-prices and their changes over time, and clearly there have been opportunities for large land price gains. In general, there were large gains to be reaped between 1970 and 1985, while the opportunities have been much more limited and less certain since then.

Land purchases may also have been used as a means to secure subsidized credit. In particular, land with a proper legal title or certificate of occupancy can be used as the collateral asset required to get access to credit. Thus, when credit terms become more favorable, the value of such titled land increases and the interest rate subsidies are therefore partly capitalized into land values. This relationship is illustrated in figure 4.1[3] which presents evidence on real land prices for crop land observed in June of each year together with the average real interest rates in loan contracts of rural credits for investment and production financing.

Figure 4.1 shows the strong relationship between land prices and interest rate subsidies. The fourfold increase in land prices in the 1970s is well explained by the negative real interest rates, booming exports, and high domestic demand for agricultural goods. The gradual demise of credit subsidies combined with high real interest rates and recession during the late 1980s then led to the decline of land prices. An econometric analysis of the relationship between credit subsidies and land prices provided by Brandão (1988) shows that, even when accounting for cyclical effects and support price policies, land prices are significantly related to the volume of credit per hectare.

[3] *Source:* Reis (1996, figure 3).

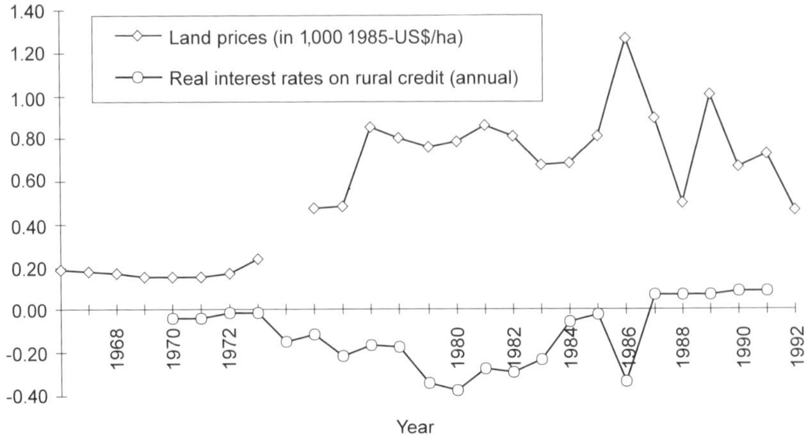

Figure 4.1 Land prices and interest rate subsidies in Legal Amazonia, 1968–1992

Other reasons for the expansion of cattle

Although land prices on average increased in Legal Amazonia, prices fell compared to land in the South. In 1970 you could buy roughly 2 hectares of land in the North for every hectare you sold in the South. By 1980 this ratio had increased to about 10 (Schneider 1992, tables 4.1–4.5). The dramatic increase in land prices in the South and Center-West was brought about by the introduction of soybeans, which allowed a big increase in land productivity. The effect of this change in relative land prices was to push land-extensive activities like cattle ranching away from the South and the Center-West towards the cheaper land in the Amazon.

While land-price dynamics acted to push cattle towards the Amazon, the expansion of local markets provided an important pull factor. The urban population in Legal Amazonia increased from 2.7 million in 1970 to 10.8 million in 1995 at almost the same rate as the cattle herd. The model we estimate econometrically in chapter 6 lends support to the hypothesis of urban demand being an important pull factor for cattle production. Both level and growth of urban GDP are strong in-sample predictors of future herd growth at the municipality level. In addition, we find that both level of roads and new road constructions (i.e. growth of roads, especially paved) are positively correlated with future herd growth. This is all consistent with the idea that local demand for cattle products is a driving force behind herd expansion.

The relative cost of serving the local versus international or national markets is also favorable towards cattle ranching. One of the advantages of selling meat and milk locally is that it does not require much marketing expertise or overhead costs. Exporting sustainably harvested chocolate-covered nuts to rich foreigners, on the other hand, requires a professional marketing and distribution organization.

There are numerous other reasons why cattle ranching is attractive to farmers in the Amazon. First, cattle are a highly liquid investment and can readily be sold when a crisis or opportunity occurs. Second, cattle can reach the market even when roads are impassable by trucks. Third, sales can be delayed without major losses. Fourth, the marginal costs of establishing pasture after cropping is low for small-holders. Fifth, ranching is a low-risk operation compared with crop farming. Sixth, cattle produce milk, skins, manure, and offspring as very useful by-products. Seventh, cattle are often a more secure and familiar investment than banks, whose interest rates do not always accompany inflation. And eighth, cattle raising is not labor-intensive, an important consideration in rural Amazonia where the shortage of labor is a perennial complaint (Smith *et al.* 1995, p. 162). The fact that cattle ranching is a prestigious activity, which brings social status and political influence, may also help tip the balance in favor of cattle ranching.

In sum, while government policies both directly and indirectly did contribute significantly to the growth of cattle ranching in the Amazon, the rise of urban centers and economic development throughout the region has been able to generate endogenous economic and social forces strong enough to sustain and promote cattle ranching even after the government incentives have been removed.

Small- and large-scale agriculture

After cattle ranching, annual crops (rice, maize, beans, potatoes, sugarcane, soybeans, manioc, corn, wheat, tobacco, and others) take up the second biggest share of cleared land; about 10 percent. They are primarily cultivated by small farmers who practice slash-and-burn agriculture: they burn a piece of forest and grow annual crops for one–three years until the nutrients from the ashes are used up or washed away. A fallow period of about ten years is then usually required before the land can be used for crops again (Toniolo and Uhl 1995). This fallow period is rarely applied, however. Since pasture land is typically two–three times more valuable than uncleared forest (Schneider 1992, p. 40), it is more profitable for the farmer to convert the land to pasture and sell it to a nearby cattle ranch. In that way he can both make a reasonable return on his annual crops in the initial period when fertility is high and the land relatively pest-free because of burning, as well as a capital gain from the sale of the land. The capital gain can then be reinvested in new forest and the cycle continued.

On average this procedure is quite profitable, but it is also risky. Often farmers are inexperienced in their new environment, and many farmers experience crop failure. Even if the farmer gets a good harvest he may have problems selling it at a reasonable price owing to the thin markets in frontier areas. He may also run into land-tenure conflicts owing to the unclear property rights situation at the frontier. While the area dedicated to annual crops increased rapidly during the 1970s, it stagnated during the 1980s and 1990s.

In contrast to slash-and-burn farming in the forested parts of Legal Amazonia, crop production in the *cerrado* areas of Legal Amazonia is increasingly being dominated by technically advanced, highly mechanized, and very profitable soybean production. While the *cerrado* soils suffer from low natural fertility owing to high acidity and low nutrient availability as well as several other chemical problems, Brazil's Agricultural Research System (EMBRAPA), especially the Cerrado Research Center, has been highly successful in finding feasible solutions to these problems. The simple application of lime and phosphorous typically increases the productivity of soils by four–five times (Schuh 2001). In addition to research on soil improvement, EMBRAPA has also worked on improving the varieties of soybeans and making them more adaptable to the *cerrado* soils. By 1981, Brazil had almost 1,000 researchers working on soybeans (Bojanic and Echverría 1990), making Brazil the world leader in soybean research. The interaction between the two breakthroughs has been very significant and soybean production in the Brazilian *cerrado* is widely held up as one of the success stories of tropical agricultural research (e.g. Lopes 1996; Schuh 2001).

Soybean production involves major economies of scale at both the sector level and at farm level. To produce soybeans competitively, a large and modern system of processing, transportation, storage, research, and marketing is needed. Subsidized credit programmes targeted at the *cerrado* area (POLOCENTRO – Program for the Development of the Cerrado) helped get farmers started on soybean production, and once the process had begun, the economies of scale in soybean production accelerated it (Kaimowitz and Smith 2001).

The significant economies of scale combined with private and public investment in improved waterways and port facilities in the Amazon, implies that soybeans from Mato Grosso are becoming very competitive at international markets, and Brazil is rapidly gaining market share from the traditional soy producers in the United States.

Perennial crops have been actively promoted by government extensions as the best agricultural alternative for the region (Schneider 1992, p. 52). These crops (cacao, coffee, black pepper, cotton, bananas, oranges, passion fruit, etc.) offer several advantages over annual crops. In particular, they are usually better adapted to the region and therefore less susceptible to pests. They are also often less perishable and therefore imply smaller losses induced by the generally inadequate transport and storage facilities available. Finally, the value of output per hectare is higher and sustainable over a longer period, and they protect the soil better against erosion.

However, for the typical small farmer who cares little about sustainability as long as new sources of inexpensive land remain abundant, perennial crops have several disadvantages relative to annual crops. First, the initial investment required is about ten times larger (Almeida and Uhl 1995). In addition it takes more than one season to get a positive return, and thus requires more commitment and carries even greater risk. Finally, contrary to basic annual staples like rice, beans, and corn you cannot live on them if the need arises. The area devoted to perennial crops increased rapidly between 1970 and 1985. Since then the area in perennial crops has remained stable at a little below 1 million hectares.

Silvicultural plantations (planted forest) are also being encouraged as an appropriate form of development for the Amazon region (Fearnside 1996, p. 31). Plantations could potentially supply most of the country's wood and paper needs from a much smaller area than would be the case if natural forest were used. The Jari project is the most famous silvicultural experiment, and also the largest with a concession of 1.6 million hectares. It has commonly been portrayed as a failure and an undesirable development model for the Amazon (Uhl *et al.* 1982; Parker *et al.* 1983; Szultc 1986; Schmink 1988; and Browder 1989), but much valuable experience has been gained at Jari that could be useful for future environmentally sound development in the humid tropics. The consortium that took over the concession from the shipping magnate Daniel Ludwig learned from the early mistakes, and experienced positive profits after 1990. Owing to improved planning, research, and better agronomic practices, productivity has increased dramatically with yields now reaching as high as 100 m^3/hectare/year. This is far greater than the potential of tree plantations in temperate climates (Smith *et al.* 1995).

Planted forest is the smallest land-use category, but at 7.0 percent per year, it has been growing faster than both perennial crops (6.5 percent per year) and annual crops (4.6 percent per year). Importantly, the area of planted forest continued to increase between 1985 and 1995, while the growth of other types of crops stagnated as the land gave way to pasture.

The area devoted to all types of crops (annual crops, perennial crops, and planted forest) expanded rapidly from 1.8 million hectares in 1970 to 6.2 million hectares in 1985. Between 1985 and 1995 total crop area decreased to 6.0 million hectares. This may be a result of the unfavorable developments for agriculture in general during that period, but some of the apparent drop may also be owing to the change in reference period for the Agricultural Census, as explained in chapter 3.

Like cattle ranching, small-scale farming in Amazonia has been naturally stimulated by rapidly rising land prices in the South and growing local markets in the North. In addition, there has been government support in the form of agricultural credit, extension and marketing services, price support schemes, and various fiscal incentives. Unlike cattle ranching, however, crop farming seem to be more sensitive to changes in economic environment and economic policy. Whereas the number of cattle in the Amazon has continued to increase despite the deterioration in overall conditions for the agricultural sector, the growth of crop land levelled off between 1985 and 1995.

Logging

Logging in the Amazon has historically been very limited owing to difficult access and a very high level of species diversity which makes extraction of a particular variety of wood especially difficult. As commercial markets have existed only for a few, high-value species such as mahogany, this high diversity of species made intense logging infeasible. Thus, very little deforestation in this region could be directly attributed to logging before the 1980s.

Since the 1980s, however, logging activity has increased dramatically in the Brazilian Amazon. According to IBGE's Annual Survey of Extractive Vegetal Production (PEV), the production of logs increased from 7 million m^3 in 1975 to 52 million m^3 in 1995. Logging is still not very widespread, however. Almost all of the increase between 1975 and 1995 took place in the state of Pará, which accounted for 84 percent of the total logging volume in Legal Amazonia in 1995 (Otsuki and Reis 1998). Pará is a natural place for a burst of logging activity because of the good market access to wood-hungry regional markets in the North-East and Center-West regions of Brazil.

Good market access is essential for the development of a logging industry. While loggers could log for free in many areas of the Amazon, they are willing to pay around \$150 per hectare to farmers in Pará for the right to harvest timber from their land (Veríssimo *et al.* 1992; Stone 1996). This is still quite a low stumpage fee, but the farmers often accept it because of the non-monetary benefits the loggers may bring in the form of logging roads and easier subsequent clearing.

The municipality Paragominas in Pará provides a good example of how the logging industry responds to sudden improvements in market access and opportunities. When Paragominas was founded in 1966, the area was covered by forest and no saw mills were in operation. When the Belém–Brasília highway opened, however, loggers, along with many other types of entrepreneur, were attracted to the region. The number of saw mills increased from 0 to twelve in 1975, 154 in 1985, and 238 in 1990 (Stone 1996). Veríssimo *et al.* (1992) estimated that between 1970 and 1990 logging and timber processing companies in this area realized average annual profits of about US$900 per hectare logged. As land tenure rights became more securely established and areas of accessible forest receded, however, the price of clearing rights – as reflected in stumpage fees paid to land owners – rose dramatically from $84 in 1990 to $193 in 1995 (both in 1995-US$), and profit margins were reduced. This prompted a consolidation of the industry and the closure of many of the smaller mills whose owners presumably moved on to frontier areas where raw materials were cheaper. Many of the remaining mills have increased production in order to cover the high fixed investments, and some mill-owners have started investing in plantations to secure a local and economical future supply of raw materials (Stone 1996).

Pinedo-Vasques *et al.* (2001) provide another example of the course of a logging cycle in the Amazon. The authors analyzed a region in Amapá, which in 1970 had seven large saw mills and four plywood mills. Their owners quickly exhausted the six high-value timber species that interested them, however, and by the early 1980s they had shut down all of their mills. Consistent with boom–bust patterns, there were many fewer jobs after the boom and economic activity was considerably lower. Nevertheless, there were some positive benefits. Twelve of the mills' former employees established their own small family-run saw mills. With no more high-value timber to work with, these saw mills broadened out to a much wider range of timber species. Local and regional markets also emerged for poles and firewood. As a result, there are now markets for thirty-six different tree species. Some local farmers responded to the new market opportunities by managing their fallow areas, forests, and home gardens to produce poles, firewood, and timber. Now when the farmers clear new plots for agriculture they first harvest the timber. Then after growing crops for a couple of years they leave the land fallow and use those fallow areas to produce wood. This new approach to forestry has proven both sustainable and profitable. Farmers now devote a lot of time and energy to nurturing their forests. Previously exhausted high-value timber species have begun to make a comeback in farmers' home gardens. The farmers earn money in the short term from selling poles, firewood, and timber from fast-growing species, and the slower-growing species serve as a form of savings. The incomes they earn far exceed the minimum wage. The way their activities complement each other lets them use their labor more efficiently and by selling such a diverse set of forest and agricultural products they reduce their risks.

Many authors are critical of the boom–bust cycle that too intense logging can create in a frontier region and would prefer to see a more even flow of timber over time. This may not be desirable in practice, though, for simple economic reasons. If a new area is opened up where all the timber is mature, as in the case of Paragominas, the region may lose a lot by not harvesting timber as soon as possible. Unless stumpage values are expected to increase substantially over time, the net present value (NPV) of rapid harvesting would be much higher than the net present value of even-flow harvesting (Vincent 1997). A simple example may illustrate. Consider the case of 100,000 hectares of mature forest, where the optimal rotation age is fifty years and the discount rate is 12 percent. Under even-flow harvesting 2,000 hectares (1/50th of the forest) should be cleared each year. The net present value of an indefinite stream of timber profits would then be $\frac{1}{0.12} \cdot$ 2,000 hectares $\cdot$ \$900/hectare $=$ \$15 million, if the annual profits stayed constant at \$900/hectare. An alternative strategy is pulse harvesting, where all timber is harvested immediately, and again at fifty-year intervals. This strategy yields an NPV of more than \$90 million, i.e. at least six times more than the even-flow scenario.

If per hectare profits from logging are expected to rise over time, this may make it worthwhile to delay harvesting some mature stands and smooth the flow of timber somewhat, but probably not to the extreme of even-flow harvesting. Vincent (1997) points out that the most fundamental reason for not attaching too much importance to even-flow harvesting is that, despite its appearance, it is not a sufficient condition for ensuring sustainability. Ensuring that requires regeneration of the forest after logging. Without adequate regeneration, even-flow harvesting will ensure constant timber production only during the first cycle of harvesting.

To ensure real sustainability and reduce the extent of illegal logging, increased government planning and regulation is necessary. Research has shown that many loggers would actually prefer to operate within a stable system of defined rules and secure land tenure (Schneider *et al.* 2000) which would allow them to establish stable and legal enterprises. The Brazilian government is increasingly responding to this demand by creating National Forests where managed timber extraction is permitted. The amount of managed timber lands rose from almost nothing in 1993 to nearly 1 million hectares in 1999 and in the year 2000, the Ministry of the Environment launched a new National Forest Program with the goal of establishing at least 400,000 km^2 of new National Forests in the Brazilian Amazon (Veríssimo *et al.* 2002).

Using a Geographical Information System approach, Veríssimo *et al.* (2002) identified public forested areas that were sufficiently close to existing infrastructure to allow profitable timber extraction and at the same time not under immediate demand for other land uses. They show that there are still sufficient unoccupied and unprotected forested areas in the Amazon to establish a network of Natural Forests that would be capable of supplying enough managed production to meet present and expected demands for Amazon timber. If the Brazilian government acts now to incorporate these areas into its system of Natural Forests, it can do so with a minimum of social conflicts or protests from conservationists. Furthermore, by acting now, the government can capture a greater portion of the rents for extracted resources and put in place the control and management measures needed to sustain these vast natural resources (Veríssimo *et al.* 2002).

The creation of 400,000–700,000 km^2 (8–14 percent of Legal Amazonia) of Natural Forests for sustainable timber harvesting combined with Brazil's other conservation lands, would easily make Brazil one of the foremost conservers of natural resources in the world (Veríssimo *et al.* 2002).

Mining

The mineral wealth of Legal Amazonia is estimated at US$3 trillion with deposits of gold, bauxite, tin, copper, uranium, potassium, iron ore, rare earths, niobium, sulfur, manganese, schist, diamonds, and other precious stones (Schneider 1992, p. 68).

Mining activities can be divided into two categories: (1) large-scale, highly mechanized, government-supported mining operations and (2) traditional placer mining.

Large-scale mining

Mining is one of the most intensive land uses possible in the Amazon, and little deforestation is directly attributed to corporate mining. Hoppe (1992) estimates that at most 4,500 km^2 of forest is likely to have been cleared to gain access to all known exploitable mineral deposits in Amazonia. This is less than 0.1 percent of the total area of Legal Amazonia. However, substantial indirect deforestation may have been caused through the development booms that mining has caused in the mineral growth poles of Legal Amazonia.

Pará is the state with the greatest intensity of mining activity. Within Pará, the largest currently identified area of mineral wealth is the Carajás range which holds one of the world's largest iron-ore reserves as well as large deposits of manganese, copper, nickel, bauxite, and gold. In 1980 the government created an overall development plan for the Carajás region, named the Greater Carajás Program (PGC), of which the Carajás iron ore mine was to be the centerpiece. The objective was to develop the region into a major center for mineral resource-based industries. As one of the growth poles in the POLOAMAZONIA program, it was granted exemptions from income tax, manufactured products tax, and import duties. In addition, the region enjoyed intensive infrastructure investments including the construction of 890 km of railway and a deep-water port capable of handling ships of up to 350,000 dead weight tons. Total project design and execution costs were assessed at $2.8 billion, of which the World Bank financed roughly $240 million and other international lenders $914 million (Schneider 1992, p. 69). The direct environmental impact of the PGC has been relatively limited. This is partly because the World Bank and other lenders required that environmental planning become an integral part of the overall development program. Thus 2.2 percent of total PGC project costs were devoted to zoological, archaeological, and botanical research, pollution control, and regeneration of degraded areas (Schneider 1992, p. 70).

The sizable investments made in the PGC spurred a general development boom which had a large indirect impact on deforestation in the Carajás region. However, at the level of Legal Amazonia as a mega-region, it may actually have slowed down deforestation, because it absorbed labor in a very land-intensive activity. This labor might otherwise have been engaged in land-extensive agricultural activities elsewhere in the region where it would have caused more deforestation (Reis 1996).

Placer mining

It is difficult to get reliable data on placer mining activities in the Amazon. The National Department of Mineral Production (DNPM – *Departamento Nacional de Producão Mineral*) estimates that real gold production is between three and five times larger than official figures. They estimate that Legal Amazonia produced around 1,100 tons of gold worth $13 billion between 1980 and 1988. This represents over 80 percent of the Brazilian national gold production for that period (Schneider 1992, p. 57).

The number of placer miners (*garimpeiros*) is estimated at around 400,000 with about the same number providing general services to the mining camps (transportation, sales of basic goods, entertainment, and prostitution). A 1989 study by DNPM found the biggest *garimpeiro* populations in Pará (530,000), Mato Grosso (170,000), Roraima (100,000), and Rondônia (60,000) (Schneider 1992, p. 58).

Since mining is one of the most intense activities with respect to land-use, it causes very little direct deforestation. But where it happens, it involves a major disruption of the soil in a way which makes forest regeneration extremely difficult. In addition, the profits generated from mining may be invested in cattle ranching, thus indirectly contributing to deforestation (MacMillan 1995). However, the most severe environmental impacts probably arise from the resulting siltation and pollution of rivers.[4]

Hydroelectric dams

More than 90 percent of the electricity in Brazil comes from hydropower, which is a relatively clean and sustainable form of energy. Two of Brazil's 600 large dams (defined as higher than 15 m) are located in the Amazon basin.[5] In addition, there are two smaller dams and five very small dams. Table 4.7 provides a summary of the four existing dams in Legal Amazonia with an installed capacity larger than 10 MW.

The total area flooded by these dams amounts to approximately 5,537 km^2 or around 0.1 percent of the total area of Legal Amazonia. The efficiency, measured as capacity per area flooded, varies enormously between the dams, however. By far the most efficient dam is the large Tucuruí dam located on the Tocantins river 300 km south of the city of Belém. Completed in 1984, it was the first large dam built in a tropical rainforest and its reservoir is the largest artificial lake created in such a zone. It has a generating capacity of 6,600 MW, and the total cost of construction was an estimated US$5.5 billion.[6] It supplies electricity to

[4] Despite the well-known dangers of mercury poisoning on both the environment and human health, mercury is still used in several stages of the gold mining process. DNPM estimates that for each gram of gold extracted, 2 grams of mercury are released into the river system (Schneider 1992, p. 60). This implies that about 2,000 tons of mercury has been dispersed in the Amazon basin in the period 1980–1988.

Furthermore, the process of gold washing empties large amounts of dirt into the river. This causes an increase in suspended particles which, in turn, reduces the amount of sunlight available for organic life in the rivers. Other pollutants include motor oil and the detergents used by the miners to remove oil from the water because it reduces the amalgamating action of mercury on gold.

[5] World Write 2001 (http://www.worldwrite.org.uk/site/brazil/dam.html).

[6] World Commission on Dams 2001 (http://www.dams.org/studies/br/background.htm).

Table 4.7. *Existing dams in Legal Amazonia, selected years*

Dam	Year flooded	State	Installed capacity (MW)	Flooded area (km^2)	Efficiency (MW/km^2)
Tucuruí	1984	Pará	6,600	2,430	2.7
Balbina	1987	Amazonas	300	2,360	0.1
Samuel	1988	Rondônia	200	645	0.3
Curuá-Una	1977	Pará	100	102	1.0
Total			7,200	5,537	1.3

Source: Authors' elaboration based on information in Fearnside (1995a).

the aluminium processing plants near Belém and is also connected to the national electricity network.

The other three dams are all small in terms of generating capacity, but the area flooded by the Balbina dam on the Rio Uatumã north of Manaus almost matches the area flooded by the Tucuruí dam. This implies that the efficiency in terms of energy generated per area flooded is almost 90 percent lower than the efficiency of the Tucuruí dam. The Balbina project is officially acknowledged as an environmental disaster, and Fearnside (1989a) shows that the carbon emissions from that dam are much larger than the carbon emissions that would have been emitted from similar amounts of fossil-fuel-based energy.

Plans for further dam construction in the Amazon basin are meeting substantial resistance both locally and internationally, because the relatively flat relief and wide flood plains in the Amazon make it difficult to limit ecological damage from dam construction. In special locations, however, it is possible to exploit the power from falling water without creating dams. To supply power to the pulp mill at Jari, for example, a proposed hydroelectric plant at the San Antonia Falls will divert part of the river through a turbine and will thus not involve any flooding (Smith *et al.* 1995). In addition, planned natural gas imports from Bolivia during the coming decades has relieved some of the pressure to construct further dams, so further deforestation from dam construction is likely to be limited, at least for the immediate future.

Property rights

A large and growing body of research in economics focuses on the role of institutions and transaction costs in economic life. The "new institutional economics" puts a particularly large emphasis on the role of property rights as a key institution. Indeed, the lack of well-defined property rights and its relationship to deforestation and wasteful use of land in the Amazon has been explored by a number of researchers including Mahar (1989); Almeida and Uhl (1995); Alston *et al.* (1996); Faminow (1998); and Alston *et al.* (1999, 2000). Without secure property rights the incentive to invest in more intensive land uses is greatly diminished. Furthermore, in such a case the forest can be perceived as an open-access resource, leading to excessive clearing and deforestation.

Alston *et al.* (1999, 2000), in particular, has documented how some peculiar inconsistencies in Brazilian property law may at once incite violent land disputes, as well as increase the incentive to clear land beyond what would otherwise be economically optimal. On the one hand civil law protects the traditional private property rights of title-holders, while on the other hand constitutional law outlines an aggressive land reform agenda in which, through specific procedures, squatters can obtain legal title to both government and private land. As Alston *et al.* (2000, p. 16) explains:

> The difficulty these constitutional land redistribution provisions bring for the security of title is obvious. Essentially, they authorize the invasion of private land if it is not placed in "beneficial" use, however defined. Typically, uncleared forest land in the Amazon is prima facie evidence of a lack of beneficial ("adequate and rational") use, but any definition will be arbitrary and invite disputes. As a squatter in the municipio of Conceição do Araguaina in Pará stated: "Here the best title is the biggest ax."

These conflicting laws[7] strongly increase incentives to clear for both title holders and squatters alike. However, the actual extent to which the land reform regime has contributed to clearing is hotly disputed as it is very difficult to actually differentiate "economically appropriate" clearing from excessive, pre-emptive clearing. One 1997 government report attributed up to 30 percent of deforestation between 1964 and 1977 to land reform programs, but others claim the real figure is either higher or much lower (Alston *et al.* 2000). In their survey, Alston *et al.* (2000) find that in fact land-owners do confess to clearing more of their land than strictly necessary in order either to stave off would-be squatters or increase their compensation in the case of expropriation. However, in their quantitative analysis they find no statistically significant relationship between the number of land reform settlements between 1987 and 1990 and the extent of clearing in 1985. If agents are forward-looking and have good information about the future, this result could suggest that

[7] The situation is made even more confusing by laws requiring up to 80 percent of private land to be kept in a natural state (see description and analysis in chapter 6).

pre-emptive clearing is not as much a problem as some believe, but of course a more fully dynamic estimation strategy with clearing as the dependent variable would be the more appropriate way to examine this particular question.

Regardless the actual extent of deforestation attributable to poorly defined and/or conflicting property rights, there seem to be potentially large gains to be had from reforming property laws to better achieve the goal of land redistribution without the negative side effects of excessive land clearing and violence. Alston *et al.* (1999), discusses some approaches to legal reform that have been tried and suggest some alternatives, and while a full discussion of the merits and dismerits of these proposals is beyond the scope of this book we believe that this is an important area for further research and legal work.

Secondary forest growth

When a relatively low number of farmers practice slash-and-burn agriculture in a forest, deforestation of most plots is only temporary. Most plots will be abandoned or kept in fallow and will grow back into forest again with little harm done. As the density of farmers in the forest increases, however, some of the deforestation will turn out to be permanent. If a plot happens to be located near a road with good access to rapidly increasing urban markets, the farmer is likely to settle down, get a formal title to his land, and intensify his agricultural practices. The probability that such a piece of land will turn into forest again is very low.

Some areas of the Amazon are still so thinly populated that most deforestation there is of the temporary kind. Other areas, however, are so densely populated and have such good access to local and regional markets, that deforestation is predominantly permanent.

There is very little concrete evidence on the extent of secondary forest in Legal Amazonia, since the two main sources of deforestation information neglect this issue.

Agricultural surveys capture only short and long fallow, both of which we call "cleared," since we know they have been recently cleared and we expect them to be used for active agriculture again within a few years. The agricultural surveys do not include abandoned land, since nobody is claiming it. It is thus counted as public land and is likely to feature some kind of secondary forest growth, but the agricultural surveys say nothing about the extent of this area.

Satellite data from INPE, on the other hand, consider all clearing permanent, and if an area was identified as cleared in 1978 it will automatically be counted as cleared in all subsequent years, even if the area shows such advanced secondary regrowth that it looks indistinguishable from primary forest on later satellite pictures.

This means that neither the land survey data nor the satellite data can give us any information about the extent of secondary forest regrowth. However, by combining the two sources, we may get a rough idea about the extent of secondary forests in Legal Amazonia. If we assume that the only reason for the discrepancy between deforestation estimates based on satellite and the estimates based on land surveys is the differential treatment of secondary forest regrowth, we can conclude from table 3.5 (p. 42) that 3.89 percent of Legal Amazonia was featuring secondary forest regrowth in 1995. This corresponds to almost 200,000 km^2. A similar calculation made for 1985 shows an area of secondary forest regrowth of 75,000 km^2.

This definition of secondary forest is relatively narrow, however, since it includes only abandoned land. Other authors also include private fallow lands, which amount to about 90,000 km^2 in 1995 according to table 4.1. Yet other authors include areas that have been logged over, since they exhibit similar features of regenerating forest although they have never been fully converted.

In addition to secondary forest regrowth, there would also be extensive regrowth of other vegetation types, such as savannah, bush vegetation, and low-density forest.

The expansion of abandoned land and secondary regrowth areas indicate that human intervention in natural forests of the Amazon region is in many cases of a temporary nature, the aim of which is to reap transitory benefits, rather than a permanent, planned conversion to alternative uses. These benefits may involve cashing in rich timber or mineral resources or a mining of nutrients. Ultimately, the destiny of these transitory intervened areas may be affected by factors such as fire, invasion of pioneer species, or land occupation by squatters. The expansion of extensive and transitory uses of forest land is thus yet another indication of the fact that land is still widely perceived as an abundant resource in Legal Amazonia.

Although secondary forests are frequently perceived as indicators of land abandonment following shifting cultivation or pasture degradation, they are in fact used and managed within a wide variety of rural communities (Dubois 1990). In chapter 5 we will see that most non-timber forest product extraction is actually carried out in secondary forests rather than in primary forests, as secondary forests often have a much higher density of economically useful species. A dramatic example of this is the "babaçu belt" in Maranhão where secondary forest with high densities of babaçu palms now cover approximately 100,000 km^2 of land that was once cleared for agriculture. The babaçu palm serves multiple purposes for the local population at the subsistence level and in the market economy. The fruit kernels are utilized by local industries for the production of vegetable oil, soap, and margerine. After the oil is extracted, industries use the pressed kernels to make feedcakes for cattle and nitrogen- and phosphorous-rich fertilizer. The residues are also transformed into charcoal providing the main source of cooking fuel in regions where babaçu forests abound (Dubois 1990).

Another example of economically important secondary forests is the "açaí belt" located near Belém in the Amazon floodplains. The açaí palm is used both for its fruits which are processed into a popular drink in Belém as well as to make Palmito (heart of palm).

5 Alternatives to deforestation: extractivism

Plant extractivism is a sub-sector of agriculture that has received considerable international attention, owing to its alleged potential for promoting the sustainable use of tropical forests and other natural ecosystems, e.g. through the harvesting of non-wood products in extractive reserves. In this chapter[1] we will concentrate on non-wood forest products like nuts, latex, and fruits. Sustainable timber management could in principle provide an important alternative to deforestation, but in practice the link has been the reverse: unsustainable logging enables the process of deforestation. Wood extraction, which was discussed in chapter 4, is thus not included here.

In the writing on the economic history of Brazil, plant extractivism – a production system based on human's removal of biomass from natural ecosystems – has consistently been equated with backwardness. A classical Brazilian historian like Buarque de Holanda sees historical extractivist systems, adapted by the Portuguese colonists from indigenous traditions, as a logical response to a land-abundant physical environment with constrained tropical soils, abundant plagues, and labor scarcity. However, to him it is also a system led by the Iberian *conquistador* spirit of resource mining and commerce, permitting a harvesting of the fruits of nature without the organized and laborious effort of land cultivation (Buarque de Holanda 1978). On the other hand, the contemporary Gilberto Freyre actually credits the Portuguese for their pioneer efforts to shift from "pure extraction" to agriculture. The creation of a plantation colony for him entails the "local creation of wealth," and "the use and development of plant richness by means of capital and individual effort" (Freyre 1977). This inferiority view on extractivism *vis-à-vis* agriculture is shared by later economic historians, such as Furtado (1970) and Prado Júnior (1978), and refined for a current setting in the theory about a product-wise, stage-led rise and decline of extractivism (see Homma 1993, 1994, 1996).

[1] This chapter is based on Wunder (1999).

Nevertheless, extractivism has received a new impetus since the 1980s, backed by those concerned with the sustainability of production and the conservation of biological diversity. In this discussion, Brazil, with its large share of the Amazon, has been a strategically important case. While timber extraction is recognized by most as ecologically damaging, the extraction of non-wood forest products was seen as a socially, economically and ecologically viable alternative to widespread forest conversion, especially in the Amazon (see Allegretti 1990, 1994; Nepstad and Schwartzman 1992; Ruíz and Pinzón 1995; Broekhoven 1996). Other observers have viewed the scope for extractivism with a certain hesitation (e.g. Fearnside 1989b; Glüsener-Godt and Sachs 1994; Assies 1997) or outright pessimism (e.g. Browder 1992; Richards 1993; Coppen *et al.* 1994; Chomitz and Kumari 1998).

The belief in the economic viability of non-wood extraction *vis-à-vis* converted land uses had been fortified by a number of pioneer, influential forest valuation and income generation studies from the Amazon, such as Anderson and Jardim (1989), Peters *et al.* (1989), and Anderson and Ioris (1992). It was thus sought to create an appropriate institutional framework for extractivism by promoting the land rights for traditional forest-extracting populations, such as indigenous groups and rubber tappers. Their social struggle was brought to the forefront of international attention with the assassination of the rubber tapper leader Chico Mendes. Extractivism also received international financing, culminating in the creation of the Resex project in the PP-G7 Pilot Program.

Consequently, there has been ample debate about the potential of extractivism as a tool for integrated conservation and development, but the economic–quantitative side of the issue has been somewhat under-researched. Homma (1993) provides a thorough analysis of Amazon extractivism, with a particular strength in the long-run historical analysis of different Amazonian products. Allegretti (1994) gives a static summary description of the extraction data in the 1980 IBGE Agricultural Census, but little analysis of the data. Two works by Instituto Sociedade, População e Natureza (ISPN) (Sawyer *et al.* 1997; Pires and Scardua 1998) deal specifically with the Brazilian *cerrado* (savannah) region. The studies by Peters *et al.* (1989) for the Peruvian Amazon, Anderson and Ioris (1992) for the Amazon estuary, and even Anderson *et al.* (1991) for the babaçu production zone in Maranhão already mentioned all represent case study settings which are perfectly justifiable in their own right. However, as will be argued below, the selected sites are by no means representative of the Amazon, or for tropical forests in a wider sense.

In the light of this panorama of existing research, the objective of the present chapter is to analyze the main determinants of extractive value generation: Why are some extraction areas economically far more important than others, and what are their special characteristics? Why are some products widely cultivated, and others not? Are the same change factors at work for wood and non-wood products? What is the role of different types of soil and vegetation?

The data

In case studies across the world, non-timber forest products have proven to generate very different levels of economic returns, differences that were often co-determined by the variability in data and methods (Godoy *et al.* 1993). It is thus important to make a thorough and honest assessment of the advantages and drawback that each source presents. The main source used in the following is also IBGE's Agricultural Census, which includes a questionnaire section about plant extraction. The latest census is from 1995/1996, published in 1998 (see IBGE 1998), but selected data will be drawn from previous Censuses, back to 1920. IBGE defines plant extraction as "the process of exploration of native plant resources which entails the harvesting or collection of products . . . either in a rational way that allows for a long-run sustainable off-take, or in a primitive and itinerant manner which generally allows for only one single production cycle" (IBGE 1998, p. xi, our translation from Portuguese). The IBGE Census also makes explicit reference to "plant extraction . . . from non-planted (native) species." By current definition, the origin of plant extractive production is thus native, natural vegetation, the main category of which is forests. The term "extraction" will be used for the economic activity that appropriates a physical value; the term "extractivism" will be used for the wider description of the mode and framework of this productive activity.

Data on current production, costs, income, etc. refer to the period from August 1, 1995 to July 31, 1996; data on land area, ownership, and employment to end-1995. Gross income from different types of production and products (annual and perennial crops, animal husbandry, plant extraction, forestry, processing activities) is registered. Cost elements are not dealt with on a product-specific basis, thus making it impossible to explicitly compare the profitability across different types of products and activities.

A key question for the interpretation of the Agricultural Census results is thus to what extent marginal, forested areas and their inhabitants, from *caboclos* to *caiçaras* and inhabitants of indigenous reserves, are well represented in the census sample. If they are, another critical issue is the duration and quality of the interview, *vis-à-vis* different purposes of data collection. In general, one–three daily interviews per inquirer are carried out, including transport time, which indicates the limits for the normal range of time spent on each questionnaire. The Agricultural Census includes questions on all economic aspects of the establishment's farming system. Individual, fully structured interviews of the person "responsible for agricultural production" are usually carried out at the farm, although an overall assessment at the village level in some cases (e.g. indigenous communities) may be preferred.

For the specific issue of plant extraction, production quantities during the last twelve months are inquired, according to the memory of the respondent. No pre-defined production area with a predictable productivity exists for extraction, so it may be difficult to cross-check the validity of the given information. Harvested and sold quantities are distinguished in the questionnaire, and a uniform price per quantity unit is applied to compute gross production values. The eight most common extraction products (both wood and non-wood) are pre-printed in the questionnaire; a supplementary list of 82 different plant extraction products is at the disposal of the inquirer, together with a detailed manual (IBGE, no year).

What are the comparative advantages and disadvantages of the Agricultural Census for an assessment of the economic values generated by plant extraction? The overwhelming advantage is the alleged full geographical coverage of the Agricultural Census, which should eliminate those sample representativity biases that are so common in the site selection and data interpretation of the literature on Amazonian non-timber forest products. Much investigation has been carried out in natural environments that are particularly favourable to high-value extraction, such as oligarchic forests or dense stands of palm trees producing commercial fruit. At the same time, the selected areas are often close to large urban markets, thus generating elevated per hectare and per household incomes that are not representative for rural areas in a broader sense. In comparison, the Census should allow for a more generalized picture.

On the other hand, the large geographical coverage, combined with budget constraints, jointly determine the main weaknesses of the Agricultural Census: a rapid, somewhat superficial assessment, which may not capture the full range of diverse uses in households living close to natural forests, not to speak of the intricate patterns of seasonal and yearly fluctuations characteristic for many plants in the wild. A head of a rural household cannot reasonably be expected to record *ex memoria* the consumption of, in principle, up to 82 extractive products over the last twelve months. In spite of the long list of products, certain uses (e.g. medicinal plants) are only sporadically represented in the product sample, and the true size of products with some economic importance is likely to be much larger. Illegality of exploitation (e.g. of wood products in protected forests) may be an additional reason for (deliberate) understatement. The interview of only one household member may also imply that gender-specific extraction patterns are overlooked. In general, experiences with tropical forest valuation studies have shown that more sophisticated techniques (*in situ* observation, diaries, etc.) need to be employed, preferably over a longer time span, to give a more accurate picture (see Godoy *et al.* 1993; Gregersen *et al.* 1995).

One advantage of the Agricultural Census over other statistical sources is that it aims at a distinction of product origin between native, natural vegetation (extraction) and planted, cultivated resources (agriculture, animal husbandry, or plantation forestry). However, this also leaves some "grey," intermediate areas of "soft management" techniques, which it may be difficult to classify correctly in an interview of reduced length. Some domestically consumed products, such as firewood, may originate from both planted and native resources. The use of popular plant names with many local variations may lead to confusion when the same plant is identified by various names, or vice versa. Also, the Agricultural Census does not distinguish product origin in terms of different biomes. This means that products collected from non-forest native vegetation forms are also included. In particular, it is important to note the case of a relatively large range of products that are fully or partially extracted from the Brazilian savannah (*cerrado*), including the transition zones between forest and cerrado, such as some semi-deciduous forests.

The agents and harvesting areas included in the Agricultural Census may imply additional omissions. Some products may actually not be harvested by a "rural establishment," but rather by landless workers that are employed by those establishments. Case study examples in this regard are pequi nuts (*Caryocar brasiliense*) harvested in Minas Gerais State (O. Chevez Pozo, personal communication), or Brazil nuts (*Bertholletia excelsis*) collected by land clearing workers in Pará state (see Clay 1997). Related to this is the question of land tenure. The Census should, in principle, count only those products that are harvested from the area owned, leased, or occupied by the individual establishment, but not those that come from state lands or other open-access areas. In practice, many of the non-timber forest products registered in the Census are likely to be harvested from open-access areas outside the proper establishments; again, Brazil nuts are a good example (see Clay 1997).

Furthermore, and perhaps most important, the Census is generally confined to plant resources so that, in terms of an interpretation towards total non-timber forest extraction values, the non-registration of game constitutes a severe limitation for some geographic areas. Consequently, both the range and quantities of plant extraction are likely to be underestimated in the Agricultural Census, especially in those regions where multi-product extraction for auto-consumption is predominating. Having said that, it should be noted that some of the most common subsistence products are in fact registered in the Census data, such as firewood and wood posts, or non-wood product like buriti palm fruits (*Mauritia exuosa L.*).

However, a bias of the opposite sign applies to prices, where an overestimation of extraction values occurs. The Agricultural Census registers just one set of (market-derived) prices, to be applied both to auto-consumption and to product sales. First, this leaves an open question as to what valuation technique was applied for auto-consumption products where there was no local market, as occurs in some locations for firewood, wood poles, locally abundant fruits, etc. Secondly, even in the presence of such markets, commercialized products will often be of a superior quality, compared to the ones that are consumed directly at the site. Thirdly, and most important, any transaction-based price from farm-gate prices to urban consumer prices may be used in the questionnaire, but the difference between the two extremes may be extensive, owing to the inclusion of transport costs and middlemen profits in the latter. Only farm-gate prices truly reflect the value to the specific rural productive establishment. Applying village or, at worst, urban product prices may result in a significant overestimation of auto-consumption uses: many natural forest products currently consumed in remote areas would be so costly to bring to urban markets that their commercialization would yield net losses. Often, this is exactly why their marketing does not occur, in spite of their local abundance.

Finally, it should be noticed that other statistical sources in Brazil also assess plant extraction values, but they do generally not provide attractive alternatives for our research purposes. IBGE also publishes the annual PEV survey (Produção Extrativa Vegetal); since the mid-1980s, the survey has been renamed PEVS (Produção da Extração Vegetal e da Silvicultura) because it pools extraction and plantation forestry data. Unfortunately, this means that it becomes impossible to distinguish between a native and a plantation forest origin of the respective product. The latest PEVS version covers data for 1995, with a three-year publication lag (see IBGE 1998). The survey always uses the latest available Agricultural Census (here, from 1985) as a base, and projects changes on the basis of a network of variable types of informants at the municipal level. It thus does not represent a set of primary data, but rather individual experts' "best guesses" or subjective observations on local market trends. Obviously, data origin makes the annual survey an inferior type of source, compared to the more direct and objective information collected in the

Census. Furthermore, abrupt and inexplicable year-to-year changes occur, possibly because of discontinuities in the type of informant. As will be shown below, the highly fluctuating character of most non-wood markets over time makes the PEVS an unreliable source in assessing extraction quantities.

Mapping extractive value densities

Figure 5.1 shows the value of non-wood products in each municipality within the area of Legal Amazonia. For each municipality, the registered value of non-wood extraction of all agricultural establishments was divided by the municipality's total land area. The map thus expresses differences in the land density of value generation. Some of the main roads, rivers, and cities have been sketched to allow for easier orientation.

Before turning to the map interpretation, it may be useful to provide some summary characteristics on extraction in the Legal Amazonia area. Total extraction value in 1995/1996 was US$373.7 million, of which US$118.2 million (31.6 percent) is non-wood and US$255.5 million (68.4 percent) wood values. The first impression from the non-wood values in figure 5.1 is one of extreme economic concentration. In some municipalities, extraction values are zero, for instance in areas where deforestation has progressed heavily: south-eastern Pará, Tocantins, parts of Mato Grosso, and in general some other areas near the main roads

Figure 5.1 Value of non-wood extractive products per hectare in Legal Amazonia, 1995/1996 Agricultural Census
Source: BCE.

(BR 010, BR 174/364). However, some of the municipalities registered with zero extraction also cast inevitable doubts about the quality of the data collection process (see discussion on pp. 45–46). Two more light-coloured categories represent areas with minor extraction activity (ranges US$0–0.8/hectare and US$0.8–0.15/hectare), which embrace most of the remaining Amazonian territory.

In economic terms, significant value generation occurs only in the two core categories, marked by the darkest areas in figure 5.1 (0.15–10 US$/hectare; more than 10 US$/hectare). High-value areas can even be labeled by products. In Pará state (eastern Amazonia), in the vicinity of the large capital Belém, one finds what may be called the "açaí belt" (or the "fruit belt"). These areas are dominated by the extraction of açaí palm fruits and palm hearts (*Euterpe oleracea*). Açaí fruit juice is a product that has greatly increased its market share, also in Southern Brazil. However, açaí palm hearts are often harvested in a manner that destroys the palm. Açaí grows preferably in intervened, seasonally flooded riverside areas, where, owing to human intervention, they may occur at great densities.

In the Belém region, other important fruits are e.g. bacuri (*Platonia insignis Mart.*) and cupuaçu (*Theobroma grandiflorum*). Two factors seem to make the area "special": the previously intervened Amazon estuary environment that is particularly favorable to dense stands of açaí palms, and the closeness of the area to a large market for açaí fruits (processing and consumption) in Belém.

The second high-value area is the "babaçu belt" in Maranhão State (also Eastern Amazonia). Oil from the fruits of the Babaçu palm (babaçu, *Orbygnia martiana*) is the economically most important non-wood extractive product in Brazil. The "comparative advantages" of the geographical area seem to be of the natural type, with soil and climatic conditions, combined with the impact of previous land degradation: Babaçu favors degraded landscapes. Owing to its fire resistance, it tends to be a dominant element in pioneer vegetation regrowth after burning. Also in this case, babaçu palms occur in areas with high density of this one commercial palm, but low frequency of other species.

It is thus worth noticing that the ecological characteristics of both the identified high-value extraction areas, the açaí and babaçu belts, are highly distinct from the biologically diverse, primary, closed *terra firme* rainforest. A large part of these production belts tends to be previously intervened areas characterized by a large frequency of dominant, commercialized palms, sometimes occurring in almost monotonous stands ("quasi-plantations").

Table 5.1 permits a closer look at the eighteen non-timber high-value municipalities with a per hectare extraction superior to US$10. Of these "special" municipalities, seven are in the state of Pará (açaí belt), seven

Table 5.1. *High value non-wood extraction municipalities: main characteristics*

State	Municipality	Area (ha)	Non-wood value (R$)	Non-wood density (R$/ ha)	Main product
Pará	Abaetetuba	161,390	1,899,560	11.77	Açaí palm fruit
Pará	Acara	436,360	6,244,311	14.31	Açaí palm fruit
Pará	Anajas	702,220	7,422,465	10.57	Açaí palm fruit
Pará	Barcarena	131,620	4,155,243	31.57	Açaí palm fruit
Pará	Cameta	312,200	4,383,288	14.04	Açaí palm fruit
Pará	Igarapé-Mirim	200,970	10,341,916	51.46	Other products
Pará	Inhangapi	473,200	4,746,196	10.03	Açaí palm fruit
Pará	Ponta de Pedras	338,030	3,468,188	10.26	Açaí palm fruit
Tocantins	Axixa do Tocantins	10,480	105,534	10.07	Babaçu almonds
Tocantins	Sítio Novo do Tocantins	27,910	324,593	11.63	Babaçu almonds
Maranhão	Bacabal	174,400	2,399,744	13.76	Babaçu almonds
Maranhão	Cajari	42,140	839,429	19.92	Babaçu almonds
Maranhão	Igarap' Grande	64,350	873,873	13.58	Babaçu almonds
Maranhão	Lago do Junco	55,230	1,109,018	20.08	Babaçu almonds
Maranhão	Lago Verde	41,460	568,417	13.71	Babaçu almonds
Maranhão	Pio XII	54,460	648,074	11.90	Babaçu almonds
Maranhão	Poção de Pedras	5,260	114,563	21.78	Babaçu almonds
Maranhão	São Luiz Gonzaga	108,750	1,137,525	10.46	Babaçu almonds
Total	18 municipalities	3,340,430	53,613,901	16.05	Açaí palm fruit
Total	Legal Amazonia	507,545,390	112,504,935	0.22	Babaçu almonds

in Maranhão and two in Tocantins (both babaçu belt). With a combined extraction value of US$47.5 million, they unite no less than 42.2 percent of all non-wood extraction in Legal Amazonia. Their weighted-average value-density (US$16/hectare) is 73 times higher than that of all the Amazon (US$0.22/hectare).

In addition to the areas of highest value, there are a number of secondary areas, with per hectare extraction values in the range of 0.15–10 US$/hectare. First, this refers to the large peripheral zones of the babaçu and açaí belts. Secondly, it concerns a number of more isolated areas: in the state of Acre and Rondônia (dominated by rubber), and in Amazonas state near the city of Manaus (where piassava is an important product).

The map thus underscores the centers of extractivist activity already mentioned: the entire northern part of Pará State (timber and açaí belt), the babaçu belt in Maranhão and parts of Tocantins (kernels and charcoal), plus high-value "islands" in Mato Grosso, Acre and Amazonas states. It also seems to document that, like for other economic activities, closeness to the larger cities (Belém, Manaus, São Luís, Rio Branco), rivers (the Amazonas) and roads (BR-010, BR-364, part of BR 230) increases the options for value generation, as market access is facilitated. In turn, some of the large, isolated municipalities in the central and northern Amazon generate little extraction value, if credit is to be given to the IBGE figures.

One potential point of criticism *vis-à-vis* the usefulness of figure 5.1 refers to the general relevance of per hectare values. The typical Amazon frontier may be characterized as a land-abundant environment (see Schneider 1995). Hence, land would not be any serious constraint to extractive production, and economic agents would be inclined to base their land-use decisions on comparative per capital and per labor returns to the establishment's assets (see Young and Fausto 1997). This critique would also apply to the econometric analysis in the following section. Lacking appropriate data on the activity distribution of financial capital, figure 5.2 at least partially meets this concern, by calculating the value of non-wood extraction per number of establishments, which may serve as a proxy for labor availability in the respective municipality. Roughly speaking, values are being related to population rather than to land size.

Figure 5.2 shows that the geographic distribution of non-wood extraction value per establishment is even more skewed than the corresponding

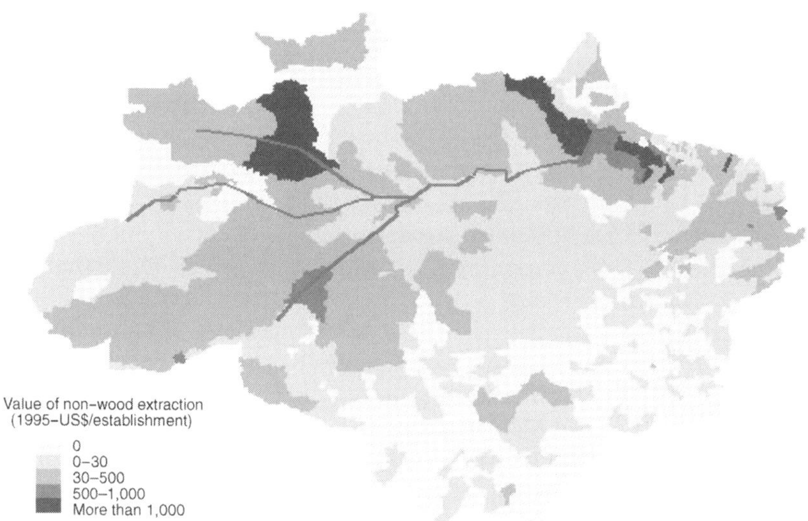

Figure 5.2 Value of non-wood extraction per establishment in each municipality of Legal Amazonia, 1995/1996 Agricultural Census
Source: BCE.

per hectare values. Municipalities with an average yearly value of more than US$500 per establishment are limited to some high-value units in northern Pará and Amazonas.

An interesting observation is that some thinly populated areas in the northern and western Amazon, which were described as low-value per hectare in figure 5.1, come out with intermediate values per establishment (US$30–500). At the same time, more populous areas in Maranhão and Acre states, which had relatively high per hectare values, score only intermediate values in figure 5.2. The values per establishment thus add another dimension to the description of extraction values.

Explaining spatial differences in extraction values

This section will try to elucidate the 1995/1996 inter-municipal differences in extraction value that have been observed for Legal Amazonia in the previous section. In prolongation of the visual analysis of maps, this econometric cross-section exercise will hopefully shed further light on the determinants of extraction value. What type of economic and biophysical scenario is favorable to extractivism and, vice versa, what factors tend to act as obstacles to the generation of high extraction values? First, a regression model with an economic rationale will be applied, testing *a priori* hypotheses regarding extractivism. As a second step, the economic model will be combined with different biophysical variables, using stepwise selection procedures that maximize the explanatory power of the regression model, for a pre-determined significance level of the selected variables.

The dependent variable of the analysis will be the extraction value density per hectare of municipal area, i.e. the study unit is the spatial distribution of non-wood extraction value density, as depicted in figure 5.1. Correspondingly, the absolute value of the independent variables will be "normalized" by dividing by municipal land area: all variables are expressed either in land densities or in percentages. Normalization of variables is desirable because municipalities differ markedly in size, so that the direct use of absolute variables in the regression model creates a spurious correlation. Normalization alternatives to land densities exist; for instance, the World Bank uses land size, population size, and national income size as denominators in cross-country comparisons (see World Bank 1998). In theoretical terms, pros and cons can be mentioned for the use of different densities, but the final choice of land area as denominator was empirically determined.

The units of our analysis are the 256 Minimum Comparable Areas (MCAs) discussed in chapter 3. We will first look at an economic model,

Table 5.2. *Economic explanations of spatial variations in extraction values*

Dependent variable:	Non-wood value	
Constant	−0.40	
	(−0.61)	
Establishment density (no./ha)	126.2	
	(5.36)	***
Natural forest share (%)	7.93	
	(2.06)	**
High-fertility soil share (%)	0.04	
	(2.91)	***
Wage labor share (%)	−4.11	
	(−1.69)	*
Public credit share$_{t-1}$ (%)[a]	−1.52	
	(−0.71)	
Road density (km/ha)[b]	8.95	
	(0.54)	
River density (km/ha)	80.81	
	(3.42)	***
Share of establishment's land occupied (%)	−0.25	
	(−0.02)	
Share of establishment's land leased (%)	6.24	
	(0.11)	
Average size of establishment (%)	0.0004	
	(0.38)	
Number of observations	256	
R^2	0.2456	

Notes: Numbers in parentheses are *t*-values.
*Coefficient significant at the 10% level.
**Coefficient significant at the 5% level.
***Coefficient significant at the 1% level.
[a] The share of financing from Banco do Brasil and from the government in gross monetary agricultural income.
[b] Federal and state roads, both paved and non-paved in 1993.

where the explanatory variables have been chosen according to theoretical hypotheses about the nature of the extractive economy. The results of the economic model are shown in table 5.2. Three different types of independent variables are distinguished, as described below.

The first three variables approximate typical production function elements. As the number of agricultural establishments per hectare can serve as a crude approximation of the density of labor inputs into production. These variable results are highly significant (at a 1 percent significance level) implying that the higher the density of establishments, the higher the extraction densities. Second, the density of natural forests (establishments' natural forest area divided by total area) must also be expected to be highly correlated with extraction values, as it represents the main native ecosystem from which extraction by definition occurs. Also this variable is highly significant: the higher the forest density, the higher the extraction densities. Third, one may expect that, for an activity based on vegetation growth, the size of the area not only matters, but also the quality of soils. The percentage of high-fertility soils proves to be significant for non-wood extraction. The question of different soil and vegetation types will be more fully explored below.

The second group of variables refers to market and infrastructure development. Two opposed theoretical expectations may apply here. On the one hand, like for any other economic activity, better infrastructure and market mediation would *ceteris paribus* tend to increase the options of value generation. Contrary to this view, one may conjecture that when markets and infrastructure are well developed, extractivism as an alleged "inferior" production mode will decline, in favor of competing economic activities, i.e. extractivism will tend to survive only in areas of economic backwardness.

The average wage–labor cost share may be seen as a proxy for the development of labor markets: the lower this share, the more the emphasis on household establishments characterized by self-employment. The variable is estimated with a negative sign, but not significant at the 5 percent level. Similarly, the share of public credits in agricultural income may be taken as an indicator for the importance of credit markets for value generation. Again, the variable is estimated with a negative sign, but not at a significant level. In other words, high-value extractivism tends to occur more in areas with underdeveloped labor and credit markets, though for credits not in a significant manner. An interesting third variable in this segment is the municipal density of roads (km/hectare of both federal and state roads, both paved and unpaved); often, the vital importance of road infrastructure for the economic viability of agricultural production in rural areas is recognized. Somewhat surprisingly, road density is insignificant.

A second infrastructure variable is river density; navigable rivers may be important transport arteries in many forested areas where little road construction has occurred. The river variable is estimated with a positive, significant sign for non-wood extraction. Rivers would thus appear to be a more important means of transport than roads in the context of extraction activities. However, as a note of caution, the river density correlation may reflect not only the importance of rivers for transport, but also to a certain extent the type of soils and vegetation that predominates riverside environments (see below). On aggregate, the coefficients estimated in this second part of table 5.2 thus lend moderate support to the "inferiority hypothesis": extraction per hectare values tend to be slightly higher in areas with limited input market development (labor, credits) and with natural, river-based transport systems, rather than roads.

The third group of variables concerns the institutional framework, in particular questions of land tenure. Does the predominance of certain types of land tenure and land-owners favor or disfavor extractivism? In table 5.2, both the average share of municipal establishments' occupied lands, the share of leased lands, and the medium size of the establishments were investigated. For non-wood extraction, none of the tenure variables has any significant influence.

In summary, the ten explanatory variables included in the economic model, reflecting production function, infrastructure, and land tenure conditions, are able to explain about one-fourth of the spatial variation in non-wood extraction values ($R^2 = 0.246$). This value may be considered intermediate for this type of cross-section analysis. Notably, the production function variables proved to be the most significant, complemented by various additional factors. Both soil fertility and natural forest density proved to be highly significant. Considering the variable ecological requirements for the large array of products concerned, it was thus decided to attempt an explanation of the same dependent variables by a more detailed biophysical analysis of disaggregated soil and vegetation types, the results of which are reproduced in table 5.3.

The approach taken here was somewhat different from the economic model, in the sense that no theoretically founded *a priori* expectations existed on which types of soils and vegetation would be particularly favorable to extractivism. Consequently, instead of starting out with a pre-established set of variables, a stepwise regression procedure[2] was used to discriminate between significant and insignificant variables, using a cut-off entry level of 15 percent.[3] The tested variables included twenty-seven soil classifications and fifteen vegetation types, supplemented by

[2] Specifically, the Forward Selection procedure in the statistical software package SAS was applied.

[3] The decisive statistical criterion for entry of a variable is the F-test, testing if the specific independent variable could be excluded from the model without deteriorating significantly the model's ability to explain the variation in the dependent variable. Alternative criteria may be the "adjusted R^2" (R^2 corrected for the growth in the number of explanatory variables), or "Mallows $C(p)$," a measure which relates to the skewness of estimates and the power of prediction of the model – factors which are of little relevance to our case, where we simply seek to identify a set of variables that reasonably explain value variations.

Table 5.3. *Biophysical explanations of spatial variations in extractivism values*

Dependent variable:	Non-wood value	
Constant	−0.39	
	(1.01)	
Density of establishments (no. /ha)	117.71	***
	(29.65)	
High-fertility soils with excess humidity (%)	0.07	***
	(15.19)	
Medium-fertility soils with excess humidity (%)	0.20	***
	(42.52)	
Low-fertility, latericious soils with excess humidity (%)	0.04	**
	(5.9)	
Saline soils of restricted use with excess humidity (%)	−0.04	**
	(4.8)	
Areas with water cover (%)	−0.16	**
	(3.7)	
Number of observations	241	
R^2	0.3714	

Notes: Numbers in parentheses are *t*-values.
*Coefficient significant at the 10% level.
**Coefficient significant at the 5% level.
***Coefficient significant at the 1% level.

the eight remaining variables from the economic model above.[4] The total of fifty variables is too large for a simultaneous computation, so the analysis was divided into two stages. First, the eight economic variables were re-examined together with the fifteen vegetation variables. The selected significant variables were then scrutinized together with the remaining twenty-seven soil variables. Table 5.3 thus shows the selection procedure's "end model" for each of the three value categories, showing those among the fifty investigated variables, which are significant at the 15 percent level.

An initial observation is that the only "surviving" variable from the economic model in table 5.2 is the density of agricultural establishments.[5] Two soil categories come out with significantly positive coefficients:

[4] The variable from table 5.2, "high-fertility soils (%)" was replaced by the more disaggregated soil and vegetation variables. The source of these variables was the SIG-AML project, the results of which are included in IPEA's DESMAT data base (see above).

[5] Direct comparison between the two models (tables 5.2 and 5.3) might have been restricted by the fact that, owing to lack of data, the number of observations in the latter was only 241, i.e. fifteen MCAs fewer than in the regressions of table 5.2. A control regression was run for the economic model, deleting those fifteeen MCAs where no disaggregated

high- and medium-fertility soils, both with excess humidity. The share of low-fertility latericious soils with excess humidity is also a significant explanatory variable, with a positive coefficient. On the other hand, the share of saline, humid soils of restricted use – the less apt soils – is estimated with a negative, significant coefficient. The same applies to a high share of areas covered by water (lakes, swamps, dams, etc.), which, naturally, goes along with lower value generation. Note that the forward selection model reaches a higher R^2 value than the economic model in table 5.2, explaining about 37 percent of the variation of the dependent variable.

How is this pattern of selected soil and vegetation categories to be interpreted? The positive, significant coefficient for three of the soil classes with excess humidity is probably explained by the high extraction of both fruits (like açaí) and timber from riverside environments (várzeas, igapós, estuaries) where soils are seasonally inundated or otherwise subject to a high water exposure.[6] The two types of vegetation that are selected in the computation provide an interesting supplement to this picture: a high share of pioneer formations goes along with high non-wood extraction values.[7]

To understand the implications of these results, one should bear in mind the distribution of soil and vegetation types in the entire region. The three soil categories with excess humidity that were estimated with a positive sign occupy together 9 percent of the area of Legal Amazonia, according to the SIG-AML figures. Correspondingly, pioneer vegetation occupies only 2.5 percent of the Legal Amazon, whereas closed rainforest covers 43.9 percent of the area. This provokes thoughts not only on the poor representativity of the high-value areas, but also on the link to biodiversity. It is recognized that, on average, dense *terra firme* dry-land rainforest holds a higher biological diversity and species endemism than both várzea and pioneer vegetation types. Unfortunately, the lack of full municipal coverage on biodiversity data made it impossible to include this aspect explicitly in the regression analysis, yet more restricted evidence indicates that there may be a negative correlation between high-value non-wood extraction areas and high indices of biodiversity.

soil/vegetation data were available. The exclusion of the fifteen MCAs causes no significant changes in the estimates, confirming that a direct comparison between table 5.2 and 5.3 can legitimately be made.

6 Note that the navigable river density from table 5.2 does not come out as significant in the stepwise selection procedure, denoting that its original correlation is probably absorbed by the corresponding soil variables.

7 The significance level of pioneer vegetation in the "end model" is 11 percent, i.e. it is significant at the 15 percent, but not at the 10 percent level. However, this changes when the set of independent variables is changed.

The results suggest that non-wood extraction at an economically significant scale tends to occur mostly from restricted niches, which indeed are little representative of the Amazon forest as such. They are characterized by a high frequency of commercial species (especially palms), and they often have a history of notable previous anthropogenic modifications. Prominent areas here are different pioneer vegetation types and riverside ecosystems, neither of which are characterized by the same average biological diversity as the *terra firme* rainforest, but which hold a high frequency of commercial species.

Conclusions and discussion

According to the IBGE data, plant extractivism is a minor productive sector. Even minor is the particular value of non-wood plant extraction products. These products may often be harvested in an ecologically more benign manner than wood, but in the 1995/1996 Census they only made up US$189 million, about one-fourth of the total extraction value. Other plant extraction values fall mainly on three wood products: timber, charcoal, and firewood. Many individual non-wood products registered increased quantities and values up to the 1985 Census, although with marked fluctuations over time, but absolute values declined during the 1990s. In relative terms, the decline has been even more pronounced, compared to the expansion of cultivated agricultural production. In 1939, extraction value in Brazil made up 6.2 percent of total agricultural production (see IBGE 1950, p. 3) while in 1995/1996, total extraction corresponded to only 1.6 percent of total agricultural production values. A shift from extraction to cultivation has been an integrated feature of long-run structural change in the agricultural sector, supporting those who, in a historical perspective, view extractivism as a transitory, "inferior" production type.

A critical issue for the interpretation of the presented results is the validity of the IBGE data: are there structural biases in the agricultural census which cause an undervaluation of extraction in particular, i.e. more than is the case for agricultural production? Indeed, such factors are present:

- The focus, duration, frequency and level of detail of the Agricultural Census interviews do not permit a full appreciation of minor but multiple uses of forests and other natural ecosystems
- Census coverage is probably more restricted in forest – near agricultural frontier settings
- Illegality of forest extraction causes deliberate omission and understatement in some regions

- Landless producers (who are not proper "agricultural establishments") are excluded
- Game and other animal resources are not included.

An extremely scrupulous interpretation would thus state that the Agricultural Census is generally more representative of "formal" (legal, commercial) than of "informal" (illegal and/or subsistence) production. On the other hand, that seems overcautious in the light of the actual registration of many auto-consumption uses, from wood (e.g. firewood) to non-wood products (e.g. buriti, assai, ciruella, etc.). For a product like babaçu, cross-checking with detailed case studies showed that auto-consumption is well registered in the Agricultural Census. Hence, a key question is in how many municipalities the value of neglected multiple but minor auto-consumption uses adds up to something which is significant, as a share of total production value. At the aggregate level of Brazil, some undervaluation indeed occurs, with significant errors for several federal states, but the Census is still an extremely valuable tool, which contributes vitally to a general overview. This is badly needed, in order to avoid the erroneous extrapolation of highly site-specific case study evidence.

The regression analyses confirmed that extractivism is highly dependent on labor inputs and, to a certain extent, on river transport. The statistical results lend moderate support to the "inferiority hypothesis," stating that extractivism is more likely to survive in areas with underdeveloped input markets and poor road infrastructure.

In spite of the large number of non-wood forest products that are included in the census, non-wood extraction values occur in an extremely concentrated way: diversity in use does not preclude compression in values. Concentration refers both to products and to geographical areas. Eighteen high-extraction municipalities, distributed on the "açaí belt" (Pará state) and the "babaçu belt" (mainly Maranhão, marginally Tocantins state), concentrate an astonishing 42 percent of total non-wood extraction values in Legal Amazonia, although they cover less than 1 percent of the area. It is noteworthy that four of the five high-value extraction plants in Brazil are palm trees, and none of the products traditionally associated to rainforests, like tapped rubber or Brazil nuts, currently enters the top-five list.

What are the general characteristics of these geographically defined product belts? Most of them are situated in market-near areas, in ecological niches with specific soil and vegetation types. Notably, most are previously intervened or degraded areas that now are covered by pioneer vegetation, as well as várzeas and other riverside areas with high humidity. These environments are characterized by dominant commercial species, sometimes up to the point of becoming "quasi-plantations."

This feature is inherent to the succession dynamics of natural re-growth, but it is often combined with management practices to deliberately eliminate competitive vegetation, e.g. by the repetitive use of fire. The high site-specific concentration of commercial species reduces harvesting and management costs, and thus markedly increases the economic viability of extractivism.

However, it is equally clear that the characteristics of these areas are little representative of Brazilian tropical forest biomes in a broader sense, neither of the Atlantic nor the Amazon forests. Most of all, this observation refers to the ecological setting: biological diversity tends to be much higher in *terra firme* dry-land, closed forests, which cover almost half of the Amazon's land area. The fact that large household incomes are derived from a single-species (or handful of products') harvest in market-near várzeas or pioneer vegetation areas says just about nothing about the income-generation options from highly diverse tropical forests. Even worse, if such results are extrapolated carelessly by overenthusiastic forest conservationists, they may raise highly unrealistic expectations about the profitability of non-wood forest-product harvesting – a boomerang which is certain to rebound once disappointing field results begin to speak for themselves.

High biodiversity also means a lower frequency of single commercial species per land unit, which drives up harvesting, transport, and management costs – and increases the temptation of overharvesting (see Peters 1994, p. 6). In such a scenario, only the most valuable products (such as precious timber species) are worth extracting. This means that per hectare extraction values in remote, biologically diverse, and abundant forest environments will almost inevitably be low, thus limiting the economic potential of sustained forest extraction from those sites (see Southgate 1998). To a certain extent, an insoluble conflict rules in most tropical forests between biodiversity and the long-run feasibility of commercial direct uses, between ecology and the economics of sustained market-oriented product extraction. More generally, a characterization by Curtis H. Freese may apply: "Natural ecosystems and commercial markets are uneasy bedfellows" (see Freese 1998, p. 134).

In general, some of the results in this study have confirmed the so-called "inferiority" of forest extractivism. However, this finding does not mean that extractivism should be neglected across the board, or even actively discouraged. It still facilitates a steady flow of new products that are gradually integrated into the market economy, as an intermediate phase between biodiversity's "option values" and the stage of full commercial (domesticated) integration. It also provides some complementary income for highly capital-scarce producers in land-abundant environments – a setting that is applicable to many marginal or frontier areas. However, a gradual transition from extractivism to cultivation is likely to occur for most products, and even for most places of extraction. It is difficult, if not impossible, to swim against this tide. Barriers to cultivation often appear to be technical, but the real decision parameters tend to be deeply embedded into the sphere of economic incentives: if sufficient profitability and market prospects exist, investments in research and development (R&D) of cultivation techniques will often solve what previously was perceived as an insurmountable technical hurdle. For instance, this is why cashew and rubber are now cultivated on a large scale, while Brazil nuts, for example, are not.

Although many products pass on to cultivation phases, new ones will arise from the pool of resources that the forest and other natural ecosystems continue to provide, whenever niches in the market are identified and exploited. It is important to consider these "option values" provided by the reservoir of biological diversity in natural forests in an economic sense, as an externality to the economic returns of exploitation here and now. In many forest-rich and agricultural-frontier type areas, even apparently small per hectare returns from large forest extraction areas may provide valuable partial contributions to households' livelihoods and to the economic feasibility of forest conservation strategies. On the other hand, based on the present findings, it would indeed seem unlikely that such strategies can use plant extractivism as a sustained economic cornerstone.

6 Modeling deforestation and development in the Brazilian Amazon

[I]t is now time for those interested in deforestation to shift the direction of research away from descriptive accounts and *a priori* reasoning and toward the careful empirical analysis needed to document the relationships involved and to measure their magnitudes.

(Robert T. Deacon 1995)

Previous studies

This chapter will describe our econometric model of land clearing and economic development in the Brazilian Amazon. First, however, we briefly review some of the methodological approaches that have been used in previous empirical studies of the topic and discuss the strengths and weaknesses of each. These studies can be broadly categorized as cross-country studies, regional-level analyses (such as our own), Geographical Information System (GIS) studies, and micro-level studies. For a more in-depth discussion of alternative models of tropical deforestation, we refer readers to Barbier and Burgess (2001), who also provide an excellent bibliography of recent studies.

In principle, cross-country analyses permit investigations into the relationships between the rate of deforestation and macroeconomic and institutional factors such as economic growth, population growth, openness, trade policies, political regime, indebtedness, devaluation rates, inequality, education, inflation, etc. Many of these factors vary only at the national level, and thus can be analyzed only in a cross-country context. However, serious problems beset these models, including the poor quality of data and the heterogeneity between countries. Most of these analyses are based on FAO estimates of forest cover or forest loss. These data, however, are considered highly unreliable (e.g. Rudel and Roper 1997; Kaimowitz and Angelsen 1998) and alternative estimates vary greatly. For example, the FAO estimates and the World Bank estimates of the rate of deforestation in Indonesia during the 1980s differ by a factor of 3. Furthermore, many countries reported no loss of closed-canopy forest at all during the 1980s. In a 1990 FAO Assessment, only twenty-one out of ninety estimates were based on two or more national forestry inventories. For the remaining countries, deforestation rates were extrapolated from a single data point using a simplistic model with population density and ecological classes as its only explanatory variables (Kaimowitz and Angelsen 1997, p. 11).

Another major problem with cross-country deforestation regressions is heterogeneity. Even when estimating a fixed-effect model, which allows for variations in the intercept across countries, it is doubtful that the relationships of interest are the same across all countries. While firewood collection, for example, appears to be an important source of deforestation in many African countries, it has practically no significance in Latin America, where the main source of deforestation appears to be demand for agricultural land. In Asia, logging appears to be relatively more important. If the homogeneity assumption is in fact not correct, it can lead to severely biased estimates, as shown, for example, by Andersen *et al.* (1997) for a simple model of changing land uses in the Brazilian Amazon. For a more comprehensive review of cross-country deforestation analyses, see the excellent review by Kaimowitz and Angelsen (1998).

For analyses at the regional level, it is presumably impossible to investigate the effects of variables that are identical across the whole country or region. This holds for factors such as indebtedness, devaluation rates, and many national policies. However, local government bodies can often significantly influence the manner in which national policies are implemented. For example, credit and infrastructure can be distributed differently across regions. Differences in population characteristics, internal migration, and population densities can also best be analyzed at this level.

Although the results from country-level analyses can usually not be generalized to other countries, such analyses have several significant advantages over cross-country studies. Bilsborrow (1994) mentions five such advantages: (a) more detailed data can be obtained, permitting better specified statistical models, (b) country-specific historical factors can be taken into account; (c) there is a much closer geographical match between deforestation rates and the variables of interest (population density, road density, etc.); (d) dynamic relations over time can be more readily investigated; and (e) the results generally have more obvious policy implications, which the country may choose to act upon.

Quite a large number of studies have been carried out for Latin American countries (and we review some of these when we discuss our results on land clearing below), but none has available data of the same quantity and quality as we will use for our estimations later in this chapter.

Micro-studies at the household or farm level are particularly useful because households are the actual decision makers with respect to migration, land clearing, land-use, choice of technology, etc. Such studies can potentially help provide answers to the questions about the underlying causes of deforestation, because they allow detailed information from the farmers on their place of origin, why they migrated, their current land-use practices and the reasons for them.

The primary drawback of this kind of micro study is the large costs of conducting household surveys in the vast rainforest, and the limited generalizability across sub-regions. These studies, however, are very important for complementing and validating larger-scale models, and we should be delighted to see more of them.

Finally, deforestation is an inherently spatial phenomenon and more and more researchers have recognized the need to be spatially explicit when modeling deforestation. GIS analysis makes it possible to analyze deforestation and its causes at pixel level (for example, sample points at 1 km intervals). Typical variables in GIS models include land-use type, distance to road, distance to market, and soil quality. However, other important variables do not easily lend themselves to geo-referencing and are therefore often ignored in these models. These include population variables, income variables, and credit extension.

Thus, there are many different kinds of empirical models, all with different inherent advantages and disadvantages, that yield insights into different aspects of the economic and ecological processes. The data we employ in this book is the most comprehensive regional-level data set yet compiled on the Brazilian Amazon. The present book represents a good first pass at analyzing this rich resource, but undoubtedly more insights will come in the future. Ultimately, a comprehensive understanding of the dynamics of land-use in the Amazon will also require different kinds of studies, especially micro-level and GIS research, to fill in the picture.

Model specification

The processes of growth and development in the Amazon are clearly complex and in addition they are evolving over time as the role of government policy changes and the frontier advances. A good structural (i.e. a "theory-based") model of these processes requires a comprehensive theoretical knowledge of the possible important relationships; leaving out any one of them could significantly bias the results if the processes under study are correlated with the omitted variables. However, identifying all the dynamic and spatial interactions and feedback relationships that could be expected to play an important role in the evolution of these processes may be virtually impossible at this point in time. We therefore estimate a "reduced-form" model in which we start with an initial (large) set of variables which *may* play a role and let the data itself decide which of those should be included in the model: the so-called "general-to-simple" modeling strategy (for a complete discussion see Hendry 1995, pp. 344–368). Thus, our model will give us an idea of general relationships in the data; it will not tell us the specific functional form that these relationships take. The advantage of this approach is that we can start with a larger set of possibly important variables and so are more likely to be successful at controlling for omitted-variable bias. In turn, if the data do not choose a particular variable as being important then we have added confidence in that result; a structural model that forcibly included a variable while leaving out myriad other relationships may well find that the variable of interest is significant for no other reason than that it is picking up the effects of the omitted variables. This is especially important when it comes to our policy variables such as roads.

Nevertheless, the "general-to-simple," data-based estimation strategy does have its own drawbacks, some of which we can try to avoid and some of which we must live with. In particular, a principal drawback of the sort we can try to avoid is that the "reduction" stage of a traditional estimation process (where the researcher removes variables from the analysis that are not deemed statistically important) can potentially be somewhat arbitrary. The order in which variables are eliminated may have a significant impact on the final specification and thus there is always the possibility that the researcher herself may have a subtle influence on the direction of the modeling. In other words, given a certain criterion for determining a "final" model, the data-based approach may theoretically be able to generate a number of models, each equally "good" by the researcher's criteria. These multiple alternative models may or may not yield differing policy implications.

A primary drawback of this approach that is more difficult to avoid is that despite the large number of control variables, ultimately the model still estimates average relationships across time and space. The assumption that most of the important differences among the municipalities are captured in our set of control variables is quite heroic, so there is always the possibility of important omitted variables that could be biasing the results. In particular, for the analysis of roads a critical piece of information missing from our model is whether the roads in a certain municipality are leading to specific locations. In the history of the Amazon, as discussed earlier in this book, there are dramatically different effects from different road projects depending on the start and end points of the road in question. Thus roads from one project going through a municipality could have dramatically different effects than from the same length of road associated with another project and headed towards a different destination. Our model cannot capture these distinctions: it estimates an overall average effect from all road projects. We do attempt to control for the fact that roads built through virgin areas will have different effects from roads built through more established areas, however.

In addition, while our model does include state dummies, distance to market variables, soil and climatic data correlated with location, and neighborhood effects of a sort (described below), it is not a completely specified spatial model in the GIS tradition by any means. Thus, our model should be seen as complementary to, but certainly not a substitute for, other types of macro-models. In particular there is an acute need for more studies of potential migratory and market effects of proposed roads projects and more detailed GIS studies that include economic, as well as environmental, data.

Modified "general-to-simple" modeling: random reduction

While we cannot completely eliminate the possibility of omitted-variable bias and our framework and data do not allow us to trace the destination of roads, we nevertheless attempt to minimize the possibility of arbitrariness or bias in the selection of the final model by developing a modification to the standard "general-to-simple" approach. In particular, we use an iterative procedure in which the variable that is to be removed from the analysis is randomly chosen from among up to three (statistically insignificant) variables with the lowest degrees of statistical significance, a procedure we call "random reduction." This random reduction proceeds until all variables in the model fulfill a particular criteria (see the Technical appendix for a full accounting of how this was applied in our case) and is thus chosen as a "final" model. However, as pointed out above this "final" model is not unique among all possible models fulfilling our criteria. Thus, we repeat the process, again randomizing the elimination choice across the lowest significance variables, and come up with a second "final" model, and so on. For this book we have repeated each random reduction 100 times and then examine how many times each variable ended up in the final model, what the average coefficient estimate was, and what the spread of the coefficient estimates (highest and lowest value) was across all models in which that variable appeared. We call variables that made it into the final model frequently "robust." We can also see if the spread of coefficient estimates is relatively tight or spread out – another indication of how reliable the mean coefficient value is.

Using the random reduction method ensures that our results are a function only of the initial set of possible explanatory variables and the chosen functional form of the regression, not of any pre-existing researcher bias about which variables should remain in the analysis. We further reduce the possibility of conscious or unconscious researcher bias by relying on a series of objective out-of-sample forecasting exercises developed in Granger and Huang (1997) to determine the specification and sample time-span of the estimated models (see the technical appendix for more detail).

Because our methodology differs from the standard one-shot-only regression analysis, the summary statistics presented in the tables also differ slightly. In particular, while we do provide an indicative, representative goodness of fit (R^2) measure for each model, we do not report *t*-statistics in the standard fashion as they would be uninformative. All the variables that make it to a "final" model do so because their respective *t*-statistic is over 2 in absolute value. However, given that our model uses an iterative search for the final model specification, these *t*-statistics are not associated with the same statistical size as would be expected from a standard set of statistical tables and correctly calculating them would require a bootstrapping approach that would take many weeks even on today's fastest computers. For the purposes of constructing our simulation model below we consider all variables that reach the "final" model at least 50 percent of the time to be statistically important, but in the statistical appendix we report the number of "hits" for all variables so that readers can impose their own criteria if they believe our framework to be too liberal or too conservative.

Model specification and variables

Our six endogenous (dependent) variables are land clearing, rural and urban GDP growth, rural and urban population growth, and cattle herd growth. In addition we include models of paved and unpaved roads to get an idea of the driving factors behind their expansion.[1] We exclude a separate equation of land prices from the analysis only because we do not have complete data for 1995. Since we have data for all other years, however, we can control for the lagged values in the other equations.

We model the growth rates, rather than the levels, of our endogenous variables, for several reasons. First, the levels are highly trending in most of our variables and thus a model in levels would be highly susceptible to spurious correlation. Second, by taking growth rates we effectively eliminate the municipality-specific "fixed effects" from the analysis. In other

[1] We do not endogenize the roads equations in the later *Avança Brasil* simulations, however, as in those exercises we wish to exogenously vary the roads to see their effects on other variables.

words, all the time-invariant municipality characteristics that influence, say, the level of cattle herd, are present in both the start and the end period, so the change between periods cancels them out. In this way we effectively control for an enormous host of unobserved time-invariant variables that could bias the analysis if omitted from consideration. Controlling for the fixed effects also controls for the overall average level of spatial correlation in the data, thus cutting down considerably the scope for spatial correlation becoming a problem in the estimation.

Some time-invariant municipality-specific characteristics could still play a role if they are important determinants of the *growth* of our endogenous variables, not just the levels (i.e. "fixed effects" in growth rates). This could be the case if there is a direct effect, but also if they are correlated with more municipality-specific spatial correlation that remains in the data. Given that we want to allow for time-heterogeneity of the models (see below), we do not have enough data to control for these fixed-effects-in-growth completely. Nevertheless we do include a number of time-invariant variables including a full set of state dummy variables, measures of the original natural vegetation and soil type of each municipality, distance to state and federal market, length of navigable river, variables on the average monthly temperatures, and a dummy variable for high rainfall. These variables will enter only if important for the *growth* of the dependent variable; many variables may be important for the level but not the growth rate and so do not appear in the final models.

While we have controlled as much as is feasible, given our data, for both unobserved and observed time-invariant municipality characteristics that could affect the levels and growth rates of our dependent variables, there still remains the question of time-varying omitted variables. Thus, we include a lagged dependent variable (i.e. lagged growth rate of the dependent variable) and a twice-lagged initial level of each endogenous variable in the specification. These variables embody all the information that was important for determining the endogenous variable at that time, including time-varying unobservables. In as much as those time-varying unobservables are themselves correlated across time, then, the lagged dependent variable can serve as a partial control for them as well (the lagged level will also control for time-invariant effects).[2]

Another important advantage of including lagged dependent growth rates and lagged levels is that we can investigate one of the most important characteristics of a growth process: the dynamic path over time

[2] Statistical estimation of dynamic models with few time periods can be tricky (see the technical appendix). However, we discuss below why we have chosen (via our forecasting criteria) to separate the model by years rather than pooling. Thus, our final specification is actually a cross-section (albeit with a lot of time-series information included) rather than a panel, which has the advantage of avoiding some of these statistical problems that arise with very short dynamic panel estimation.

that it seems to be following. Many processes have some intrinsic dynamic structure apart from the effects of exogenous forces; for example, as GDP gets higher the marginal returns may diminish and slow growth, or as land becomes more cleared the remaining forest becomes increasingly protected by law or the remaining land may become less attractive for agrotechnical reasons. In addition, there is a natural limit on the extent of clearing, which secures that clearing cannot continue linearly indefinitely. In other cases we might see explosive growth (perhaps as a result of increasing returns) in which a high growth rate one period would lead to high growth the next. An advantage of our model specification is that we can check for these kinds of relationships and take them into account when projecting into the future. A model which generates predictions by simply extrapolating from current trends and growth rates could be badly biased and could overestimate or underestimate the trajectory of variables that display either of these kinds of internal dynamic structures.

Another issue that is important is that the six variables of interest are all *endogenous* in that the direction of causality between them could go in either or both directions. For example, including the growth of cattle herds in a model of the growth of cleared land could lead to bias because it could be that cattle ranchers clear land directly, or are attracted to areas that are already cleared. Theory provides us with some good hypotheses but the resolution of this question will ultimately be an empirical issue. If causality goes in both directions, any model that does not control for this endogeneity will produce biased estimates and incorrect policy conclusions. Thus, in our model we attempt to minimize this possibility by including only the time-lags of all endogenous variables on the right-hand side.[3]

As we have discussed above, in the frontier environment of the Amazon spatial location can be extremely important in determining economic activity. In a standard regression analysis it is assumed that all the observations are independent, but this is clearly not the case in the Amazon; it matters a lot what is going on in neighboring municipalities. Pfaff (1996), using very similar data to our own, finds that the spatial distribution of both roads and people are very important for the modeling of deforestation processes in the Amazon. In fact a whole category of empirical models of deforestation focus on geographical location as the primary determinant of many economic activities. Some of these models are based on adaptations of the theoretical framework of von Thünen (1966) in which the location structure of different economic activities is described as functions of the distance from a central market. Deforestation adaptations of the von Thünen model have been used by Cline-Cole

[3] In that sense our model looks almost like a vector autoregression (VAR) model, except that, as mentioned above, we do not technically use a true panel estimation.

et al. (1990), von Amsberg (1994), Schneider (1995), Chomitz and Gray (1996), and others. Another broad category of spatially intensive models are GIS models which include information on topography, land quality, road networks, population densities, and agricultural prices (e.g. Ludeke *et al.* 1990; Liu *et al.* 1993; Nelson and Hellerstein 1995; Chomitz and Gray 1996; Mertens and Lambin 1997). The Brazilian Institute of Geography and Statistics (IBGE) is in the process of creating a large GIS system for the Brazilian Amazon and it will soon be possible to start modeling on a scale that is useful for sensible location of roads, forest reserves, logging and mining concessions, and for other planning purposes.

Unfortunately the municipality-level data set that we currently have available is not sufficiently detailed for this type of GIS modeling. As discussed above, in our model we rely to a certain extent on the fact that while levels of variables may be very spatially related, the growth rates should be somewhat less so (since location is, after all, a time-invariant characteristic). Of course we cannot exclude the possibility of spatial correlation in the growth rates as well – and our story of an evolving frontier would strongly suggest that such relationships could be important. Some of our time-invariant municipality characteristics may help to indirectly capture some of these relationships, but we also want to directly incorporate a spatial dimension in the model. Thus, we include additional spatial variables which measure the state of affairs along a number of dimensions in nearby municipalities. In particular we control for the (lagged) level of all of the endogenous variables, normalized by land area where appropriate, as well as the density of paved and unpaved roads and the average land price in surrounding regions. Each spatial variable is constructed by taking the weighted average value across the five closest neighbors, with the weights inversely proportional to the distance between them.

The policy variables that we include are lagged growth and level of land prices and paved and unpaved federal and state roads. We do not include municipal roads as we suspect these (even lagged) are highly endogenous to the processes under study. We also include SUDAM government credit through 1985, and federal government transfers in 1985.

As the discussion above has made apparent, the initial list of potential explanatory variables is extremely important. It must balance the need to span as much of the information set as possible without being too large; with too many explanatory variables the initial model may not be estimable or may have such low power that the initial steps of the reduction process become almost completely arbitrary. Our list includes (twice) lagged growth and levels of the endogenous variables, a set of municipality-specific characteristics, a set of spatial terms and roads and land-price data for a total of seventy-four initial variables. With a sample size of 257 it is clearly impractical to include all the variables in a final regression; and any smaller sub-set of these variables chosen from theory would run the risk of omitting potentially important factors. By employing a "general-to-simple" methodology we allow the data to tell us what sub-set of our initial list is important, and by iterating this process many times via the random reduction strategy we can tell how robust any given final model specification is.

Timeframe of the analysis

Given the DESMAT panel data set we have a choice of whether to pool all the years together or to estimate models across differing time spans. The first complication we face is that our final time period spans ten years, rather than the five-year periodicity of the rest of the data. While we can attempt to deal with this by modeling average annual growth and assuming that this was constant over each period (as well as controlling for heteroskedasticity), this assumption may be problematic. Nevertheless, if the true model is relatively consistent across time, we might gain more power despite this problem by pooling the data. However, if the relationships under study are changing significantly over time then pooling may impose unrealistic homogeneity restrictions on the model specification and coefficients.

There are good reasons to suspect that there has been considerable change over time as the settlement process evolves in Legal Amazonia. In particular, while early in the colonization process such activities as land clearing, population growth, and cattle ranching may have been driven primarily by government policies and exogenous external forces, as the region's economy matures many endogenous internal forces may in fact have become the more powerful, driving forces behind the development process. In addition to a natural dynamic evolution of development, a number of more exogenous forces came to bear on the region in the late 1980s and early 1990s that could easily have changed the structure of the underlying process as well. Within the period from 1985 to 1995 Brazil suffered a significant economic downturn, and although economic activity picked up after 1993, real urban GDP *per capita* was, on average, lower in 1995 than in 1985. At the same time, after 1985 the Brazilian government reduced or repealed many of the pro-development policies it had pursued up to that point (see chapter 2 for a more complete discussion).

Thus, in building our model we first wish to check for parameter stability over the sample period, in particular between the 1980–1985 and the 1985–1995 periods. As discussed in the technical appendix, we compare the out-of-sample forecasting performances of models estimated using both pooled and non-pooled data over different time spans. Even the non-pooled data has significant time-series information in it in the form of lags of the endogenous and exogenous variables, but the data itself is a cross-section (i.e. 257 observations). For the purposes of forecasting 1995 values we found that the non-pooled model did best; in other words there was evidence that the relationships had changed significantly over time.

This conclusion is further borne out when we compare two non-pooled regressions for 1980–1985 and 1985–1995 and find that the models are quite different, in some cases dramatically so.[4] While limited degrees of freedom in the regressions could cause some parameter heterogeneity, the difference in the two model estimates, presented in the technical appendix, clearly indicates structural changes in the underlying driving forces behind our eight endogenous variables. Many of the coefficient estimates change signs and some variables that are important in 1985 are not in 1995, and vice versa. Given the striking heterogeneity between the two time periods it is clearly incorrect to pool the data and instead we estimate two models, one for the growth from 1980 to 1985 and a second for growth from 1985 to 1995.

Care must be exercised when comparing the two models, for several reasons. First, as we mentioned above, the time spans are different with the former modeling five-year growth from 1980 to 1985 and latter growth over ten years from 1985 to 1995. Owing to data limitations we can allow up to two lags of each growth rate in the 1995 model, but only one in the 1985 model. Furthermore, the latter model is averaged across ten years during which there was a serious economic recession and recovery. As we do not observe the dynamics over these ten years, the model can capture only the average relationships over the period. Finally, as discussed in chapter 3, the 1995/1996 Agricultural Census was taken during a different part of the year from previous Censuses and we cannot be completely sure of the consequences of this change.

On the other hand, the ten-year span in the latter model could prove an advantage in other ways. For example, the longer period minimizes the problem of endogeneity bias by increasing the chances that the explanatory variables are truly exogenous (as they are further in the past). In any case, given the rapidly evolving nature of development in the Amazon we believe that the more recent 1985–1995 model should

[4] The two models presented in this book differ in that the 1995 model includes two possible lagged values of each growth rate, while owing to data limitations the 1985 model can include only one lag. However, when the number of lags in the 1995 model is constrained so that the potential dynamic structures are identical the same parameter instability is observed that is reported here. Thus we feel very confident that this is a robust finding and not an artifact of the different dynamic structure of the two models.

provide us with better estimates of current relationships than the older model. An analysis of both sets of results is indeed relatively consistent with the view that the earlier model reflects relationships much earlier in the process of frontier development, while the model of economic processes suggested by the latter model has matured and evolves more endogenously. Thus, it is the later 1985–1995 model that we analyze more intensively and use for policy simulations as well.

The full specification of the 1985–1995 model takes the following form:

$$gY_{kit} = \alpha + \beta_{1j} \sum_j X_{1i} + \beta_{2k} \sum_k gY_{kit-1} \tag{6.1}$$

$$+ \beta_{3k} \sum_k gY_{kit-2} + \beta_{4k} \sum_f lY_{kit-3} \tag{6.2}$$

$$+ \beta_{5h} \sum_h S_{hit-1} + \epsilon_{it} \tag{6.3}$$

where gY_k correspond to the $k = 1 \ldots 8$ growth rates of our endogenous variables, and lY_k correspond to the log-level of those endogenous variables. Thus, the growth rates of endogenous variables appear lagged twice on the right-hand side, whereas the log-levels, lY_ks appear with a three-period lag. The X_{1j} are the $j = 1 \ldots \mathcal{J}$ time-invariant variables including state dummy variables and ecological, weather, and distance to market indicators, and S_{2h} are the $h = 1 \ldots H$ spatial neighborhood variables, which are log-levels (weighted and normalized as described above and in the technical appendix) lagged once.

In the 1980–1985 model we include only one lag of endogeneous variables and the second lag of endogenous log-levels of the variables, so the model structure becomes:

$$gY_{kit} = \alpha + \beta_{1j} \sum_j X_{1i} + \beta_{2k} \sum_k gY_{kit-1} \tag{6.4}$$

$$+ \beta_{3k} \sum_f lY_{kit-2} + \beta_{4h} \sum_h S_{hit-1} + \epsilon_{it} \tag{6.5}$$

For both sets of equations, the reported results below include only those variables that were statistically significant in at least one of the final models after 100 iterations of random reduction, so the actual model specification for any given equation will be a sub-set of those outlined above.

Estimation results

As discussed above, a result of the random reduction strategy is that we end up with up to 100 different models (in practice the same model may be repeatedly derived) that are all "good" by the criteria we have specified. We have found this approach complementary to the ideas of "thick" modeling presented in Granger (2000, p. 2), where he comments:

> a combination of forecasts is often a better procedure than using the individually best forecast. Similarly, a portfolio of assets is usually better than investing in a single asset, even if it is better than any other single alternative in comparisons of pairs. Thick modeling consists of using many alternative specifications of similar quality, using each to produce the output required for the purpose of the modeling exercise . . . and then combine or synthesize the results.

Thus, in the spirit of Granger (2000) we present our results as follows. For each variable we calculate the number of times it ended up in the "final" model and present the average coefficient value over all these cases. In the technical appendix we also present the spread (minimum and maximum value). To save space and keep things tidy in this chapter we present only an abbreviated version of the 1980–1985 and 1985–1995 model results; namely, the coefficient estimates of the endogenous and policy variables while excluding most of the time-invariant variables. The complete results of both the 1980–1985 and the 1985–1995 models are presented in the technical appendix.

The tables should be interpreted as follows. Information about the lagged values of each of the main endogenous variables (as well as paved and unpaved roads, land prices, and policy variables) comes in at least one of three possible forms: as lagged growth rates, as lagged (log) levels and as lagged spatial neighborhood variables. The exact definition of each variable can be found in the technical appendix, along with the complete results from each model. The tables each correspond to one endogenous variable and succinctly indicate which factors were found to have significant explanatory power for that endogenous variable in both the 1980–1985 model and the 1985–1995 model. These possible explanatory factors (the lagged endogenous and policy variables) are listed down the left-hand column. Across the row appear the corresponding average coefficient estimates for the possible forms it could take: growth, level, or spatial variable.[5] In parentheses below the coefficient estimates are the number of times out of 100 that the particular variable "made it" into the final model in the random reduction process as explained above. As a rule of thumb, we generally consider those variables that have counts of at least 50 as being reasonably robust, although that is an arbitrary rule of thumb that is open to question. By reading across the row for each explanatory

[5] Where there are two (lagged) growth rates, tables 6.1–6.8 present the sum of the coefficients.

factor, then, it is quite easy to see whether it entered significantly, and with which sign, in each model. In the final row of each table we have listed the adjusted R^2 (goodness of fit) statistic for the model made up of all explanatory variables that made it at least 50 times out of 100 into the final model, which are also the specifications used later in the simulation exercises.

Growth of cleared land

The evolution of cleared land is clearly an immensely important variable of interest to policy makers and environmentalists alike, and an understanding of how and why land is cleared is a central question addressed by this book. Numerous other studies have also attempted to characterize the primary determinants of land clearing (or deforestation), with mixed success. In this section we shall first discuss the results of our random reduction model, and then compare our results with those found in the literature.

Perhaps the most remarkable characteristic of our model of the growth of cleared land is how exceptionally stable the specification is: most of the robust variables made it into the final model for all 100 iterations (see table 6.1, p. 125, and table A.2 in the technical appendix, p. 217). In addition, the dynamics are similar across the 1980–1985 and 1985–1995 models: from these highly robust models we observe that the growth of cleared land within a municipality clearly displays leveling-off effects in which areas that were cleared especially quickly in the past are cleared less rapidly, and those that are already highly cleared have a lower rate of clearing growth. There is a positive correlation between growth of cleared land and past neighbors' cleared land density, which could be interpreted as a frontier effect in which land is cleared more quickly in areas near already highly cleared areas.

However, in other aspects the clearing pattern in the 1980–1985 and 1985–1995 models is quite different. In the early model, rural population patterns were important with land being cleared fastest where there was high rural population growth, but slowing down in already highly settled areas. In the 1995 model we also see an impact from fast-growing rural populations, but now the growth of urban populations is also important. So too is the growth of cattle herds, a result consistent with the literature indicating cattle ranching as one of the major contributors to land clearing (see, for example, Harrison 1991; Faminow 1998).

In this 1985–1995 model clearing growth is also negatively associated with both neighbors' rural population and cattle herd density. Given that the model is also controling for neighbors' cleared land density, one interpretation of this result is that for a given amount of cleared land in

Table 6.1. *Estimation results: growth of cleared land*

	1980–1985			1985–1995		
MODEL:	Growth[b]	Log-level[b]	Spatial[b]	Growth	Log-level	Spatial
Variable	(All variables lagged*)			(All variables lagged*)		
FINAM[a] credit		−0.121[c]				
		(34)[d]				
Cleared land	−0.3013	−2.9708	8.6995	−0.5414	−2.7312	15.6622
	(100)	(100)	(100)	(100)	(100)	(100)
Rural GDP						−1.3596
						(3)
Urban GDP						0.8545
						(3)
Urban pop.				0.2593		4.4992
				(100)		(97)
Rural pop.	0.3829	−3.127		0.5255		−13.86
	(100)	(100)		(100)		(100)
Cattle herd				0.1316	0.9071	−17.977
				(100)	(99)	(100)
Land price	0.1115	3.4032	−3.0165		0.8269	
	(100)	(100)	(100)		(99)	
Paved roads				0.4227	4.2762	
				(79)	(100)	
Unpaved roads		−6.0947		0.0471	0.5227	
		(100)		(89)	(97)	
Interact (unpaved*clear)		0.5878		0.0041	0.0477	
		(100)		(8)	(1)	
Interact (paved*clear)				−0.0375	−0.399	
				(88)	(100)	
Adj. R^2:		0.4617			0.6002	

Notes: [a]FINAM and federal transfers from 1985 only.
[b]A full definition of the growth, level, and spatial version of each variable can be found in the technical appendix, along with the full results of all regressions.
[c]Figures are mean coefficient estimates from the random reduction estimation method described in this chapter and in the technical appendix.
[d]Numbers in parentheses are the number of times a respective variable made it into the final model (i.e. with a t-statistic over 2) out of 100 iterations.

the neighboring regions, the more established the rural activity, the lower the new clearing in the surrounding regions – again, a result consistent with an evolving frontier view of the process and one in which established areas prove relatively more attractive. At the same time, urban demand (as measured by urban population) from neighboring municipalities is positively associated with increased clearing. Taken together, these results show the increasing importance of local urban demand on the more recent clearing patterns.

In terms of the policy variables the results are also illuminating. In particular, federal transfers are never significant, and FINAM credit is not robust, even in the 1980–1985 model. In the 1980–1985 model, the coefficient on the level of unpaved roads is negative, but this must be taken into account with the positive coefficient on the interaction of unpaved roads and cleared land. In other words, in municipios with relatively high proportions of cleared land, increased levels of unpaved roads increased the growth of cleared land. We find no impact of paved roads in this earlier model.

In the 1985–1995 model, on the other hand, the effect of roads is quite different. *Ceteris paribus*, both the growth and existing level of both paved and unpaved roads increases the growth of cleared land. Moreover, the interaction between growth and level of paved roads and cleared land is negative, indicating that in those areas with relatively less cleared area, the rate of clearing owing to paved roads is higher. Thus, in highly cleared areas we would not expect new paved roads to have much of an impact on clearing rates while the impact could be quite dramatic in relatively uncleared areas.

The results on roads are worth stressing for two reasons. First, it has very important implications for government policy in the region. Second, other authors (e.g. Ferraz 2001) have have found a somewhat different result, namely that cultivated area and cattle head density are positively correlated with the lagged density of paved roads but not the lagged density of unpaved roads. Theoretically, our results seem more sensible. Unpaved roads tend to be built through virgin areas where they open up new agricultural frontiers and drive land prices down everywhere. This would tend to cause an increase in extensive land-use, such as cattle ranching. Paved roads, on the other hand, tend to be constructed in more established areas and cause a dramatic increase in land prices owing to better market access. This would tend to encourage more intensive farming methods and displace the extensive ones. Thus, theoretically one would expect federal and state unpaved roads to cause agricultural extensification (additional clearing), whereas paved roads would tend to cause an intensification of agriculture, i.e. an increase in GDP but not much additional clearing. Our empirical model of clearing is generally consistent with this story, and thus lends some support to the recent modifications of Brazil's infrastructure plans for the Amazon. Almost all road projects described in *Avança Brasil* are about improvements to existing roads, and only a few small stretches of new road are being planned with the purpose of connecting existing roads. This should theoretically encourage agricultural intensification and relieve the pressure for new land clearing (see further discussion of this program below). Nevertheless, our findings also caution that construction of paved roads into or through less established areas could indeed cause new land clearing, so that careful planning is necessary to gain the greatest benefit at the lowest environmental cost to the forest.

There are other explanations for why our findings differ from those in Ferraz (2001) as well. In particular, Ferraz uses annual state-level data, rather than municipal-level data, which means that the geographic units are rather coarse and the correspondence between the location of roads and the location of cattle and crops thus quite weak. The effect of roads is really best analyzed at pixel level, like the studies of Chomitz and Gray (1996) and Alves (1999, 2002). Ours is at an intermediate level between the pixel and the state level. Perhaps more importantly, however, unlike us Ferraz (2001) includes municipal roads, which must be considered highly endogenous, especially since Ferraz's lags are of only one year. Since municipal roads completely dominate state and federal roads in terms of extension, they have the potential to seriously bias any estimates of the effect of roads.

Finally, we should also point out that our model says something about the effects of state and federal road building, the grand projects, and over a relatively long time period. We estimate the effect of roads built up until 1985 on clearing between 1985 and 1995, and find that even relatively old unpaved roads keep causing new clearing, probably through the local road networks that build up around them. Paved roads through relatively unspoiled areas can precipitate new clearing as well, although paved roads through established areas in general do not lead to continued high clearing rates. Thus we capture the long-run effects of grand road building (including their indirect impact through the effect on land prices and local road building), whereas in Ferraz's estimates, given the specification, one could expect the short-run effects to dominate.

Rural GDP growth

The dynamics of rural GDP growth display robust signs of leveling off in both the 1980–1985 and 1985–1995 models, with those municipalities experiencing faster than average growth in the past growing more slowly, and vice versa (table 6.2, p. 128). Rural GDP growth depends on urban GDP and population; municipalities with historically high urban growth rates display higher rural growth, as do those with relatively wealthy urban neighbors (in the later model). These results indicate strongly that some of the primary determinants of rural GDP are local urban demand factors.

In the 1985–1995 model, rural GDP growth is higher in areas whose neighbors have a high density of cleared land, and higher where land prices have been high. Rural GDP growth also is higher in areas which

Table 6.2. *Estimation results: growth of rural GDP*[a]

	1980–1985			1985–1995		
MODEL: Variable	Growth[b]	Log-level[b] (All variables lagged*)	Spatial[b]	Growth	Log-level (All variables lagged*)	Spatial
Cleared land	0.1225[c]	4.6662		0.1313	3.3713	11.717
	(100)[d]	(100)		(100)	(100)	(100)
Rural GDP	−0.5699	−11.926		−0.6244	−8.0112	−3.0021
	(100)	(100)		(100)	(100)	(100)
Urban GDP	0.1103	1.9769	−0.7776		1.0052	1.9815
	(50)	(11)	(1)		(93)	(100)
Urban pop.	0.5886	−1.3401		0.3119		
	(100)	(36)		(100)		
Rural pop.		4.6783	11.1348	0.3232		
		(100)	(100)	(100)		
Cattle		1.0471		0.0349		
herd		(100)		(92)		
Land price	0.062	1.7883		0.1353	2.76	
	(25)	(80)		(7)	(100)	
Paved roads			−101.67	−0.0346		
			(88)	(100)		
Unpaved roads						−96.922
						(100)
Interact				0.0104		
(paved*clear)				(77)		
Adj. R^2:		0.3053			0.5893	

Notes: [a] FINAM and federal transfers from 1985 only.
[b] A full definition of the growth, level, and spatial version of each variable can be found in the technical appendix, along with the full results of all regressions.
[c] Figures are mean coefficient estimates from the random reduction estimation method described in this chapter and in the technical appendix.
[d] Numbers in parentheses are the number of times a respective variable made it into the final model (i.e. with a t-statistic over 2) out of 100 iterations.

have seen higher than average growth of cattle herd. In the 1985 model, growth depends on the level of existing herd, rather than the growth rate. Importantly, we note that unpaved roads has no direct impact on rural GDP growth. Suprisingly, the coefficient on paved roads is negative. Upon closer inspection of the complete results in the technical appendix, it is apparent that this is the sum of a positive coefficient on the first lag, and a negative coefficient of slightly larger magnitude (but less robust) on the second lag. However, the interaction of the growth of paved roads and cleared land is positive. In other words, in those municipalities with a relatively large proportion of cleared land, the gains from paved roads are larger. This is significant; it indicates that the returns to paving roads are higher in areas that already have significant economic activity. Any extension of paved roads into relatively untouched areas is thus unlikely to result in the same economic benefit.

Urban GDP growth

The model of growth of urban GDP also shows the leveling-off effects (table 6.3, p. 130). Unlike the rural GDP model in which rural population never entered, the growth of urban population is an important positively related determinant of urban GDP growth in the 1985–1995 model, although not in the 1980–1985 model. The growth of urban GDP also depends on indicators of the scale of rural activity. In particular, there is a positive association with the level of cattle herds in both the earlier and the later models. Finally we find that the level, growth, and spatial effects of paved roads, and the level of unpaved roads, are important determinants of urban GDP in the 1985–1995 model. In the 1980–1985 model we find that there is some benefit from paved roads in areas with relatively high proportions of cleared land. This result is not repeated in the 1985–1995 model; in fact where it does appear the sign is negative (although not robust). Finally, in the early model we find a very strong positive effect from federal transfers. However, as this variable is not lagged there is a possibility of endogeneity; in other words the federal transfers could be directed towards those areas that are growing strongly and thus a causal relationship is impossible to infer from this model alone. In fact, since 1985 federal transfers are not significant in the 1985–1995 model the reverse causality argument is made even stronger.

Urban and rural population growth

While urban population growth is slower in municipalities with relatively high existing populations, we find that growth from 1985 to 1995 is positively correlated with past growth (tables 6.4 and 6.5, pp. 131–132). Hence population movements in this period seem to display a certain amount of hysteresis, with more migration towards those areas which have already received relatively higher rates of recent migration. In addition, urban population movements in the 1985–1995 model display a significant amount of spatial influence. We find urban population growth is faster in areas whose neighbors have high rural population densities, low land prices, and large paved road densities. In areas that have already been cleared, the growth of unpaved roads seems to facilitate the growth of urban populations. However, we do not observe this effect for more unspoiled areas.

Table 6.3. *Estimation results: growth of urban GDP*

	1980–1985			1985–1995		
MODEL:	Growth[b]	Log-level[b]	Spatial[b]	Growth	Log-level	Spatial
Variable	(All variables lagged*)			(All variables lagged*)		
% Indian reserve					−6.101 (40)	
Federal transfers/ GDP(−1)[a]		45.862[c] (100)[d]				
Cleared land	−0.1204 (2)	−2.1329 (2)				7.6477 (9)
Rural GDP			2.077 (9)	0.0761 (8)		
Urban GDP	−0.2653 (100)	−2.4044 (99)		−0.4856 (100)	−3.9853 (100)	
Urban pop.			6.692 (81)	1.1956 (100)	5.6671 (100)	6.4512 (100)
Rural pop.	0.3963 (1)	−3.1577 (88)	15.3972 (16)			
Cattle herd	0.0924 (3)	0.8924 (97)			1.7289 (100)	−17.602 (73)
Land price		2.0611 (97)			1.5811 (1)	3.8978 (100)
Paved roads	0.0366 (4)		−101.16 (5)	0.205 (74)	1.1472 (95)	51.1586 (22)
Unpaved roads	0.0441 (2)	0.7774 (13)			3.0663 (93)	−92.768 (47)
Interact (unpaved*clear)	0.0039 (14)				−0.2825 (94)	
Interact (paved*clear)	0.003 (58)			−0.006 (12)	0.0941 (5)	
Adj. R^2:		0.3735			0.5083	

Notes: [a]FINAM and federal transfers from 1985 only.
[b]A full definition of the growth, level, and spatial version of each variable can be found in the technical appendix, along with the full results of all regressions.
[c]Figures are mean coefficient estimates from the random reduction estimation method described in this chapter and in the technical appendix.
[d]Numbers in parentheses are the number of times a respective variable made it into the final model (i.e. with a t-statistic over 2) out of 100 iterations.

The pattern of urban population growth is quite different in the earlier model, however. Spatial variables are not quite as important; instead, there is a clear dynamic in which highly populated areas grow more slowly, and there is urban migration from neighboring areas with high population densities. In addition those areas that experienced the highest urban GDP

Table 6.4. *Estimation results: growth of urban population*

	1980–1985			1985–1995		
MODEL:	Growth[b]	Log-level[b]	Spatial[b]	Growth	Log-level	Spatial
Variable	(All variables lagged*)			(All variables lagged*)		
% Protected					−6.804 (88)	
Federal Transfers/ GDP(−1)[a]		6.222[c] (60)[d]				
Cleared land	−0.0313 (93)	−0.5384 (12)	−2.4992 (1)	−0.0095 (49)	−0.1727 (5)	0.8123 (8)
Rural GDP			0.832 (61)	0.008 (1)		
Urban GDP	0.0694 (100)	1.2682 (100)	−0.5791 (53)			−0.1198 (62)
Urban pop.	−0.1025 (9)	−2.204 (100)	3.8237 (100)	0.5029 (100)	−0.3584 (100)	1.0009 (1)
Rural pop.	0.1508 (92)	0.8763 (86)	−4.6667 (40)		0.2894 (48)	1.7092 (79)
Cattle herd	0.0531 (100)		4.3097 (2)			1.0642 (6)
Land price			−0.6394 (11)	−0.0091 (83)		−0.5619 (98)
Paved roads	0.0116 (1)					11.19 (90)
Unpaved roads		−0.7012 (16)	25.7761 (6)	−0.0991 (92)	−0.3511 (21)	
Interact (unpaved*clear)		0.0551 (35)		0.0093 (93)	0.0359 (16)	
Adj. R^2:	0.5389			0.8430		

Notes: [a] FINAM and federal transfers from 1985 only.
[b] A full definition of the growth, level, and spatial version of each variable can be found in the technical appendix, along with the full results of all regressions.
[c] Figures are mean coefficient estimates from the random reduction estimation method described in this chapter and in the technical appendix.
[d] Numbers in parentheses are the number of times a respective variable made it into the final model (i.e. with a t-statistic over 2) out of 100 iterations.

growth over the previous periods attract the biggest population increases (an attractant force we do not see in the later model at all). These forces are all more important than roads as we find no robust effect of these at all in the early model.

Neither of the models for rural population growth are very robust; few variables make it consistently into the final model, leading to very unstable final specifications across iterations. This indicates that our model

Table 6.5. *Estimation results: growth of rural population*[a]

MODEL: Variable	1980–1985 Growth[b]	Log-level[b] (All variables lagged*)	Spatial[b]	1985–1995 Growth	Log-level (All variables lagged*)	Spatial
% Indian reserve					1.797 (91)	
% Protected		13.060[c] (82)[d]				
Cleared land	0.0206 (2)		−1.8929 (59)	−0.0183 (94)	−0.2915 (3)	−1.5339 (94)
Rural GDP	−0.0337 (81)	−1.0481 (100)	0.4903 (99)	0.0256 (6)		
Urban GDP	−0.026 (2)					
Urban pop.	0.0634 (67)		−2.0932 (100)	0.0514 (9)	0.332 (94)	
Rural pop.			14.9627 (100)	0.6684 (100)		
Cattle herd	0.022 (36)	−0.1883 (2)				−2.4401 (3)
Land price		0.458 (68)	0.5286 (22)	−0.0126 (14)		
Paved roads	0.0081 (1)			−0.0153 (22)	−0.1732 (3)	8.777 (1)
Unpaved roads	−0.0598 (2)	−0.831 (4)		−0.0057 (1)		
Interact (unpaved*clear)	0.0027 (5)	0.0855 (4)		−0.0005 (1)		
Interact (paved*clear)	0.001 (96)					
Adj. R^2:		0.3743			0.7134	

Notes: [a]FINAM and federal transfers from 1985 only.
[b]A full definition of the growth, level, and spatial version of each variable can be found in the technical appendix, along with the full results of all regressions.
[c]Figures are mean coefficient estimates from the random reduction estimation method described in this chapter and in the technical appendix.
[d]Numbers in parentheses are the number of times a respective variable made it into the final model (i.e. with a t-statistic over 2) out of 100 iterations.

likely does not capture all the important factors driving rural population patterns and that there are significant omitted variables still to be discovered. Thus, we hesitate to interpret the results too strongly, and indeed it is hard to make sense of some of the results. In the 1985–1995 model, rural populations grow more rapidly where they have been historically growing and in areas with established urban populations. In the 1980–1985

Table 6.6. *Estimation results: growth of cattle herd*[a]

	1980–1985			1985–1995		
MODEL:	Growth[b]	Log-level[b]	Spatial[b]	Growth	Log-level	Spatial
Variable	(All variables lagged*)			(All variables lagged*)		
Cleared land				−0.1628		4.2823
				(100)		(5)
Rural GDP		3.5236[c]				−1.1513
		(100)[d]				(21)
Urban GDP	0.1578	−1.4656		0.1262	0.5103	0.9245
	(97)	(84)		(100)	(8)	(100)
Urban pop.	0.3605			0.0931		
	(100)			(100)		
Rural pop.		−2.5931		0.2482		−10.322
		(2)		(99)		(100)
Cattle herd	−0.1337	−3.5003	15.9188		−1.1923	11.2088
	(90)	(100)	(10)		(100)	(95)
Land price			−1.1309			
			(1)			
Paved roads			−120.49			
			(7)			
Unpaved roads		−3.5334		0.0357	1.0008	−48.382
		(84)		(86)	(100)	(93)
Interact		0.3645		0.0029		
(unpaved*clear)		(80)		(14)		
Adj. R^2:		0.2155			0.5827	

Notes: [a]FINAM and federal transfers from 1985 only.
[b]A full definition of the growth, level, and spatial version of each variable can be found in the technical appendix, along with the full results of all regressions.
[c]Figures are mean coefficient estimates from the random reduction estimation method described in this chapter and in the technical appendix.
[d]Numbers in parentheses are the number of times a respective variable made it into the final model (i.e. with a t-statistic over 2) out of 100 iterations.

model we find rural populations growing faster in areas that have been cleared with a high growth of paved roads. Rural population growth is also higher in municipios whose neigbors have relatively high rural population densities and rural GDP, or lower urban population densities.

Growth of cattle herds

As cattle herd growth has been indicted in both the existing literature as well as our own model as being a significant determinant of land clearing, it is important to consider the underlying forces driving it (table 6.6). It is interesting to note that despite the aggregate high growth rate in the Amazonian herd, at the municipal level herd growth dynamics also have some robust leveling-off properties in that areas with particularly large herds have slower growth. High levels of urban GDP and population growth are important precursors of increased cattle herd growth, again consistent with the idea that local urban demand is an important driving force behind the expansion of the herd. In the 1985–1995 model rural population seems also to have become important with herd growth following in areas that had seen high rural population growth. This effect is partially mitigated by the finding that there is slower growth of cattle herds where neighbors' rural population density is relatively high.

While paved roads do not seem to affect the growth rate of cattle herds, unpaved roads significantly increase the rate of cattle herd growth, especially in the later model. In the earlier model, unpaved roads encourage cattle herd growth only in relatively settled areas, not in more virgin areas.

Finally, it is perhaps surprising that neither government subsidies, credit nor land prices play any significant role in predicting the growth of cattle herd across municipalities. Even in the 1980–1985 model in which the government transfer variables are contemporaneous they do not enter into any of the final models.

Paved and unpaved roads

Our data on roads include those planned and built at the state and federal level, but do not include the many smaller, informal, and unpaved roads that are created locally (tables 6.7, 6.8, pp. 135–136). The nature of the roads data thus clearly limits our analysis in some ways, but perhaps not quite as much as one would initially think. One of the most important issues surrounding the construction of paved roads is the proliferation and branching off of many smaller unpaved roads as a consequence. Thus, if we could account for all the unpaved and paved roads perfectly and try to attribute some percentage of clearing to each, it still would be a tricky job to ascertain what deforestation was due to paved roads directly, and what was due to paved roads indirectly via their effect on increased unpaved roads in their vicinity; and in fact whether this distinction is meaningful at all is debatable.

Owing to the nature and timing of our data we have to approach this problem in a slightly different way. In particular, in the case of paved roads the model asks: controlling for important characteristics, how can the variation in the levels and growth rates of paved roads across municipalities through 1985 explain the subsequent clearing over the next ten years? We then ask the analogous question for unpaved roads (note again

Table 6.7. *Estimation results: growth of paved roads*

	1980–1985			1985–1995		
MODEL: Variable	Growth[b]	Log-level[b] (All variables lagged*)	Spatial[b]	Growth	Log-level (All variables lagged*)	Spatial
% Protected					93.751	
					(76)	
FINAM credit[a]		−0.131[c]			0.269	
		(87)[d]			(6)	
Federal transfers/ GDP(−1)		−7.820				
		(1)				
Cleared land		0.8465	−7.3996		1.6036	
		(75)	(69)		(5)	
Rural GDP		0.9476	−0.8399	0.1339		
		(32)	(1)	(63)		
Urban pop.		1.0118	−5.6617	0.4147		
		(44)	(99)	(100)		
Rural pop.			12.8816		2.5031	
			(95)		(72)	
Cattle herd	0.0239					
	(34)					
Paved roads	0.5184	−8.1986		−0.3749	11.7294	159.063
	(100)	(95)		(100)	(76)	(100)
Unpaved roads	−0.0346		124.137	−0.8256	−13.269	110.606
	(10)		(48)	(78)	(100)	(94)
Interact (unpaved*clear)	−0.0035	−0.0711		0.1033	1.321	
	(81)	(91)		(52)	(100)	
Interact (paved*clear)	−0.0306	0.6869		−0.0319	−1.0757	
	(100)	(94)		(100)	(100)	
Adj. R^2:		0.3152			0.4427	

Notes: [a]FINAM and federal transfers from 1985 only.
[b]A full definition of the growth, level, and spatial version of each variable can be found in the technical appendix, along with the full results of all regressions.
[c]Figures are mean coefficient estimates from the random reduction estimation method described in this chapter and in the technical appendix.
[d]Numbers in parentheses are the number of times a respective variable made it into the final model (i.e. with a *t*-statistic over 2) out of 100 iterations.

that our unpaved roads do not include locally created smaller unpaved roads, only the larger state and federal projects).

Since we do not control for the simultaneous creation of roads we minimize the possibility that we would attribute clearing to road building, when in some cases the reverse could be true: new clearing causing roads to be built. This is a potentially serious problem in the analysis of the effects of roads and thus our lagged estimation strategy has a distinct

Table 6.8. *Estimation results: growth of unpaved roads*

	1980–1985			1985–1995		
MODEL: Variable	Growth[b]	Log-level[b] (All variables lagged*)	Spatial[b]	Growth	Log-level (All variables lagged*)	Spatial
% Indian reserve					11.229	
					(2)	
FINAM credit[a]		−0.114[c]				
		(88)[d]				
Federal transfers/ GDP(−1)		−19.24				
		(18)				
Cleared land				0.2614		
				(4)		
Rural GDP	0.0755	1.1297			5.308	
	(26)	(54)			(100)	
Urban GDP		−1.4437			−1.9572	
		(88)			(27)	
Urban pop.	−0.4152		−4.4082		2.1332	
	(100)		(83)		(50)	
Rural pop.						−10.713
						(100)
Cattle herd				0.2305		
				(100)		
Paved roads	−0.03	7.5012		1.0411	7.3309	
	(1)	(100)		(65)	(67)	
Unpaved roads	0.1939	−10.919	108.225	−0.0945	−2.7289	
	(100)	(100)	(72)	(43)	(100)	
Interact (unpaved*clear)		1.0047		−0.0546		
		(100)		(100)		
Interact (paved*clear)	−0.0032	−0.6649		−0.0995	−0.6988	
	(6)	(100)		(67)	(67)	
Adj. R^2:		0.3349			0.4806	

Notes: [a]FINAM and federal transfers from 1985 only.
[b]A full definition of the growth, level, and spatial version of each variable can be found in the technical appendix, along with the full results of all regressions.
[c]Figures are mean coefficient estimates from the random reduction estimation method described in this chapter and in the technical appendix.
[d]Numbers in parentheses are the number of times a respective variable made it into the final model (i.e. with a t-statistic over 2) out of 100 iterations.

advantage. Furthermore, we control for the amount of unpaved (state and federal) roads in 1985, but not their contemporaneous creation over the next ten years. Nor do we control for the creation of smaller local unpaved roads over the next ten years. Thus, if increased paved roads through 1985 led to increased unpaved roads, both local and at the state and federal level and then increased clearing, and if these unpaved roads and clearing were *caused* by the paved road construction such that variation in paved roads explained their growth better than other variables, then our model will attribute the growth in cleared land from all the newly spawned unpaved roads to the paved roads, which is exactly what we would want it to do.

Thus the fact that we notionally differentiate between paved and unpaved roads in the model does not imply that we are leaving out the effects that paved roads have on spawning new unpaved roads when we talk about their impact on clearing. In fact we would attribute *all* the clearing due to newly spawned unpaved roads to paved roads (if those newly spawned unpaved roads were entirely due to the paved road construction, that is). On the other hand, for those interested in the precise breakdown of clearing caused directly by paved roads and then the clearing caused by the new unpaved roads, our analysis cannot shed any light on this question.

So what does our model say about road building? For both the roads models most of the robust variables are lagged endogenous variables themselves; in other words the models are picking up dynamics which, most likely, are themselves functions of variables not captured in the initial variable set. Compared to our other six models, the roads models are relatively unstable with the specifications of the final models varying considerably from one to the next; very few variables consistently make it into most final models. Taken together these observations are consistent with the fact discussed above that our data reflect road building during the development of Amazonia that was due to federal and state policy initiatives rather than directly from local demand. Nevertheless, by looking at the models of paved and unpaved roads we can gain some insight into what was driving the pattern of road creation, whether from the local or the national perspective.

In particular, for the 1980–1985 model of paved roads we see there is a leveling-off pattern, but we also see clearly that paved roads are more likely to be built in areas that have a relatively high proportion of existing cleared land. In the 1985–1995 model we see paved roads being driven much more by the past growth of urban populations. There is still a relationship between paved road construction and the proportion of cleared land, but it is not as strong as in the 1980–1985 model. Paved roads seem to be being built where there is already an established network of paved roads (i.e. not leveling-off so much any more, at least with respect to levels) but this growth is actually less in highly cleared areas, which have perhaps already fully matured. Growth of paved roads is also highly influenced by spatial effects, with new roads being constructed in areas surrounded by municipalities with well-established road networks existing already.

The unpaved roads models are even less robust than the paved roads models, and are almost entirely driven by endogenous dynamics. One exception to this is that rural GDP and the growth of cattle herds have an important role in determining the pattern of unpaved road construction in the 1985–1995 model.

The relationship between road building and clearing is very complex and a great deal of further research is needed. As discussed, our analytical approach has some advantages, but also disadvantages, and certainly ours will hardly be the last word on this topic. In particular, more careful GIS and local-level studies should be done to illuminate the myriad relationships between official and local roads, economic activity and clearing. This book spans a wide range of topics surrounding deforestation; further research that focuses specifically on the role of roads could, by definition, design the methodology and collect data more directly suitable to the task, and we look forward to seeing such work done.

Policy simulations

What destiny awaits the Amazon forest over the next couple of decades? It appears that, after a halt to expansionary projects over the last decade, the Brazilian government now plans to resume a more aggressive development of the Amazon region, including road paving, waterways, mining, logging, and hydroelectric initiatives, etc. under the *Avança Brasil* plan and a new proposal to relax the limits on the proportion of private land that must be kept in a natural state.

These projects, and in particular the accompanying road infrastructure, will further open up the Amazon to forest conversion and degradation, which in turn paves the way for wildfires and further forest degradation. In a much-noticed article published in *Science*, Laurance *et al.* (2001a) have made a provocative prognosis on the expected deforestation impact of *Avança Brasil*, combined with two other plans (*Programa Brasil em Açao* and Eletrobrás' Ten-Year Expansion Plan B 1998–2007). Extrapolating the observed impact of such infrastructure from the 1980s–1990s, two scenarios derived by the authors from map overlays show that between 28 percent and 42 percent of the area will be deforested or heavily degraded in 2020. Another 24–28 percent of the remaining forest will be lightly degraded; only between 5 percent and 28 percent will remain pristine forests.

While the article rightly points to the dangers of a renewed expansion into the Amazon, a couple of qualifying comments seem in place. First, past experience shows that it is unrealistic to expect all existing infrastructure plans to be implemented in practice, especially if they require substantial financing from foreign creditors that are increasingly sensitive to environmental impacts. As the current political discussions around *Avança Brasil* show, such plans are part of a political play, not a true reflection of expected reality. Second, the definition of "deforested and heavily degraded areas" includes a natural forest cover that is reduced to less than 85 percent (see Laurance *et al.* 2001a, supplementary material) – a definition that is fundamentally different from FAO's definition of less than 10 percent tree cover. According to the latter criterion, the immediate risk of extensive forest degradation is much greater than that of large-scale deforestation. Ongoing research will have to clarify how these two phenomena are interrelated in the longer term.

Furthermore, the projections in Laurance *et al.* (2001a) are based on assumptions of unchanged "economic pressures" over time, and this may prove a significant overestimation. In particular, during the earlier settlement period in the Amazon large development projects were often "the only game in town" for new migrants to the region. Now there are multiple established urban areas (or rural areas surrounding urban areas) providing attractive alternatives for would-be residents. Between our 1980–1985 model and our 1985–1995 model, for instance, there is evidence that local urban demand is becoming a more important determinant of land-use. Furthermore, the latest Population Census showed that Legal Amazonia's rural population actually declined in absolute terms over the 1990s – thanks to both an accelerated demographic transition in Brazil and to rapid urbanization of the Amazon region. Thus, there are fewer people with more choices, and it seems likely that the prospect of roughing it in uncleared and unpopulated regions will prove less attractive than in the past.

Besides the planned development projects mentioned above, additional factors shaping economic pressures for land conversion are the expected growth of urban and rural income, market distance, and the development of land prices inside and outside the Amazon. Our models estimated above capture many of the important links between clearing, population increases, and changes in economic policies. Within the context of this model, then, an interesting exercise is to simulate the effects of both the *Avança Brasil* plan as well as the effects of relaxing the clearing constraints on private land. For the former, because roads play an integral role in the model, we can exogenously manipulate the respective lengths of paved and unpaved roads and then trace through both the direct and indirect effects of these changes, over time, on the endogenous variables. Thus, we predict the net effect of any given road change without the simplifying and probably unrealistic assumption of constant economic pressures in the region. For the latter, we can impose any constraint we wish to explore on the amount of new clearing and compare the trajectory of the model with a baseline in which no constraints are imposed.

In these simulations we first estimate the model as described above and choose a set of explanatory variables based on the criteria that each should make it into the "final" model at least 50 times out of the 100 iterations of the random reduction process. We then generate coefficient estimates for all the variables in each of these models and save them. Then, taking as a starting point the state of Legal Amazonia as measured in our data set in 1995, we forecast what the model would predict for 2000. Using these predictions to generate new predicted levels of our variables, we continue this process until we have projected the model ten years into the future,[6] predicting the evolution of the six endogenous variables (eight when we endogenize paved and unpaved roads in the simulations with clearing limits) as they interact dynamically and spatially as the model evolves. We then compare alternative policy scenarios for the future and analyze their projected differential regional effects.

Avança Brasil

The *Avança Brasil* plan calls for investments during the 2000–2007 period of R$24.1 billion in the western and northern parts of Legal Amazonia (Acre, Amapá, Amazonas, Roraima, and most of Pará) and of R$49.8 billion in the border areas to the east and south of the heart of the Amazon (Rondônia, Mato Grosso, Maranhão, Tocantins, the most eastern part of Pará, and areas bordering Legal Amazonia). These amounts cover mostly infrastructure projects (road improvements, bridges, airports, ports, channels, floodgates, railways, terminals, powerplants, natural gas pipelines, telephone lines, etc.) but about a third cover social development projects (education, health, housing, water and sanitation) and 5–8 percent are intended for environmental projects and information collection.

For the purposes of this simulation, we will focus only on the projects that have to do with roads in Legal Amazonia. Virtually all projects are paving of unpaved roads or improvements to already paved roads. Very few new roads are being planned. After going through the plans we find that *Avança Brasil* would cause an increase in the length of paved roads of 6,222 km and a decrease in unpaved roads of 5,812 km.[7]

[6] In our simulation this corresponds to two iterations of the model. Iterating further produces qualitatively similar results.

[7] According to the *Avança Brasil* plan, 8,479 km of roads are to be paved in Legal Amazonia. These are in various conditions. 410 km are only planned so this is going to imply 410 km of brand new paved roads. 2,257 km are already paved, so their improvement

The plan specifies in detail what stretches of road are to be considered for paving or improvements in the period 2000–2007, but this is, of course, no guarantee that they will actually be financed or implemented. If history is any guide, a number of unforeseen obstacles are likely to prevent some of the projects from being realized. The designers of the plan seem resigned to this reality, aptly naming the list of proposed projects "Public and private investment opportunities 2000–2007."

Later in this book (chapter 8, tables 8.4 and 8.5) we indirectly infer the role of paved and unpaved roads within the sample period of our model. In that exercise, we compare the actual level of 1995 clearing with that predicted under different scenarios that included more or less paved and unpaved roads than actually were built. These in-sample estimates of the effects of roads find that paved roads tend to cause increases in both rural and urban GDP, with no or negative increase in accumulated clearing. Unpaved roads, on the other hand, cause additional clearing, and are associated with a fall in urban GDP and only a slight rise in rural GDP.

In the present simulations, in contrast, we project the model into the future rather than examining in-sample effects. In the first baseline scenario we assume that no new roads will be built and allow the model to evolve given 1995 levels of paved and unpaved roads. In the second scenario, we assume that the *Avança Brasil* plan is implemented in 1995 and we then again trace the evolution of the model through time. By comparing the levels of clearing and economic activity under the two scenarios, then, we hope to get an idea of what our model predicts for the effects of the road building plans of the Brazilian government. Of course, all the caveats and potential problems of our model, discussed earlier in this chapter and in the technical appendix, apply to this simulation exercise as well. In the conclusion we discuss some of the more important caveats more fully.

The results presented in table 6.9 indicate that the 6,222 km of road paving projects in *Avança Brasil* are predicted to cause a *decrease* in total cleared area of 15,580 km^2 in Legal Amazonia after ten years, according to our model. This is owing to the reduction in the extent of unpaved roads. It will also cause \$386 million and \$1.1 billion in extra accumulated rural and urban GDP, respectively.

Table 6.10 shows the estimated effect of *Avança Brasil* by state. The states that experience the most dramatic increases in paved roads are Amapá, Acre, and Roraima. They are also the states that will gain most

will not change neither the length of paved nor unpaved roads in our simulations. The majority, 5,812 km, are unpaved and destined to become paved with the *Avança Brasil* program, which means an increase in paved roads of 5,812 km and a decrease in unpaved roads of the same size.

Table 6.9. *Simulated effect of Avança Brasil road improvements after ten years*

Scenario	Accumulated clearing (km^2)	Rural GDP (million 1995-US$)	Urban GDP (million 1995-US$)
Without *Avança Brasil*	441,550	10,096	88,065
With *Avança Brasil*	425,970	10,482	89,173
Difference owing to *Avança Brasil*	−15,580	386	1,077

Source: Authors' calculations based on the model estimated in chapter 6.

Table 6.10. *Simulated effect of Avança Brasil, by state*

State	Paved roads	Unpaved roads	Cleared area (change in %)	Urban GDP	Rural GDP
Acre	84.0	−65.4	−3.1	4.0	11.5
Amapá	148.3	−48.7	2.7	5.1	10.8
Amazonas	21.5	−13.5	−1.9	0.1	2.1
Goiás/Tocantins	0.0	0.0	0.0	0.0	0.0
Maranhão	0.0	0.0	−0.0	−0.0	0.1
Mato Grosso	47.5	−13.3	−5.8	3.4	5.1
Pará	55.3	−34.2	−4.6	0.7	5.2
Rondônia	4.2	−2.8	−0.4	0.2	1.7
Roraima	104.3	−4.0	−4.1	6.1	6.2
Total	35.7	−13.2	−3.6	1.3	3.8

Source: Authors' simulations based on the model estimated in chapter 6.

from the infrastructure improvements. Their urban GDP will be 4–6 percent higher after 10 years, and their rural GDP 6–12 percent higher, compared to the scenario where *Avança Brasil* is not implemented. Both Acre and Roraima actually enjoy less clearing as well, while that in Amapá increases.

Taken at face value, our model simulations imply there is actually no aggregate, Amazon-wide trade-off with the *Avança Brasil* plan as it simultaneously increases GDP and reduces land clearing overall. A regional exception is the state of Amapá which gets the greatest allocation of paved roads (as a percentage) and also suffers from a higher clearing rate. This is because Amapá is one of the least cleared Amazonian states, and the model predicts that road paving through such virgin areas will have a much more damaging effect on the forest cover than road paving through more settled areas. In Pará and Mato Grosso, for example, the road paving projects are predicted to reduce cleared area by 5–6 percent, as farmers get incentives to intensify their activities in already cleared areas close to the newly paved roads.

There are several caveats to this overall interpretation which must be emphasized. First, the *Avança Brasil* plan is about paving existing roads, and thus transforming their status – it is not about eliminating existing unpaved roads entirely. The simulation, however, treats the loss of unpaved roads as an actual loss, albeit accompanied by a net gain in paved roads. As unpaved roads led unambiguously to higher clearing rates in the model, while paved roads only led to higher clearing under some circumstances, in general this leads the model to predict lower clearing in most regions. Thus, the simulation and (planned) reality differ in subtle ways, and readers will have to decide for themselves if they feel it is a reasonable approximation.

Second, the model was estimated over actual patterns of paved and unpaved roads that existed in the Amazon between 1975 and 1995. If the characteristics of municipios where paved roads were built historically are quite different from where the *Avança Brasil* plan indicates, then our model will attribute to the new *Avança Brasil* roads the same costs and benefits derived from historical experience. In particular, if paved roads have historically been constructed primarily in relatively cleared areas, there may not be enough variation in the data for the model to differentiate strongly enough between the effects of roads in cleared areas versus the effects of roads in relatively less cleared areas. As discussed earlier in this chapter, we attempt to control for this as much as possible by introducing interaction terms that allow the effect of roads to vary by the amount of cleared land in the municipio (controlling for area). Indeed, the model finds much higher clearing impact of paved roads in regions that are relatively undisturbed. Nevertheless, the model may fail to completely capture the full range of actual effects if the observed range of cleared areas around observed paved roads is relatively narrow, and especially if the relationship between clearing and effect is non-linear. In addition, the true impact of roads could vary by other characteristics such as distance to markets, point of origin and destination, and a host of other characteristics not captured by interaction effects.

In order to investigate further whether the paving projects proposed in the *Avança Brasil* plan seem to follow a pattern similar to historic patterns of paved roads (in which case our model should be expected to do a better job estimating the impact), we compare the relationship between the proportion of cleared land in areas with actual paved roads, versus those with planned *Avança Brasil* paved roads.

Table 6.11. *Aggregate relationship between new paved roads and cleared land, dependent variable: growth of paved roads*

Variable	1980	1985	1995	*Avança Brasil*
Intercept	24.10	4.07	−3.48	−13.05
	(1.22)	(0.62)	(−0.45)	(−2.50)
Log(area)	−2.63	−0.79	−0.54	1.52
	(−2.28)	(−2.40)	(−0.95)	(2.26)
Log(cleared land)(−1)	2.32	0.92	1.18	−0.43
	(2.19)	(2.62)	(2.22)	(−1.11)
R^2	0.0240	0.0352	0.0146	0.0472

Note: Heteroskedasticity-consistent t-statistics in parentheses.

Several important trends immediately jump out from the results in table 6.11. First, the R^2 measures of all four regressions is very low, indicating that the variation in proportion of clearing explains only a very small amount of the variation in new paved road growth. Nevertheless, historically in all years for which we have data, the construction of new paved roads was statistically significantly positively correlated with the (past) proportion of cleared areas, and is negatively and sometimes statistically significantly correlated with smaller areas. In other words, historically new paved roads were constructed more often in smaller and more cleared municipalities. However, for the planned paved roads in the *Avança Brasil* project, we observe the exact opposite relationship. The *Avança Brasil* roads are more likely to be constructed in *larger* municipios with *less* cleared areas, although this latter relationship is not statistically significant.

In terms of cleared land, then, clearly the pattern of the planned *Avança Brasil* roads is significantly different from historical patterns. While our model has been constructed to take variation in clearing proportion into account, the change in the *Avança Brasil* pattern may be too dramatic for their effect to be adequately predicted by our model. Our model probably does a much better job of predicting the effects of paving roads through smaller, relatively cleared areas. Its prediction of the effects of paving through large, undisturbed areas is much less precisely estimated and should be taken in the context in which it was generated.

How do the results from our model compare to other studies? At least two other recent studies have tried to evaluate the impacts of road paving in the *Avança Brasil* plan. The first is the controversial study by Laurance *et al.* (2001a), mentioned above, and the other a study by Nepstad *et al.* (2001). Both make use of mechanical projections based on assumptions about what percentage of forest will be lost within a 100 or 200 km band around the paved roads. This is done under the assumption that the future effects of roads will be more or less the same as the effects of the roads built in the past, disregarding the changes in supporting policies such as subsidized credit and settlement programs and the change in monitoring and enforcement capacity.

Both studies put forward very dire predictions for the Amazon. The Laurance *et al.* (2001a) article concludes that "Under the non-optimistic scenario, few pristine areas will survive outside the western quarter of the region" and "42 percent of the region will be deforested or heavily degraded." They have a more optimistic scenario where 27.6 percent of the area will remain in pristine conditions and only 28 percent will be deforested or heavily degraded, but they "suggest that the non-optimistic scenario may better proximate reality." Although, their verbal interpretation of their simulation results seem very pessimistic, the total amount of deforestation they attribute to these development projects is not overwhelming. The effects were calculated to be 506,000 hectares of deforestation per year in the non-optimistic scenario and 269,000 hectares in the optimistic scenario (Laurance *et al.* 2001a, supplementary material). The larger of the numbers corresponds to 101,200 km^2 of additional deforested area over a twenty-year period, or about 3 percent of the forested area. Thus, their pessimistic interpretation is more due to the fragmentation and decrease of completely virgin forest than to a dramatic increase in deforested area.

The Nepstad *et al.* (2001) study predicts that within a 50 km buffer zone of the 6,245 kilometers of roads to be paved according to *Avança Brasil*, we will experience deforestation of between 120,000–270,000 km^2 within twenty-five–thirty-five years. They hypothesize that this deforestation will cause increased fire risk and reduced rainfall which will cause an additional 192,000 km^2 to become flammable. Thus, the damage to the forest as a result of the *Avança Brasil* road paving could, according to Nepstad *et al.* (2001), be as high as 462,000 km^2 or as much as 13 percent of the forested area.

This is in sharp contrast to our simulation which indicates that *Avança Brasil* will encourage agricultural intensification and urban growth and thus actually *reduce* total cleared area compared to the situation where the plan is not implemented.

There are several factors that could contribute to the dramatic discrepancies between the findings from our model simulations and the findings in the other two analyses. First of all, our model controls for the extent of existing cleared land and thus can distinguish, to a certain extent, between new road building through more pristine areas and through relatively settled areas (although the caveats discussed above apply). These two types of infrastructure projects have very different effects on land uses and productivity. While new road building through pristine areas depresses land prices and encourages extensive land uses, the improvement of existing roads drives up land prices and encourages more intensive land uses. The latter thus causes a much higher value generation per area than the former.

Another fundamental difference is that we include socio-economic variables, such as population and income. This allows for indirect effects from road building to clearing, such as the limiting effect of high population densities on clearing rates. It is important to remember also that we model growth *rates*, not levels, of cleared land, and condition only on past (lagged) values so as to avoid endogeneity bias. Thus, we capture more long-run effects and avoid attributing a causal role to variables that occur simultaneously, but at the cost that we do not identify the short-run, immediate (i.e. one-year) impact of roads as these effects are averaged into a "medium"-run, five-year impact.

Our model also allows us to control for changes in credit incentives. Subsidized credit is believed to have caused a lot of deforestation in previous decades, especially through cattle ranching, but these incentives have been dramatically reduced by now. The two other studies discussed cannot separate the effect of roads and of credit and thus attribute all deforestation to the roads. With lower credit in the future, they are therefore likely to overestimate the effect of new roads. Our model, on the other hand, can separate the effect of roads and credit, and we can therefore project the effect of roads in the future in the absence of credit incentives.[8]

Finally, our model takes into account the non-linearity of the clearing process. Our estimated models show that there are important leveling-off effects involved in the growth of all endogenous variables. This is to be expected because of both natural physical limitations and economic mechanisms. As the level of clearing increases, for example, new agricultural land will become scarcer and this will drive up land prices. Higher land prices, in turn, will stimulate a transition to more intensive land uses, such as perennial crops or mixed agroforestry systems, which will lessen the demand for new land clearing.

Thus we come back to the question posed at the beginning of this section: What destiny awaits the Amazon forest over the next couple of decades? Our econometric model can only help to guide us to make some

[8] Actually, our model does not find credit to be significant, so this particular advantage of our methodology remains hypothetical.

educated guesses, taking into account the studies of other researchers as well. If the *Avança Brasil* plan is implemented exactly as construed, we suggest that the predictions of clearing from Laurance *et al.* (2001a), and Nepstad *et al.* (2001) could be significantly overstated. We would not go so far as to claim that there will be no clearing impact, as is predicted by our model, because the pattern of new road building is likely to be of a form for which our model is not well primed to provide good estimates of the clearing impact. Nevertheless, the logic, supported by our results, of the idea that improvements of existing roads drives up land prices, encourages more intensive land uses, and generally leads to more economic value added is compelling, and should be taken into account as well.

Our econometric results indicate that the environmental cost of road improvements is likely to be relatively small, and the economic benefits relatively large, in the long run. Our analysis further suggests that the benefits from road construction could be optimized by minimizing new road building through relatively untouched areas and concentrating on upgrading existing roads in settled areas. From the simulations presented in table 6.10 it appears that there are win–win opportunities for infrastructure investments in the relatively settled states of Pará and Mato Grosso, while road paving in the relatively virgin state of Amapá would be a win–lose prescription with a trade-off between economic growth and forest protection.

Land-use regulation

In Legal Amazonia, a certain share of all private property is required to be publicly registered as areas of permanent forest cover preservation. Owing to growing environmental concerns in Brazil, this share was increased from 50 percent to 80 percent in 1996. It was not clear, however, how land-holders who had already cleared more than 20 percent of their land were supposed to comply with this regulation, as reforestation does not count towards the 80 percent supposed to be with original vegetation. The government is currently under pressure to restore the law again to only 50 percent preservation.

This section will use the econometric model estimated earlier in this chapter to analyze the impacts of both the 50 percent and the 80 percent conservation rules. For that purpose we run forward simulations with the model and impose three alternative restrictions on clearing in each municipality. The base scenario is a 100 percent limit on clearing, which corresponds to the maximum clearing that is physically possible. The second scenario is a 50 percent limit on clearing, and the third scenario

Table 6.12. *Simulated effect of land-use regulation after twenty years*

Scenario (clearing limit in each municipality)	Accumulated clearing (km^2)	Rural GDP (million 1995-US$)
100%	302,610	7,446
50%	296,670	7,400
20%	269,880	7,155
Difference owing to 50% limit	5,940	46
Difference owing to 20% limit	32,730	291

Source: Authors' calculations based on the model estimated in chapter 6.

is a 20 percent limit on clearing, corresponding to the law dictating that at least 80 percent of each land holding should be maintained with its natural vegetation cover.

This simulation differs from the one used to study the *Avança Brasil* plan in that we endogenize the construction of paved and unpaved roads, so that now we have a system with eight rather than six equations.[9] We impose the clearing constraints as follows. If existing cleared areas exceeds the limit, then no new additional clearing is permitted. If existing clearing does not exceed the limit, then new clearing is allowed up to the limit, but not beyond.

Table 6.12 shows the simulation results for the year 2015. We see that the 50 percent limit would imply a reduction in cleared area of 5,940 km^2 and a corresponding reduction in rural GDP of $46 million. This corresponds to lost rural GDP of $77 annually for each hectare of forest preserved by the 50 percent rule. The 20 percent limit on clearing would imply a reduction in cleared land of 32,730 km^2, but also a substantially larger reduction in rural GDP of $291 million. This corresponds to lost rural GDP of $89 annually for each hectare of forest preserved by the 80 percent rule.

These annual opportunity costs are converted into Net Present Values (NPVs) in table 6.13 using three alternative discount rates. We see that at the 12 percent rate the opportunity costs amount to around $700/hectare for both rules. It is slightly lower for the 50 percent rule and slightly higher for the more restrictive rule, but the differences are not large in per hectare terms.

As we will see in chapter 8, these opportunity costs appear to be larger than the NPV of standing forest for all discount rates. Thus the perception of Amazonian farmers that the 80 percent rule is too restrictive and carries excessively high opportunity costs, is supported by this simulation.

[9] Endogenizing the roads does not qualitatively change the results.

Table 6.13. *NPV of rural GDP lost owing to land-use restrictions*

Discount rate	2%	6%	12%
50% limit on clearing (1995-US$/ha)	3,872	1,291	645
20% limit on clearing (1995-US$/ha)	4,445	1,482	741

Source: Authors' calculations based on the model estimated in chapter 6.

Conclusions

Taken together, these models and the simulations derived from them yield some interesting policy implications. Of course, as with any set of econometric results, the same coefficient estimates may be consistent with multiple alternative hypotheses so we do not claim any monopoly over the interpretation. Indeed, in our concluding remarks in chapter 9 we comment on differing interpretations of this analysis even among the authors of this book. Nevertheless, taken in the light of the more recent literature reviewed earlier, our results can be seen to provide striking support for several ideas. In particular, all our results are consistent to a greater or lesser extent with the idea that, regardless how they started, many processes in the Amazon are now endogenously determined with growing centers of urban demand acting as a driving force behind many agricultural activities. We find herd growth and new land clearing determined by a combination of natural frontier spatial processes of maturation and urban demand centers, and facilitated by the existence of unpaved roads (and paved roads in areas that have already been cleared). However the presence of paved roads is more closely associated with the creation of wealth, especially urban GDP but also rural GDP in regions that have already been extensively settled. It is important to emphasize again that we find this intensification effect in areas that have been already settled and cleared, where the majority of paved roads have in fact been built. The model very clearly indicates that paved roads through relatively uncleared areas will lead to substantial clearing, greater even than a similar length of unpaved roads. In sum, we find unpaved roads associated with land-extensive activities while paved roads are associated with more land-intensive economic activities.

The effects of time-invariant explanatory variables have been delegated to the technical appendix, but some of them warrant discussion here. For example, we wished to test the impact of rainfall, since recent studies by Chomitz and Thomas (2000) and Schneider *et al.* (2000) point out that too much rainfall is a serious limitation to agricultural activities in most parts of the Amazon. Thus, we would expect a high-rainfall dummy (more than average) to have a negative effect on new clearing and a negative effect on rural GDP. This variable would thus also have a dampening effect on new clearing as the agricultural frontier moves closer and closer to the most humid part of the Amazon. However, our expectations on rainfall were not confirmed by the model. The only robust impact of high rainfall seem to be its negative effect on urban GDP. The high-rainfall dummy was negative in the 1985–1995 cleared land equation, as expected by theory, but was not particularly robust. Moreover, it was positive in the 1980–1985 clearing model and never made it into the rural GDP model. The two models where high rainfall did seem to make a difference was in the pattern of road building; for both the paved and unpaved roads models this variable was positive and robust, whatever that implies. In any case, our results do not contradict Chomitz and Thomas: their finding is obviously true since the level of clearing is substantially higher in the drier areas of Legal Amazonia. But according to our model rainfall does not have an effect on the *growth* rates of clearing and the growth rates of rural GDP.

Perhaps the most useful aspect of our system of equations is that they interact dynamically over time and across space. By estimating the models in-sample and then using the estimated coefficients to simulate how the system would evolve over time, we can exogenously change certain policy variables to see how those changes impact the final values of variables of interest such as cleared land and economic activity. For a number of reasons discussed fully in the technical appendix, we do not make specific point predictions about future levels of clearing or, say, GDP from these simulations. Rather, by comparing alternative policy scenarios, where each simulation is ostensibly subject to the same possible biases, we then interpret the *difference* between the baseline and the policy scenario.

The two policies we have examined using this approach are the ambitious *Avança Brasil* road construction plan and a new proposal to relax clearing limits on private land. Both of these policies have generated significant attention from academics and policy makers alike.

Our simulation of the effects of the *Avança Brasil* plan differ dramatically from previous studies. While we find substantial expected economic gains, we do not find *Avança Brasil* to cause an overall increase in cleared area. However, we caution that these results are subject to several important caveats, especially since the paving plans in *Avança Brasil* are significantly different from historical patterns of paved road growth. In particular, we suspect that most likely we underestimate the impact of paved roads in relatively undisturbed areas. Nevertheless, even taking this caveat into account our results still represent quite a radical departure from existing opinion. Our interpretation of the model and simulation results is that paving roads *can* be an effective policy to promote growth and even limit clearing. To derive the full benefit from such policies, however, paved roads should primarily be introduced in established, populated areas and not in relatively virgin tracts of the forest. The current *Avança Brazil* plan as it stands does not fulfill this criteria, however. In particular, on average the planned newly paved roads are through *less* cleared, rather than more cleared, municipalities. Thus, while we do not predict the same wholesale destruction that other studies do, we do agree with them that the *Avança Brasil* plan is flawed policy. The economic benefits could be enhanced and the ecological costs reduced by redirecting resources towards paving roads in well-established areas.

In our second simulation we examine a proposal to reduce, from 80 to 50, the percentage of privately held land that must be kept in its original, natural state. We find that this will encourage more clearing, but that the economic costs of maintaining the 80 percent rule are actually quite high. Comparing these costs with our valuation of forest services from chapter 8 we find that the costs exceed the benefits, and thus suggest that reverting back to the original 50 percent rule would benefit the population. Combined with the *Avança Brasil* road simulation results this would suggest that a policy combination that improves growth without causing much clearing would be to revert to the 50 percent rule, concentrate on improving infrastructure in already relatively settled areas, and refrain from building roads through more virgin, undisturbed areas.

7 Carbon emissions

It has been argued that a reduction in tropical deforestation rates would be a relatively cheap way of curbing global CO_2 emissions compared to the cost of reducing fossil-fuel consumption in the industrialized world (Nordhaus 1991; FACE 1993; Schneider 1993; Kolk 1996). To assess whether this is a reasonable argument one would need better estimates of carbon emissions from deforestation as well as better estimates of the benefits of deforestation.

In chapter 6 we tried to assess the benefits of deforestation in terms of increased rural and urban output. In this chapter[1] we attempt to provide estimates of the rate of carbon emissions arising from land use change in the Brazilian Amazon. We will show that even when we only include the period of most rapid development in the region (1970–1985),[2] our estimates are considerably lower than other estimates found in the literature. This is owing to two factors. First, we take into account the uneven spatial distribution of deforestation: lower clearing costs cause deforestation to take place in the most accessible and least dense forests as long as these are available. Second, we take into account the considerable secondary regrowth and the carbon sequestration that takes place when previously cleared land is abandoned.

The remainder of the chapter is organized as follows. The next section describes the carbon emissions model and the parameter values used for simulations. We then describe the data on original vegetation cover and changes in land use and summarize the estimated age structure of deforested land. We then summarize deforestation measures and the calculated carbon emissions and compare these to the economic activity generated by the aggressive policies. We finally discuss factors contributing to

[1] This chapter draws heavily on Reis and Andersen (1997).

[2] We do not use data from the 1995 Agricultural Census in this chapter, since the potential problems of undercounting discussed in chapter 3 could seriously bias our estimates of carbon emissions downwards. By using data only from the period of most rapid deforestation, we get an upper bound on annual carbon emissions.

uncertainty in the carbon estimates and makes several sensitivity analyses. The final section concludes.

The carbon inventory model

A typical dense forest of the Brazilian Amazon contains a biomass of about 350 tons per hectare with a dry weight carbon content of approximately 50 percent, i.e. about 175 tC/hectare. Typical agricultural land, on the other hand, contains less than 10 tC/hectare. Thus, when forests are converted to agricultural land uses, massive amounts of carbon are released to the atmosphere, thus contributing to the increasing concentration of CO_2 in our atmosphere.

Houghton *et al.* (1983) has developed a carbon emissions model that keeps track of the carbon that was originally stored in the biomass of the forest when the forest is converted to agricultural land use through slash-and-burn methods. Various versions of this model have been used by Schroeder and Winjum (1994a, 1994b) and Reis (1996) to calculate carbon emissions from changes in land use in Brazil.

The carbon inventory model has two important parts. First, there is a set of equilibrium values for the carbon content in different types of forests and in different types of land uses. Second, a set of response functions indicates how carbon is decomposed and recomposed after changes in land use. The model is a bookkeeping type of model, and is thus purely mechanical. The parameters used to run the model are compiled from the literature.

Carbon contents

Table 7.1 presents central estimates of carbon contents in different vegetation types and for different land uses in the Amazon and table 7.2 decay parameters for the Carbon Inventory Model.[3] The dry weight carbon content is everywhere assumed to be 50 percent of biomass (Brown and Lugo 1984b; Fearnside *et al.* 1993).

Aboveground estimates of carbon content are taken from Reis (1996) which is based on Bohrer's (1993) survey. Belowground carbon content is assumed to be 17 percent of aboveground carbon content for dense forest, seasonal forest, and *campinarana* (Brown and Lugo 1992a; Fearnside

[3] Carbon contents vary greatly from plot to plot and from region to region. This has resulted in a wide variation in estimates of average carbon contents. See Brown and Lugo (1984a), Fearnside (1986, 1987), Brown *et al.* (1989), Brown and Lugo (1992a), and Fearnside (1992a) for a debate about biomass content in the Brazilian Amazon.

Table 7.1. *Carbon contents for different vegetation types and land uses*

Vegetation type/Land use	Aboveground[a] (tC/ha)	Belowground (tC/ha)	Total (tC/ha)
Primary vegetation (%):			
Dense forest (62.5)	150.0	25.5	175.5
Seasonal forest (6.1)	93.0	15.8	108.8
Savannas (15.4)	37.5	60.0	97.5
Ecological transition (7.3)	65.0	104.0	169.0
Wetlands (2.5)	57.5	43.1	100.6
Campinarana (5.4)	60.0	10.2	70.2
Secondary vegetation (climax):			
Dense forest	112.5	19.1	131.6
Seasonal forest	69.7	11.9	81.6
Savannas	37.5	60.0	97.5
Ecological transition	65.0	104.0	169.0
Wetlands	57.5	43.1	100.6
Campinarana	45.0	7.7	52.7
Agropastoral land use	5.0	0.9	5.9

Note: [a] Including litter.
Source: Reis (1996) and assumptions in text.

Table 7.2. *Decay parameters for the Carbon Inventory Model*

Vegetation type	a_v	s_v
Dense forest	3.0589	0.1530
Seasonal forest	2.5518	0.1429
Savanna	2.7425	0.1468
Ecological transition	3.3194	0.1583
Wetlands	2.7758	0.1474
Campinarana	2.0701	0.1333

1992b; Schroeder and Winjum 1994a; Reis 1996). For savannah and areas of ecological transition (*cerrado* woodland), belowground carbon content is assumed to be 160 percent of aboveground carbon content (Singh and Joshi 1979; Schroeder and Winjum 1994a). For wetlands this ratio is assumed to be 75 percent (Cannell 1982; Schroeder and Winjum 1994a).

Reis (1996) assumes that all secondary vegetation is identical and reaches a modest climax carbon content of 43.9 tC/hectare after forty years. This is a simple and conservative estimate which results in a worst-case scenario for carbon emissions. In this analysis we allow for different kinds of secondary vegetation and more realistic climax values. Following Houghton *et al.* (1983), we assume that secondary vegetation in dense forest, seasonal forest, and *campinarana* areas reaches a climax of 75 percent of the original carbon content after 50 years. Secondary vegetation in savannah, wetlands, and ecological transition areas is assumed to reach 100 percent of original carbon content after 50 years (Houghton *et al.* 1983). For agropastoral land use (crops and planted pasture) it is assumed, according to Sanchez *et al.* (1989), that belowground carbon content is 18 percent of aboveground carbon content.

Carbon dynamics

Typical slash-and-burn agriculture in the Amazon involves three phases: (1) land clearing and forest burning, (2) agropastoral use of land, (3) soil exhaustion, land abandonment, and the recomposition of secondary vegetation. Figure 7.1 illustrates the carbon cycle of vegetation in this pattern of agricultural settlement.

Carbon emissions from deforestation can usefully be divided into the three phases identified for slash-and-burn agriculture. Evidence from Seiler and Crutzen (1980), Houghton *et al.* (1991), Fearnside (1992b), Fearnside *et al.* (1993), and Carvalho Jr. *et al.* (1994) suggests that about 30 percent of aboveground carbon is released in the first phase of forest burning, while belowground carbon is unaffected in this phase. In the second phase, the remaining aboveground carbon plus belowground carbon

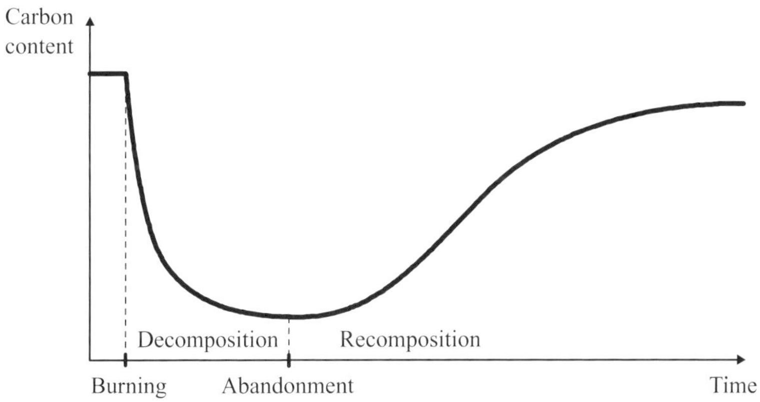

Figure 7.1 Carbon contents during a slash-and-burn cycle

is slowly decomposed. It is assumed that the decomposition follows an exponential decay function:

$$cav_{v,i} = 0.7 \cdot cav_{v,0} \cdot e^{-r_v \cdot i}$$

where $cav_{v,i}$ is aboveground carbon content in the original vegetation of type v, i periods after burning, $cav_{v,0}$ is aboveground carbon content in original vegetation type v before burning, r_v is the rate of carbon decomposition after burning in vegetation type v, and i is time elapsed since forest burning.

For belowground carbon we do not observe any immediate decline during forest burning, so the decay function for belowground carbon in natural vegetation becomes:

$$cbv_{v,i} = cbv_{v,0} \cdot e^{-r_v \cdot i}$$

where $cbv_{v,i}$ is belowground carbon content in the original vegetation of type v, i periods after burning. Reis (1996) uses the same decay rates for above and belowground carbon in which case the total carbon content in original vegetation becomes:

$$cv_{v,i} = cav_{v,i} + cbv_{v,i} = (0.7 \cdot cav_{v,0} + cbv_{v,0}) \cdot e^{-r_v \cdot i} \tag{7.1}$$

Houghton *et al.* (1991) estimate rates of carbon decompostion of 0.5 for closed forests and 0.3 for savannahs. Following Reis (1996) we assume a rate of 0.4 for other vegetation types. These rates imply that 94 percent of aboveground carbon in dense forests is released within five years, with the corresponding numbers for savannah and other vegetation types being 84 percent and 91 percent, respectively. Within fifteen years more than 99 percent of aboveground carbon will be emitted for all vegetation types.

In the third phase there will be a recomposition of biomass and carbon stock as secondary species invade the abandoned land. Recomposition will be relatively rapid in the beginning owing to the fast growth of pioneer species (Houghton *et al.* 1983; Uhl 1987; Uhl *et al.* 1988) but will then slow down and converge to a new climax. Odum (1988) suggests the following specification for the recomposition of biomass and carbon content in abandoned areas:

$$cf_{v,i} = \frac{cm_v}{1 + e^{(a_v - s_v \cdot i)}} \tag{7.2}$$

where $cf_{v,i}$ is carbon content (both aboveground and belowground) in fallow land of age i on vegetation type v, cm_v is the climax carbon content of vegetation type v, and a_v and s_v are parameters to be estimated.

To estimate the parameters a_v and s_v, we make the following assumptions: (1) the carbon content at the time of abandonment is equal to that of agropastoral land use, i.e. $cf_{v,0} = 5.9$ tC/hectare for all vegetation types; (2) fallow lands take fifty years to reach 99 percent of their climax carbon content. The climax carbon contents of different vegetation types are given in table 7.1. For most of the area they are lower than the carbon contents in the original vegetation. When combined with the assumptions above they yield the following values[4] for a_v and s_v.

Carbon stocks

The carbon stock in a given municipality at time t is the sum of the carbon stock in original vegetation, CV_t, the carbon stock in crops, CK_t and the carbon stock in fallow lands, CF_t:

$$C_t = CV_t + CK_t + CF_t$$

The carbon stock in original vegetation consists of two parts. First, the carbon stock in undisturbed areas, and second the carbon stock in the decaying original vegetation in deforested areas:

$$CV_t = \sum_v cv_{v,0} \cdot (A_{v,0} - D_{v,t}) + \sum_v \sum_i cv_{v,i} \cdot A^c_{v,i,t}$$

where $A_{v,0}$ is area of vegetation type v at time 0, $D_{v,t}$ is deforested area on vegetation type v at time t, $cv_{v,i}$ is the decreasing carbon contents of deforested natural vegetation given by (7.1), and $A^c_{v,i,t}$ is crop area of age i on vegetation type v at time t.

The carbon content in crops is assumed to be identical for all crops (including planted pasture), so the carbon stock in crops becomes:

$$CK_t = ck \cdot \sum_v \sum_i A^c_{v,i,t}$$

where ck is the carbon content of all types and ages of crops.

The carbon stock in fallow areas is the sum of the carbon stock in fallow on different vegetation types and of different ages:

$$CF_t = \sum_v \sum_i cf_{v,i} \cdot F_{v,i,t}$$

where $F_{v,i,t}$ is fallow land of age i at time t on vegetation type v, and $cf_{v,i}$ is the increasing carbon content of fallow areas given by (7.2).

The sum of crop areas and fallow areas adds up to total deforested area. Thus:

$$\sum_v D_{v,t} = \sum_v \sum_i A^c_{v,i,t} + \sum_v \sum_i F_{v,i,t}$$

[4] These parameters have no direct interpretation. They just define the shape of the carbon regeneration for each vegetation type according to our assumptions about climax values and regeneration periods.

The age structure of fallow lands

Information about the age structure of fallow lands is not available in the Agricultural Census data, but it can be estimated, if we are willing to make some assumptions. We need assumptions both about the initial age structure of fallow lands and about the dynamic process that guides the aging and use of fallow lands. To do this we will have the frontier development features of the Amazon in mind: some municipalities have only recently been exposed to agricultural development and these municipalities will therefore have very little fallow land. What fallow land they do have is likely to be very young with only the beginnings of secondary vegetation. Other municipalities experienced their most rapid agricultural development decades ago. Since slash-and-burn agriculture requires several years of fallow after a few years of crops growing, these municipalities are likely to have more extensive fallow lands and on average they are likely to be older.

To estimate the initial age structure, we thus make the assumption that the average age of fallow area in period 0 in municipality j, I_{0j}, is determined by the share of fallow in total agropastoral areas, D_{0j}, in such a way that a higher share of fallow implies a higher average age of fallow:

$$I_{0j} = K \cdot \frac{F_{0j}}{D_{0j}}$$

where K is a parameter determined by the condition that the average age of fallow over all municipalities should equal the assumed average for Legal Amazonia, I_{0A}:

$$I_{0A} = \sum_j I_{0j} \cdot \frac{F_{0j}}{F_{0A}}$$

and F_{0A} is total fallow area in Legal Amazonia at time 0, i.e. $F_{0A} = \sum_j F_{0j}$.

The dynamic changes in the age structure are believed to be well characterized by the following two assumptions. First, when fallow areas are expanding, the increase must be fallow of age 1, while the rest of the fallow area just gets 1 period older. The extent of fallow of age i at time t, in a given municipality, is thus determined by:

$$\left.\begin{array}{ll} F_{t,i} = \Delta F_t & \text{for } i = 1 \\ F_{t,i} = F_{t-1,i-1} & \text{for } i > 1 \end{array}\right\} \text{when } \Delta F_t \geq 0$$

Second, when fallow areas are contracting, it is because the oldest fallow is being converted to crop land again. This assumption can be modeled

Table 7.3. *Estimated age structure of fallow areas in Legal Amazonia, 1970–1985*

Age group (years)	Area (million ha)			
	1970	1975	1980	1985
0–5	9.2	2.4	5.0	7.4
5–10	3.8	7.1	1.7	4.6
10–15	0	1.0	5.9	1.5
15–20	0	0	0.5	5.4
20–25	0	0	0	0.4
Total	13.0	10.5	13.1	19.3

Table 7.4. *Summary statistics for the average age of fallow areas across municipalities, 1970–1985*

	1970	1975	1980	1985
Mean	3.5	6.6	8.6	9.6
Std dev.	0.8	1.7	3.2	4.0
Minimum	2.5	2.5	2.5	2.7
Maximum	5.0	9.8	14.0	18.8
Num. obs.	316	315	316	316

by the following equations:

$$\left.\begin{array}{lll} F_{t,i} = F_{t-1,i-1} & \text{for } i > 1 & \text{if } \sum_{j=2}^{i} F_{t-1,j-1} \leq F_t \\ F_{t,i} = F_t - \sum_{j=2}^{i^*} F_{t-1,j-1} & \text{for } i = 1 & \end{array}\right\} \text{ when } \Delta F_t < 0$$

where i^* is the maximum age of fallow that is not converted to crop land (as determined by the condition in the first equation).

1970 is the initial year of our analysis and the remaining observations come at five-year intervals. We assume that the average age of fallow lands in 1970 was 3.5 years and that all fallow land was less than ten years old.[5] Using that assumption and the equations above, we get an age structure as described in tables 7.3 and 7.4.

[5] Reis (1996) chose an initial average age of 2.5 in 1975, but noted that this seemed to be too low. It also seemed to be too low for 1970, so we chose 3.5 instead. The carbon emissions results are not sensitive to changes in this parameter.

Table 7.3 shows that in 1970 there was no fallow land older than ten years. This reflects the fact that significant cultivation of the Amazon began only in the 1960s. As time passes the total area of fallow lands increases and the average age of fallow land increases too. In municipalities on the agricultural frontier the average age of fallow lands will tend to be very low, whereas municipalities well behind the frontier will tend to have older fallow lands with more mature secondary vegetation. This is reflected in table 7.4, which shows that the minimum age is almost constant over time (there are still municipalities beyond the agricultural frontier) while the maximum age increases over time, as fallow lands in the early settled municipalities get older and older.

The age structure of crop lands

The productivity of annual crops on tropical forest soils is frequently very high the first couple of years while there is an abundance of nutrients from the ashes and while the land is relatively pest-free after burning. Thereafter productivity drops sharply, and a long fallow period is needed before the cultivation of annual crops can be repeated. The alternative is to plant perennial crops and supply the necessary fertilizers and pesticides.

We assume that areas with annual crops and planted pasture have been cleared for 2.5 years, on average. Areas with perennial crops and planted forest are assumed to have been cleared for 7.5 years, on average.

Clearing, carbon emissions, and economic growth, 1970–1985

Clearing

Clearing in Legal Amazonia has been very unevenly distributed across the region. People have naturally concentrated on the most accessible areas in the south-eastern part of the region, which happened to have relatively low vegetation density. This is reflected in table 7.5, which shows clearing by vegetation type. By 1985 less than 6 percent of the dense forest had been cleared, while more than 20 percent of all savannah areas has been converted for agropastoral purposes.

It is important to take into account the uneven distribution of clearing when calculating carbon emissions. In the present analysis, we assume that clearing is randomly distributed across vegetation types *within each municipality*, but because of the large variations in vegetation types and clearing rates across municipalities, we get non-randomly distributed clearing across vegetation types in the whole region.

Table 7.5. *Accumulated deforestation in Legal Amazonia, by vegetation type, by 1985*

Natural vegetation	Area (million ha)	Share deforested (%)
Dense forest	317.0	5.6
Seasonal forest	30.7	13.4
Savanna	78.3	20.4
Ecological transition	36.9	13.5
Wetlands	13.1	12.8
Campinarana	31.4	0.4
Total	507.4	8.8

Source: IBGE Agricultural Censuses.

Carbon emissions

According to our carbon emissions model, the total carbon stock in Legal Amazonia declined from 74.7 billion tons in 1970 to 72.1 billion tons in 1985, implying average annual emissions of 168 million tC. This is a net effect arising from carbon release from the destroyed original vegetation (198 million tC/year) and carbon sequestration in secondary vegetation (−30 million tC/year). Globally, annual carbon emissions amount to approximately 7.0 billion tC, implying a contribution from Amazon deforestation of about 2.4 percent. The largest emissions came from the southern and eastern states of Pará, Mato Grosso, Maranhão, and Goiás (see table 7.6). Table 7.6 also shows that the latter three states had the lowest emissions per hectare of cleared vegetation. This is owing to the generally thinner natural vegetation in these states.

The large differences in carbon emissions per hectare underline that a simple extrapolation of the high values from the center of Amazonas to the whole of Legal Amazonia would lead to erroneous results, significantly overestimating the overall level of carbon emissions.

Economic growth

Total agricultural output in Legal Amazonia increased from US$654 million in 1970 to US$2,274 million in 1985 (measured in fixed 1985-US$). Urban GDP grew even faster from US$1,522 million in 1970 to US$11,206 million. This implies an impressive average annual GDP growth rate of 12.9 percent. Table 7.7 shows the accumulated GDP over the 1970–1985 period for the nine states in Legal Amazonia and compares it with the carbon emitted.

Table 7.6. *Carbon emissions in Legal Amazonia, by state, 1970–1985*

State	Accumulated carbon emissions (1970–1985 million tC)	Carbon emissions per hectare cleared (1970–1985 tC/ha)
Acre	54.5	135.5
Amapá	31.1	119.0
Amazonas	67.1	128.4
Goiás/Tocantins	335.5	76.0
Maranhão	388.8	112.2
Mato Grosso	689.8	68.5
Pará	776.4	130.0
Rondônia	150.2	119.0
Roraima	22.8	101.0
Total	2,516.0	94.6

Source: IBGE Agricultural Censuses and assumptions in text.

Table 7.7. *Accumulated GDP in Legal Amazonia, 1970–1985*

State	Accumulated GDP 1970–1985 (billion fixed 1985-US$)	Average GDP per ton carbon emitted 1970–1985 ($/tC)
Acre	2.8	50.9
Amapá	2.1	67.1
Amazonas	25.5	379.4
Goiás/Tocantins	4.5	13.3
Maranhão	18.9	48.5
Mato Grosso	13.9	20.1
Pará	35.8	46.1
Rondônia	6.6	44.3
Roraima	1.1	47.5
Total	111.0	44.1

Source: IBGE Agricultural Censuses and assumptions in text.

On average, the states obtained an accumulated GDP of $44.1 per ton of carbon they omitted. There are big variations, however. The densely forested and largely inaccessible state of Amazonas obtained a much better trade-off between economic output and carbon emissions than the more accessible and less densely forested south-eastern states like Goiás and Mato Grosso. There are several explanations for these large differences. Goiás and Mato Grosso attracted a lot of cattle ranchers, whose activities yielded very low outputs per hectare. The activities in Amazonas, on the other hand, were much more diversified, including extractivism (mainly rubber and Brazil nuts) and a big industry related to the Manaus Free Zone (MFZ). The experience in the Amazonas state is very atypical, and now that the industries in Manaus have collapsed owing to the elimination of protection, the generation of GDP per ton of carbon emitted has probably fallen to get in line with the other states. This means that a state with a typical balance between rural and urban development generates GDP of about $40 per ton carbon emitted.

Discussion of the results

Comparisons with other carbon emission studies

Fearnside (1992b) conducted an intensive study of carbon dynamics in the Brazilian Amazon. Rather than using a bookkeeping model, as is done in this chapter, he uses a committed carbon approach, thus attributing all carbon that would ultimately be released to the year where deforestation takes place. He concludes that clearing of 1.38 million hectares per year of primary forest was responsible for the release of approximately 270 million tC/year in the period 1989–1990. This corresponds to 196 tC/hectare, which is more than twice as much as our average estimate for the 1970–1985 period (94.6 tC/hectare). The discrepancy is owing to the fact that Fearnside assumes that all deforestation takes place in dense forest and that there is no secondary re-growth at all.

Schroeder and Winjum (1994b) give a much lower estimate of net carbon emissions from land use changes in all of Brazil. Using a bookkeeping model with gradual decomposition of carbon in cleared areas and gradual recomposition in secondary forest, they get net carbon emissions for Brazil in the range of −44 to +10 million tC/year for 1990. The large discrepancy between Fearnside (1992b) and Schroeder and Winjum (1994b) is mainly attributed to the massive carbon recomposition in secondary forests in the latter study (+245 million tC/year).

Uncertainties

Biomass content

The biomass contents of Amazonian forest patches vary greatly owing to differences in soil characteristics, rainfall regimes, altitude, and previous natural and anthropogenic disturbances. In addition, there is a large statistical variation when sampling forest patches, because biomass content is very sensitive to the presence of large trees.

There has been a vigorous debate on the forest biomass in the Brazilian Amazon (Brown and Lugo 1984a, 1992a, 1992b; Fearnside 1985, 1986,

Table 7.8. *Biomass sensitivity analysis*

	Low biomass content	Central biomass content	High biomass content
Average annual emissions (million tC)	128	168	207
Average emissions per ha cleared (tC/ha)	72.2	94.6	117.0
Average GDP per tC emitted (1985-US$)/tC	57.8	44.1	35.7

1987, 1992a; Lugo and Brown 1992; Brown *et al.* 1989). Brown *et al.* (1995) note that the estimates during the 1990s differ by more than a factor of 2. They provide a new study for biomass content in Rondônia and give an estimate of the uncertainty associated with the biomass estimate. Through Monte Carlo simulation they find that measurement errors are approximately ± 20 percent around the mean (for a 95 percent confidence interval).

If we use carbon contents that are 20 percent lower than our mean values we get a lower estimate of annual carbon release of 128 million tC per year or 72.2 tC per hectare cleared. Similarly, we get a high estimate of 207 million tC per year or 117 tC per hectare cleared (see table 7.8).

Forest fragmentation and edge effects

Another issue that should be taken into account is forest fragmentation. As a part of the world's longest-running and most comprehensive attempt to assess the effects of forest fragmentation,[6] Laurance *et al.* (1997) studied the effect of forest fragmentation on biomass content on experimental plots 80 km north of Manaus. They found that the death of large trees close to forest edges caused significant additional biomass losses in the first few years after fragmentation. On average, plots within 100 m of edges lost 3.5–4.1 tons/hectare per year during the first ten–seventeen years after fragmentation, with the biggest losses taking place during the first four years. A significant increase in growth of lianas and new trees was observed, but not sufficient to offset losses caused by the increased mortality of large trees, at least not within the study period. Laurance *et al.* (2000) state three main reasons why large trees, which store a disproportionate amount of carbon, are unusually vulnerable in fragmented rainforest. First, because of their tall and inflexible trunks, large trees may

[6] See Bierregard *et al.* (2001).

be especially prone to uprooting and breakage near forest edges, where wind turbulence is increased. Second, large, old trees are particularly susceptible to liana infestation, which reduces tree survival. Third, because the crowns of large trees are exposed to intense sunlight and evaporation they are sensitive to droughts and may thus be vulnerable to increased desiccation near edges.

In a related study, Laurance *et al.* (1998) estimate the amount of carbon emissions that can be attributed to forest fragmentation in the Brazilian Amazon over and above the emissions from regular deforestation. Using a variety of assumptions about the pattern and extent of deforestation, they conclude that carbon emissions from forest fragmentation would range from 0.8 to 4.1 percent of what is caused by forest clearing *per se*. Large-scale cattle ranching tends to create less fragmentation effects than small farmers, and highly cleared areas obviously have less room for edge effects than moderately cleared areas.

Steady-state assumption

The calculations presented in this chapter assume that undisturbed primary forest, which still accounts for the major part of the Brazilian Amazon, is in a steady-state equilibrium with no net carbon gain or loss. Lugo and Brown (1992) question this assumption of a steady-state equilibrium, arguing that the rate of biomass accumulation of tropical forests is changing over time as a result of natural climatic changes, catastrophes, and past human disturbances. They cite plot-level field data from Venezuela and Puerto Rico that show mature forests accumulating carbon at rates of 1–2 tC/hectare/year (Schroeder and Winjum 1994b).

A possible explanation for the increase in steady-state carbon levels is CO_2 fertilization. Studies of agricultural and wild plant species have shown typically 20–40 percent higher photosynthesis and growth under doubled CO_2 conditions (Körner and Arnone 1992; Rochefort and Bazzaz 1992; Idso and Kimball 1993). This effect suggests faster forest re-growth and can also help explaining a possible increase in steady-state carbon stocks. Schimel (1995) notes, however, that long-term ecosystem responses may be substantially smaller than plant-level responses measured in laboratories.

Because of the huge area of primary forest in the Amazon, even the slightest change in biomass per hectare would result in significant effects on total carbon storage. If the approximately 350 million hectares of primary dense forest in the Brazilian Amazon, for example, increased its biomass with just 0.5 percent per year, then about 300 million tC would be sequestered every year. This number is larger than our estimate of annual carbon emitted from deforested areas. That makes it difficult to say anything certain about the net emissions from the whole of Legal Amazonia. Our analysis applies only to the net contributions from disturbed areas.

Conclusions

The calculations in this chapter indicate that average annual carbon emissions from deforestation in the Brazilian Amazon fell in the range 128–207 million tC/year during the rapid-development period 1970–1985. This corresponds to 1.8–3.0 percent of global carbon emissions from fossil-fuel combustion and deforestation. The estimated range is within the range provided by other studies, but falls in the low end. This is owing to two factors. First, we take into account the uneven spatial distribution of deforestation: lower clearing costs and closeness to large urban markets cause deforestation to take place in the most accessible and least dense forests as long as these are available. Second, we take into account the considerable secondary re-growth and the carbon sequestration that takes place when cleared land is abandoned.

During the same period, the Amazonian economy grew rapidly resulting in average annual GDP growth rates of 12.9 percent. On average during the period, there was generated \$44 of GDP per ton carbon emitted, but with big variations across states. The state of Amazonas was an atypical outlier, caused by temporary protection and subsidies, which probably cannot be replicated. Even apart from Amazonas, there were big variations in the gains achieved in relation to carbon emitted. The main cattle ranching state, Mato Grosso, did not obtain a very good ratio. With only \$20 per ton carbon emitted its efficiency was less than half the efficiency of the states with more diversified industrial and agricultural activities.

Since \$20 per ton carbon is less than what the most generous developed countries appear to be willing to pay in carbon tax,[7] there may theoretically be room for mutually beneficial agreements between fossil-fuel users in these countries and cattle ranchers in Mato Grosso. In most Amazonian states, however, the local gains seem to be higher than what most fossil-fuel users would be willing to pay in carbon emissions tax.

[7] Judged from actual carbon taxes in Scandinavia.

8 The costs and benefits of deforestation

> In terms of world systems, the rainforests are basically irrelevant. World weather is governed by the oceans – that great system of ocean atmospherics.
>
> (Philip Stott, cited in *The New York Post* 2000)

Chapter 6 of this book showed that there is a trade-off between economic growth and forest conservation, and that this trade-off can be affected by economic policy. The benefit side of deforestation shows how much extra regional GDP is obtained by converting 1 extra hectare of forest into agricultural land. However, there are also some significant and potentially large costs associated with forest clearing. Most of these costs are external to the farmer, in that they are not costs that he must bear himself out of his own pocket. Thus, they are unlikely to be taken into account when he makes the clearing decision. Multiplied over many farmers and land clearing decisions, the presence of these external costs will cause forest conversion to proceed more rapidly than is globally optimal. However, the existence of externalities does not automatically imply that forest clearing exceeds the socially optimal rate. The basic logic can be applied to make the opposite argument as well; imperfect capital markets, the lack of local governments to provide necessary public goods, and other market imperfections may lead to underutilization of the forest from a social cost-benefit perspective.

The global costs and benefits of Amazon deforestation

It is the purpose of this chapter[1] to provide an estimate of the global costs of Amazon deforestation and compare these with the estimated benefits. The costs are divided into private costs, local public costs, and global public costs, because it is important to understand what kind of services the forest brings and who benefits from them. Only with that understanding can we design policies to conserve forest services in an

[1] This chapter is based on Andersen (1997, 1998, 1999).

efficient way. For example, if one of the principal services of standing forests turns out to be carbon storage to mitigate global warming, then it is possible to maintain this service while also allowing some direct use of the forest, for example through sustainable logging. Sustainable logging does not cause significant net carbon emissions, since the forest will absorb carbon during the regeneration phase, and this absorption is likely to offset any carbon emissions associated with the waste products from timber productions. If we find that watershed protection is one of the most important services of the forest, then we might ban clearing near rivers and streams in order to preserve that service, while allowing clearing in areas where it will not affect the siltation of rivers. If we find that the existence value of pristine forest is very important, then we have to ban virtually all economic activities in the forest. The latter option is obviously more expensive in terms of forgone opportunity costs. In order to maintain a high level of forest services at a low cost, it is important to understand what services are really important to us, and then design efficient policies to protect these services.

Economic valuation

Putting a monetary value on a piece of rainforest is sensible only if that piece is not indisputably essential for our survival. Otherwise, the value is infinitely high and the valuation exercise futile. In a famous and hotly disputed article in the British science journal *Nature*, a group of researchers estimated that the total economic value of all the major eco-system services in the world is in the order of US$33 trillion per year (compared to global GNP of US$18 trillion per year) and the value of tropical forest services is around $3.8 trillion per year (Costanza *et al.* 1997). Many ecologists were outraged at the attempt to put a monetary value on our entire life support system, and rightly so. We cannot live without oceans, forests, and cropland, so the total value is obviously infinitely high. However, we may be able to live with a little bit less forest, especially if that forest is transformed to perform other life-support functions such as crop land. Since forests are not essential for our survival at the margin, it is conceptually valid to attach a finite marginal value to forest. In this chapter we are going to estimate an average marginal value of Brazilian Amazon rainforest, and we will assume that the marginal hectare of rainforest is not vitally indispensable at the current level of deforestation (10–15 percent). As the level of deforestation increases, we expect the marginal value to increase also. This means that the present valuation exercise has to be repeated again and again as the size of the forest shrinks and as the scientific knowledge about rainforest services develops. It is quite possible that the marginal value of forest suddenly increases dramatically if the forest size approaches some ecological threshold beyond which our life-support systems become seriously threatened. This means that it is important to understand which services the rainforest provides, and constantly check exactly how important these services are to us. In this chapter we will present a framework that allows us to do that.

We will apply the concept of Total Economic Value (TEV) (see, for example, Johanssen 1990 or Pearce 1993) to assess the value that different categories of stake-holders put on standing Amazon rainforest. The TEV concept is supposed to capture the full economic value that people attach to each type of land-use. It can be expressed as:

$$\begin{aligned} TEV &= \textit{Direct use value} + \textit{Indirect use value} \\ &\quad + \textit{Option value} + \textit{Existence value} \end{aligned}$$

For a standing rainforest the *direct use value* would, for example, stem from sustainable harvesting of timber and non-timber products (nuts, fruits, latex, etc.), tourism, and genetic material. *Indirect use values* refer to the "ecological functions" performed by the forest. These include soil and watershed protection, fire prevention, water recycling, carbon storage, and biodiversity protection. *Option values* represent the insurance premium we are willing to pay to secure that the forest, its biodiversity, and its ecological services are available in the future. *Existence value* is unrelated to both current and optional use. It arises because people are willing to pay for the existence of an environmental asset without ever taking part in the direct use of it (for example, through recreation). The existence value includes the value we are willing to pay to secure the survival and well-being of other species.

In practical applications it can be quite difficult to separate the last three categories, and great care should be taken not to double count or to leave major components out.

It is important to point out that the estimation of many of the components of the value of a standing forest is subject to considerable uncertainty. Many of the services of a rainforest are still very poorly understood, and estimates are bound to change over time as more empirical and scientific evidence becomes available. Successive versions of this valuation exercise (Andersen *et al.* 1996; Andersen 1997, 1998, 1999) have generally seen a fall in the estimated value of most services over time, one notable exception being the value of the fire-protection service which has increased in response to research by Cochrane and others (see Cochrane *et al.* 1999; Cochrane 2000). The value of the water-recycling component has dropped dramatically compared to previous versions. This is mainly due to the thorough survey made by Chomitz and Kumari (1996) on the topic, as well as the belated realization that too much rainfall, rather than too little, is generally more of a problem for farmers in the Amazon. The estimated value of the carbon storage service has dropped most dramatically. This is owing to the dramatic improvements in global, but regionally differentiated, climate–economy models which were motivated by the initial concerns about global warming.

Another problem with the analysis in this chapter is that it treats the Amazon forest as homogeneous and calculates an average marginal value across the whole region. In fact some parts of the economic value will vary substantially from area to area. For example, in chapter 5 we showed that the value of non-wood extractive products varies tremendously from area to area, with particularly high values being found in secondary forests. The carbon storage service also varies considerably across vegetation types, as shown in chapter 7. The watershed protection service is obviously higher for forest close to rivers, and there are bound to be some particularly spectacular spots with extra high existence value. It is obviously infeasible here to attach a different value to each of the several hundred million hectares of Amazon forest. In practice, however, zoning efforts at the local level should try to make sure that areas with particularly high forest service values receive better protection.

Valuation of forests is inherently a controversial exercise, and is made all the more so by the degree of uncertainty surrounding many of the "facts." People with differing preferences and tolerance for risk can have dramatically different ideas about the relative importance of various forest services. On top of this there are a number of serious challenges to the underlying methodology itself. Graves (2001) has argued that the traditional approaches to economic valuation of public goods has tended to be biased by failing to take into account the behavioral effects that the actual creation of heretofore hypothetical markets could have on peoples' choices. Others disagree with the concept of marginalist economic approaches to biophysical systems entirely. For example, David Kaimowitz[2] has argued that these are inappropriate for these systems that "probably do not operate in that way." As Kaimowitz continues:

> Most of the low estimates for biodiversity values come from the fact that reducing one marginal hectare has almost no likely affect on extinction rates (and we have little ability to value intra-species genetic variation). Island biogeography models are not very useful for understanding extinction under current circumstances. It seems likely that many systems will seem to go along relatively well and then all of a sudden collapse when they get beyond a certain threshhold. Marginalist economics does not deal with such discontinuities very well. (Personal correspondence)

[2] From personal correspondence.

Nevertheless, a feeling about the magnitude of these values is necessary in order to assess who is benefitting and who is harmed from deforestation, and what transfers should ideally be made in order to achieve a level of deforestation that is more beneficial for all, at the local, national, and global level. One approach to generating the necessary intuition about trade-offs would be to rely on people's values as reflected via democratic institutions. While many economists have argued that such an approach may end up providing valuations that are very arbitrary, arguments such as those represented by Kaimowitz (personal correspondence) and Graves (2001) suggest that the case for economic valuations being less arbitrary than democracy, at least in the case of public and environmental goods, has not yet by any means been universally accepted.

While we cannot settle this dispute here, we can attempt to provide the most comprehensive economic valuation possible and leave it to the reader to decide what to take from it and how valid the exercise may be.

Choosing a discount rate

Since a large part of the benefits of a standing rainforest will accrue to future generations of world citizens, it is important to consider their interests. It is customary, however, to attach less weight to costs and benefits materializing in the future than to those materializing today. A common justification for discounting that is often made is to point out that future generations will be better off because of general economic growth and technological progress, and they will therefore attach less value to an extra dollar of income than the current generation (because of the diminishing marginal utility of income). They may also be better equipped to counteract any bad effects of the current generation activities that spill over to them (Pearce 1993, p. 55). Another way of thinking about discounting is to consider that the amount of money needed today to pay a one-period-ahead (assuming a 6 percent interest rate) future generation \$100 is only about \$94. So, if future generations require a \$100 compensation for lost ecological services to maintain the same level of utility (their willingness to accept, assuming they have an implied property right to the service), then today's generation must put aside \$94 if they consume the ecological service. To make comparisons economically meaningful it is thus only logical to discount the values of all benefits to future generations, not just purely monetary payments.

A standard formula for discounting future consumption is:

$$d = \sigma + \mu g$$

Table 8.1. *TEV of standing Amazon forest at current forest stock levels*

	TEV (1995-US$/hectare)		
Discount rate (%)	2	6	12
Local private benefits	**1,425**	**475**	**237**
Sustainable timber supply	1,400	467	233
Non-timber products	25	8	4
Local public benefits	**590**	**163**	**74**
Water recycling	0	0	0
Nutrient recycling	0	0	0
Protection against fire	550	150	67
Watershed protection	0	0	0
Tourism	40	13	7
Global benefits	**1,120**	**540**	**120**
Carbon storage	1,000	500	100
Biodiversity protection	30	10	5
Recreational value	40	13	7
Existence value	50	17	8
Total Economic Value	3,135	1,178	431

Source: Authors' estimates. See derivations on pp. 169–189.

where d is the social discount rate, σ is the "rate of pure time preference," μ is the elasticity of the marginal utility of consumption function, and g is the growth rate of *per capita* consumption (Pearce 1993, p. 58). If the function linking utility to consumption is logarithmic, then $\mu = 1$. If, in addition, the pure time preference rate is set to zero on ethical grounds, then $d = g$. The discount rate becomes equal to the expected rate of growth of *per capita* consumption. Some empirical work suggests that μ may be a little higher than unity (Fellner 1967; Scott 1989), and that the rate of pure time preference may be slightly above zero (Pearce 1993, p. 59). Taking historical growth rates as a guide, this suggests reasonable discount rates in the range of 2–6 percent.

These discount rates may seem small compared to what is usually applied in cost-benefit analyses of investment projects, and there are probably several billion people on earth who would be willing to pay 12 percent interest on a loan. We will thus report results for three different discount rates, 2, 6, and 12 percent in table 8.1 and let the reader choose which one s/he finds most appropriate. In the text we will go through the calculations only for the 2 percent discount rate, though, which is the most conservative from a conservationist perspective.

The value of intact Amazonian forests

Table 8.1 summarizes the estimated economic value of a standing rainforest. The subsequent subsections explain how the individual components are estimated.

The classification of values into local private, local public, and global benefits is made to provide some indication of what transfers should take place to obtain the optimal amount of forest preservation.

Local private benefits

The private benefits derived from a standing forest consist of the profits derived from the timber and non-timber forest products that can be sustainably harvested from the forest.

Sustainable timber production

Almeida and Uhl's (1995) calculations for the Brazilian Amazon suggest that the annual profits from sustainable logging would on average be no more than $28/hectare. While this number was presented as an average, we will adopt it as a general marginal value, taking into account that market changes and technological progress have meant that a greater amount of species is now being extracted from the forest. At a discount rate of 2 percent this value implies a NPV of $1,400/hectare.

Non-timber forest products

Besides timber, it is possible to extract a wide range of non-timber products from a standing forest. Currently, the commercially most important extractive products are açaí (fruit), babau oil, piassava fibers, palmito (heart of palm), rubber, and Brazil nuts (see chapter 5).

Besides the commercial products, forests also provide an astonishing array of subsistence products including shelter, clothing, food, beverages, oils, firewood, kitchen utensils, tools, weapons, bait, hammocks, baskets, fishing nets, brooms, ornaments, cosmetics, toys, medicine, and magical or spiritual objects (Anderson *et al.* 1991, p. 5).

Chapter 5 of this book discussed non-wood extraction in Legal Amazonia in detail and showed that these values are on average very low. According to IBGE survey data, the total annual value of non-wood extractivism in Legal Amazonia amounted to US$118.2 million in 1995, which divided by the area of Legal Amazonia amounts to about $0.24 per hectare.

In contrast to this broad average of extractive values across the region, site studies provide much higher estimates of the value of extractive products. Peters *et al.* (1989) have estimated the net value of non-timber forest products from a plot in the Peruvian Amazon (Mishana). After deducting costs of collection, transportation, and regeneration, they found a net value of \$317/hectare/year. However, using a similar methodology for another plot in the Peruvian Amazon (the San Rafael Reserve), Pinedo-Vasquez *et al.* (1992) found a net value of only \$20/hectare/year.

Murrieta Ruiz and Rueda Pinzón (1995) report the gross incomes derived from extractive activities (including some farming) in a couple of extractive reserves in Acre. The extractive reserve of Alto Juruá covers 506,186 hectares, houses 5,821 persons in 325 settlements, and produced a gross output worth US\$1,065,026 in 1994. A third of this value came from hunting and fishing, a quarter from the cultivation of maize, a fifth from rubber collection, and the remainder from small animal husbandry and other cropping activities. In total it amounted to a gross value of about \$2/hectare. Approximately the same per hectare gross value was derived in the Chico Mendez reserve, which covers 970,570 hectares, hosts 12,017 people, and produced a gross output of \$2,664,144 in 1994. Both reserves had a population density of 1.2 persons per km^2.

Allegretti (1994) reports results from a 1987 study of the Rubber Stand of Cachoeira in Xapuri, Acre. The area comprises 25,000 hectares and houses 67 families (420 people). The economic activities consisted of a mix of market-oriented extractive activities (rubber and Brazil nuts) and subsistence activities (agriculture, small-scale raising of animals, gathering, hunting, and fishing). The total annual cash income in the area was \$64,320, and if other activities were given a monetary value, this would rise to \$100,000. This implies a gross income of about \$4/hectare/year.

The broad average of extraction values from Legal Amazonia and the three surveys of extractive reserves in Acre are judged to be most representative for Legal Amazonia as a whole, while the much-criticized study from the Peruvian Amazon looks like a very atypical outlier. We do not have data on the costs of extraction, but we will assume the costs amount to about half the gross value. Considering that the IBGE extraction data from 1995 may be missing both some extractive products and some transient extractivists, a central value of extractive products of \$0.5/hectare/year seems reasonable. This implies a net present value of \$25/hectare when applying a 2 percent discount rate.

Local public benefits

The natural forest provides a range of ecological services at the local and regional level. These include water recycling, fire prevention, erosion control, and watershed protection. Very few empirical studies are available to help quantify these benefits. However, Chomitz and Kumari (1996, 1998) offer some very useful reviews of at least some of these benefits, and we will apply their framework and observations as well as we can to the Amazon basin.

Water recycling

Compared to other parts of the world, a relatively large part of rainfall in the Amazon is derived from water recycled into the atmosphere through evapotranspiration rather than being blown into the region in the form of clouds from the ocean.[3] Since evapotranspiration is roughly proportional to leaf area, the water recycled through forest is much higher than that recycled through pasture and savannah. It is therefore tempting to assume that deforestation would result in a decrease in precipitation which could harm the productivity of neighboring agricultural land. This effect would be aggravated by the rain running off compacted pasture soils much more quickly, becoming unavailable for later release to the atmosphere through transpiration (Fearnside 1995b, p. 53). Thus, deforestation could potentially cause the dry season to become longer and more severe.

However, too much rain, rather than too little rain, is the main obstacle for agricultural productivity in the Amazon. Most crops need at least a couple of months with low amounts of rainfall (less than 100 mm) for the grains to ripen and harden and to prevent rotting. A distinct dry period also helps to control pests and diseases (e.g. Sombroek and Sousa Carvalho 2000).

Chomitz and Thomas (2000) demonstrate empirically a strong negative effect of rainfall on agriculture in the Brazilian Amazon when holding other factors such as road proximity constant. This means that the water recycling service of the forest is actually a disservice for local farmers, which implies that we might include a negative value for this service.

However, the conventional wisdom that deforestation would reduce precipitation is not fully supported by the more sophisticated General Circulation Models (GCMs) which have been developed to model these relationships. Eltahir and Bras (1992) suggest, for example, that deforestation on the scale of hundreds of km^2 increases rainfall, while deforestation on the scale of millions of km^2 reduces rainfall. Henderson-Sellers *et al.* (1993) predict that complete deforestation of the Amazon would reduce rainy season precipitation by 30 percent, while Lean and

[3] Studies by Villa Nova *et al.* (1976), Lettau *et al.* (1979), Marques *et al.* (1980), Jordan and Heuneldop (1981), and Leopoldo *et al.* (1982) show that, on average, about 50 percent (and in some places up to 75 percent) of precipitation returns to the atmosphere in the form of water vapor through evapotranspiration, while the rest is discharged through the Amazon River system.

Rowntree (1993) find a total reduction of 14 percent, but an increase of 20 percent for Eastern Brazil.

The few empirical studies from elsewhere on the relationship between deforestation and precipitation do not give much clearer answers. Meher-Homji (1988) summarizes several studies for India which find concurrent forest loss and reduction in precipitation, but Bruijnzeel (1990) is critical of these studies, and argues that these findings could also be explained by observed changes in the location of the "monsoon through." Tangtham and Sutthipibul (1989) compared regionally averaged data on rainfall amounts and occurrence for 36 stations in Northeast Thailand with changes in forest cover over the period 1951–1984. On a year-to-year basis they found no correlation between either of the rainfall variables and the percentage of remaining forest cover, although annual rainfall totals generally exhibited a weak negative trend during the period under consideration (Bruijnzeel 1990). However, when using ten-year moving averages they found evidence that showers tended to become more frequent but less severe. This is the opposite trend from what was found on private rubber estates in Peninsular Malaysia (UNESCO 1978). O'Brien (1995) collected data from twenty climate stations in Mexico over twenty-two years and matched it with ground-truthed remote sensing data of deforestation in 1979 and 1989. A preliminary analysis indicates that deforestation increases minimum temperature, decreases maximum temperature, but has no significant effect on precipitation (Chomitz and Kumari 1996).

In other words, the evidence of the link between forest cover and hydrology is highly site- and scale-specific, and it seems difficult to make generalizations. There is no scientific agreement that marginal deforestation would decrease rainfall, and even if it did local farmers might in some cases actually benefit from such a decrease rather than suffer from it. We will therefore choose a zero value for the water-recycling service.

Nutrient recycling

The main share of nutrients in a rainforest is located in the biomass above ground rather than in the soil. When the forest is burned these nutrients are temporarily transferred to the soils, where some of them are captured by planted crops and pasture grasses, while the rest are washed away. The value of nutrients removed by forest clearing is calculated at \$3,480/hectare given market prices of NPK fertilizers in Brazil (Uhl *et al.* 1993, p. 244). However, this value should not be added to the other values of a standing rainforest, since the appropriation of this value would imply the elimination of the other values. A mature forest is in nutrient balance and thus does not provide any nutrient-recycling value to surrounding areas.

It is customary to attribute a benefit to the forest because it stores carbon that would do damage to other places (see below). Thus for a symmetrical treatment it would be tempting to attach a negative value to a forest that stores nutrients that could provide a benefit in other places. However, that would result in double-counting because the nutrients that are released when converting forest to agricultural land are accounted for as a benefit of deforestation through agricultural production. Consequently, we should here set the benefit of nutrient recycling to zero.

Fire control

With its humid micro-climate the rainforest provides a natural protection against wildfires. Data from charcoal studies indicate that natural fires happen only a few times during a millennium in intact lowland tropical rainforests (Sanford *et al.* 1985; Saldarriaga and West 1986; Turcq *et al.* 1998). In disturbed areas (about 25 percent deforested), on the other hand, forest fires are likely to strike three or four times per century (Cochrane 2000). In this section we will try to make a simple calculation of the order of magnitude of the value of fire-protection service that intact forest provides.

Consider a typical 100 hectare plot in the Amazonian forest where 10 percent has been cleared for agricultural land. Intact forest has a very low fire risk. Wildfires happen approximately once every 500 years on a given hectare, i.e. the probability of fire is 0.2 percent per year. For cleared land wildfire risk is much larger, let's say 5 percent per year (once every 20 years).

Additional deforestation will increase total fire risk both because the fire-resistant area is reduced and because fires are needed as part of the deforestation process. Research by Cochrane and others indicates that fire risk in the forested parts increases by at least an order of magnitude when half the forest is cleared and the remaining forest is widely affected by logging (Cochrane 2000). Their empirical evidence, however, does not show systematic differences in fire risk between areas with, for example, 41 percent and 65 percent deforested land (Cochrane *et al.* 1999, table 8.2). Their imagery analysis and analysis based on interviews also give highly disparate results. In Paragominas (64 percent cleared and one of the logging centers of the Amazon) the imagery analysis indicated fire rotations of seven–thirteen years, while interviews indicated a cycle of 125 years. Either the farmers have an interest in providing erroneous information or they do not perceive wildfires to be as significant a problem as the authors.

Given this uncertainty, let us assume that fire risk in both categories of land increases by 50 percent if an extra 20 hectares is deforested. The

Table 8.2. *Rural GDP, urban GDP, and cleared area in Legal Amazonia, by year, 1970–1995*

	1970	1985	1995
Rural GDP (million 1995-US$)	1,607	5,216	9,882
Urban GDP (million 1995-US$)	4,244	23,711	33,948
Total GDP (million 1995-US$)	5,850	28,926	43,831
Cleared area (km^2)	151,246	389,169	485,809

Source: IBGE Agricultural Censuses, 1970, 1985, and 1995.

increase in the probability of wildfire in forests is therefore 0.1 percentage point and the increase in the probability of uncontrolled fire on agricultural land 2.5 percentage points.

If wildfire consumes agricultural land, an average of about $200 worth of crops are lost per hectare.[4] If fire consumes virgin forest, the loss will amount to the services lost during the period of regeneration. Carbon will be released during burning, but an equivalent amount of carbon will be absorbed by growing trees during the period of regeneration. Since forests regenerate relatively quickly on burned land from which the nutrients have not been removed, the ecological functions will soon be restored.[5] The biggest loss will come from the loss of sustainable timber supplies, since it will take many decades before the new trees are ready for harvest. Assume that a sustainable timber supply worth $28/hectare/year is lost for fifty years. This amounts to a cost of $880/hectare at the 2 percent discount rate. The loss of other services is negligible compared to the loss of timber in the case of a temporary fire-induced reduction in forest.

Now we are ready to calculate the value of the fire-protection service. At the 2 percent discount rate a 20 hectare increase in deforestation will imply an expected loss of $212 (2.5 percent · 30 hectares · $200/hectare + 0.1 percent · 70 hectares · $880/hectare). This implies an expected annual fire-protection service of about $11/hectare, or an NPV of $1,700/hectare.

Erosion control and watershed protection

Forests protect the soil against erosion and it is conventional wisdom that the removal of the forest cover will increase erosion and siltation of

[4] This corresponds to average agricultural output per hectare cleared in 1995, according to IBGE census data.

[5] Research by Cochrane *et al.* (1999) suggests that forests are quite resistent to a single wildfire and quickly recover from the burns, but if fires are recurrent the forest will not be able to regenerate. They make the very strong claim that "Left unchecked, the current fire regime will result in an inexorable transition of the entire area to either scrub or grassland."

rivers. This is assumed to cause damage to downstream activities, such as fisheries and dams. We have not been able to find any studies that try to determine the value of watershed protection in the Amazon, but Aylward (2000) provides an excellent survey of studies from many other places in the world, and we will try to extract the experiences from these and adapt them to the Amazon region.

First of all, it is worth noticing that the protective value of forests lies not so much in the ability of the tree canopy to break the power of raindrops, but rather in developing and maintaining a litter layer on the forest floor. It has been shown by several studies that the erosive power of rain dripping from forest canopies may be substantially larger than for rainfall in the open (Bruijnzeel 1990). It is therefore the removal of the litter layer that causes increased erosion rather than the removal of tree-canopy. Mechanical methods of forest clearing are thus much more damaging in this respect than manual clearing. The latter is still by far the dominant method used in the Brazilian Amazon, which implies that the changes in erosion caused by deforestation are smaller in the Amazon than in many other regions. In addition, the Brazilian Amazon is generally very flat compared to practically all the areas that have been subject to watershed-protection studies. Since steep slopes erode much more easily than flat or gently sloping areas, we would expect erosion and sedimentation in the Amazon to be in the low end of the range observed by international studies.

Aylward compiles a list of ten types of negative externalities associated with sedimentation, but many of these do not apply in the Amazon. Of all the negative externalities listed, we would expect the loss of hydroelectric power generation owing to sedimentation of reservoirs and loss of production in fisheries to be the two biggest items. Loss of tourism revenues and loss of irrigation production owing to sedimentation of reservoirs and canals would be negligible in the Amazon.

Aylward also notes that although most valuation exercises focus on the costs of sedimentation there may also be benefits. The illegal dredging of deposited sediment in the Ping River, Thailand, demonstrates that there can also be positive externalities associated with sedimentation (Enters 1995). The fact that the seasonally flooded areas of the Amazon is among the most fertile in the region complements this observation.

There is another important hydrological effect of deforestation that is often ignored, since it tends to create positive externalities. Since tall trees act as highly effective water pumps removing water from the soil and transpiring it into the air, deforestation tends to reduce groundwater loss, raise the water table, and increase dry season flows. This would be good news for downstream hydroelectric facilities. Dozens of controlled experiments have been conducted showing that, contrary to expectations, the net immediate effect of tree removal is often a rise in the water table, and therefore a probable increase in dry-season flows (Hamilton and King 1983). Similar results have been found in studies of actual sites. Nepstad and Schwarzman (1992) compare deep-rooted evergreen forests to an adjacent degraded pasture in Pará. At the end of the dry season, the water in the top 8 m of soil available for plants was 37 cm higher in the degraded pasture (Chomitz and Kumari 1998). A case study by Vincent *et al.* (1995) on Thailand supports these findings. After a large reforestation program around the Mae Theng watershed, an analysis of monthly stream flows showed a significant decrease of water flow. These reductions resulted in the seasonal closure of one of Chiang Mai's water treatment plants, thus imposing costs on downstream water users (Chomitz and Kumari 1998).

These observations lead us to believe that the value of watershed protection in the Brazilian Amazon could be either positive or negative, but probably very small. We thus choose the convenient value zero.

Global benefits

The global benefits derived from an intact rainforest include direct use values from recreation (eco-tourism) and from the provision of genetic material for scientific research; indirect use value in the form of a carbon storage service mitigating global warming; an option value which measures the insurance premium we are willing to pay for the preservation of forest owing to uncertainty and irreversibility; and an existence value derived from the mere satisfaction of knowing that a place exists where thousands of species live in their natural environment.

Carbon storage

The concentration of carbon dioxide in the atmosphere increased steadily during the twentieth century, because carbon is released from two of the Earth's major storage depots; fossil fuels and forests.[6] The Intergovernmental Panel on Climate Change (IPCC) estimates that deforestation accounted for 1.6 $\pm$ 1.0 billion ton carbon emissions during the 1980s while fossil fuel burning accounted for 5.4 $\pm$ 0.5 billion ton (IPCC 1990,

[6] The total carbon pool, estimated at about 49,000 metric gigatons, is distributed among organic and inorganic forms. Fossil carbon accounts for 22 percent of the total pool. The oceans contain 71 percent of the world's carbon, mostly in the form of bicarbonate and carbonate ions. An additional 3 percent is in dead organic matter and phytoplankton. Terrestrial eco-systems, in which forests are the main reservoir, hold about 3 percent of the total carbon. The remaining 1 percent is held in the atmosphere, circulated, and used in photosynthesis ("Carbon Cycle," Microsoft Encarta 1994).

p. 14). With 10–35 percent of total carbon emissions, deforestation may thus be a major cause of future climate change.

Since dense tropical forests have a much higher biomass than alternative land uses, carbon will be released when forests are converted to crops land or pasture. Brown and Pierce (1994, p. 5) estimate that the conversion of 1 hectare of average rainforest will imply a carbon release of 100–200 tons. This range is supported by estimates by Houghton *et al.* (1987), the German Bundestag (1990), Fearnside (1992a), and Sombroek (1992).

Indications of the costs of an additional ton of carbon released to the atmosphere can be obtained both indirectly and directly. Indirect methods include looking at the value at which societies are willing to tax themselves in order to stabilize greenhouse emissions, or looking at abatement costs implied by various methods of reducing greenhouse emissions. The direct approach sums up all the estimated costs and benefits of climate changes over sectors and regions. Clearly, the direct approach requires much more information than the indirect approach.

Indirect approach. The indirect approach is a convenient short cut, since it requires very little information, but it also has severe problems as discussed below. Schneider (1991) provides an overview of enacted and proposed carbon taxes. Enacted taxes in Finland, the Netherlands, and Sweden are in the range $6.1–45/ton of carbon (Shah and Larson 1992). Proposed carbon taxes in the United States and the European Community (EC) are in the range $5–70/tC (Shah and Larson 1992). The US Congressional Budget Office (CBO) concluded in a 1990 study that the tax required to reduce US greenhouse emissions to 1988 levels by the year 2000 should be $10/tC in 1991, increasing gradually to $100/tC in the year 2000 (CBO 1990; Schneider 1993). Springer (2001) provides an overview of nine Top Down Climate Policy Cost Studies, which all attempt to estimate the cost of implementing policies to meet the Kyoto Protocol targets for greenhouse gas emissions. The nine studies surveyed arrive at marginal abatement costs in the range $20–770/tC. Springer's own estimates, based on a multi-region computable general equilibrium (CGE) model with trade and different degrees of capital mobility fall in the high end of this range.

The carbon-tax approach has two potential biases, which work in opposite directions. A positive bias arises from the fact that a carbon tax will have positive effects other than mitigating global warming. Considerable secondary benefits can be expected in the form of local and regional air quality improvements, reduced traffic externalities (accidents and congestion), and tax revenues which can be used to lower other distortionary taxes. A large part of the supposed willingness to pay for carbon reduction is probably owing to such immediate local benefits rather than the more uncertain future effects through global warming.[7] Ekins (1996) reviews estimates of secondary benefits of CO_2 abatement achieved through reductions in fossil fuel consumption. The estimates reviewed are in the range \$125–795/tC. These estimates of secondary benefits are all higher than the highest carbon tax implemented (\$45/tC in Sweden), so enacted carbon taxes attached to fossil fuel consumption tell us little about the true cost of carbon emissions.

A negative bias arises from the free-rider problem. In the absence of strong international cooperation, individual countries will be reluctant to impose significant costs on the national economy, since only a negligible part of the benefits of reduced emissions accrues to themselves, while the costs in terms of loss in international competitiveness may be large.

The direct cost approach. Estimating the costs of global warming directly is extremely data-demanding. Not only do we have to understand what the physical effects of the rising average temperatures will be for different regions of the world, but we also have to know how those physical changes will affect economic systems. Finally, we have to know what the economic systems will be like when the effects occur. All of this is highly uncertain, but we will try to assess the knowledge that does exist at the moment.

The IPCC is the established authority[8] on global warming. Their latest estimates say that the atmospheric concentration of CO_2 by the end of the twenty-first century will be somewhere in the range 450–1260 ppm if current emission rates are maintained. This represents a 75–350 percent increase compared to pre-industrialization levels of 288 ppm. This increase is expected to cause an increase in world mean surface temperature of 1.4–5.8°C. The higher temperatures are expected to cause an increase in the sea level of 0.09–0.88 m, mainly owing to thermal expansion. Precipitation is also expected to increase as a consequence of the higher temperatures (IPCC 2001). These averages hide substantial regional variation. The northern hemisphere is generally expected to experience higher temperature increases than the southern hemisphere,

[7] The existing taxes on fuel and other oil products already imply implicit carbon taxes of \$65/tC in United States and \$200–350/tC in Europe (Hoeller and Coppel 1992, quoted in Poterba 1993).

[8] They are hotly disputed by some, however. The IPCC's well-known "hockey-stick" graph showing dramatic increases in mean world temperatures during the last thirty years of the previous millennium is based on Mann's study of tree rings from North America (Mann *et al.* 1999). These are not backed up by the allegedly more reliable satellite measurements of surface temperatures, which show no trend over the last eighteen years (e.g. Daly 2001).

because the deep, cool oceans of the southern hemisphere counteract warming.

The biggest worry, however, are not the moderate average changes that global warming may cause, but rather the possibility of triggering catastrophic events by destabilizing the balance of ecosystems. The IPCC finds it likely that temperature changes will cause an increase in the risk of droughts and an increase in the intensity of tropical cyclones (IPCC 2001). Others (e.g. Suzuki 2001) fear that temperature changes may change the ocean currents. If the Warm Gulf stream were to change its course, it would have dramatic impacts on Northern Europe, which is currently blessed with an unusually mild climate for its latitude. There is also the possibility that many other species will not adapt as quickly and as well to climate change as humans, and that we will see a considerable increase in species extinction (e.g. Wyman 1991).

Global climate cycles of warming and cooling have been a natural phenomenon for hundreds of thousands of years and have been mainly determined by astronomical causes outside our influence (the cyclical effects of the elliptical orbit of the earth around the sun and the cyclical changes in the sun's brightness). Figure 8.1 shows that we are currently (starting about 18,000 years ago) in a warm Interglacial period, but apart from the Eemian Interglacial period around 125,000 years ago, Earth has generally been about 3° cooler than it is now, and it is destined to become so again owing to the above-mentioned astronomical cycles.

The fact that eco-systems can establish themselves after repeatedly having been demolished by ice is a testimony to the resilience of nature. Furthermore it is probably fair to say that in the very long run humans are unlikely to have a major effect on the earth's climate. However, if we can

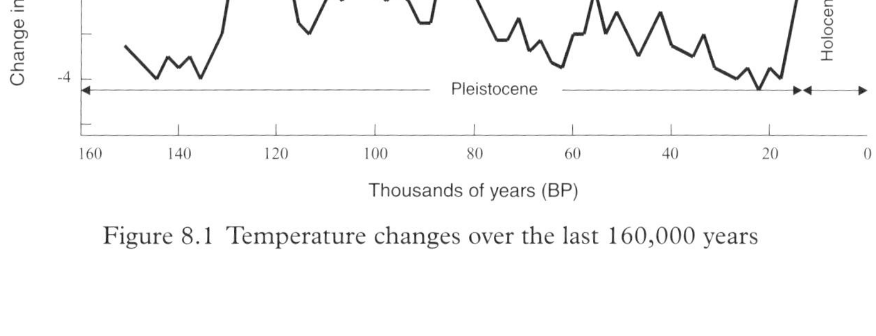

Figure 8.1 Temperature changes over the last 160,000 years

cause an increase in average global temperatures of several degrees within a few centuries, then we may experience even warmer temperatures than in the Eemian Interglacial period, and we will have to deal with those changes.

How are the physical changes likely to affect economic systems? The early studies of the economic effects of global warming used an "enumerative approach" which consisted of listing different adverse effects and summing them up into a total damage figure (e.g. Cline 1992; Fankhauser 1994, and Nordhaus 1994). Apart from the difficulty of obtaining reliable damage estimates for each item on the list, this approach ignores second-order effects. When one sector or region is affected by global warming, it will have spillover effects on other sectors and regions, through changes in relative prices, through trade, and through adaptive measures.

To capture both direct and indirect effects, a sophisticated multi-region CGE model is needed. Kurtze and Springer (1999) surveys the progress in this area, and they conclude that the CGE framework is especially qualified for the purpose of a consistent assessment of the consequences of climate change on the regional, national, and world economy, because of its capacity to represent the behavior and interrelationships of all relevant agents in the economy. Kemfert (2001) presents one of the most advanced integrated climate-economy general equilibrium models (World Integrated Assessment General Equilibrium Models, or WIAGEM). The models cover the whole world disaggregated into twenty-five regions. Each region has fourteen productive sectors, of which the energy sectors receive the most detailed attention, owing to their important impacts on climate change. The models incorporate all greenhouse gases which influence the potential global temperature, the sea-level variation, and the assessed probable impacts in terms of costs and benefits of climate change. Market and non-market damage are evaluated using Tol's damage cost approaches (Tol 2002a, 2002b). The model runs over fifty years. Model simulations using WIAGEM suggest that costs of climate change do materialize within the fifty-year horizon of the model, but that the cost of implementing the Kyoto Protocol to reduce the damages are much larger than the costs of climate change. Even regions which are not required by the Kyoto Protocol to reduce emissions suffer from it because of negative trade effects.

Nordhaus and Boyer (2000) present a simpler climate–economy model without international trade and with only one composite good. Several interesting points arise from their analysis, however. First, owing to the momentum in the built-up greenhouse gases, the temperature is going to increase by a couple of degrees over the twenty-first century even if we limit carbon emissions much more dramatically than agreed in the Kyoto

Protocol. In fact, the Kyoto Protocol reduces the temperature by only an estimated 0.03° Celcius compared to the base case of doing nothing to control global warming. This also means that the net benefits of implementing the Kyoto Protocol will be negative. A second interesting point is that the only effective measure against global warming is a technological fix.[9] A report by the National Academy of Sciences describes a number of options that provide the theoretical capability of unlimited offsets to the radiative effects of greenhouse gases at a cost of less than $1 per ton carbon (see National Academy of Sciences 1991, chapter 28). A third point is that a small delay (ten years) in action against global warming will cause virtually no increase in the NPV of damage. This means that it may be better to spend a little time getting a better handle on the problem than jumping prematurely into expensive and inefficient abatement options.

Although the CGE approach is the theoretically best way of analyzing the impacts of climate change, it suffers from the same problem as all other methods: we have only very vague ideas about how the future economic systems will be when the effects of climate change occur. The carbon we release to the atmosphere now will cause gradual warming over centuries, but to perfectly measure the effect of these changes we would have to know how the world economic systems would have developed over the next centuries in the absence of global warming. Our economic systems and the way we live and work changed dramatically over the twentieth century, and they are likely to change even more dramatically during the twenty-first century. Progress in the field of genetic engineering may well completely revolutionize agriculture all over the world, in which case a CGE model calibrated to current agricultural technology would be unable to estimate the impact of climate change. Dramatic advances in information sharing (through the Internet) may well cause an increase in the rate of innovation, which makes it very difficult for us to imagine the technology we have available by the end of this century. If we are successful in reducing poverty in the world, there will be many fewer people who are vulnerable to climate change.

Considering the enormous uncertainties on (1) the effect of carbon emissions on the climate, (2) the effect of climate changes on our future economic systems, and (3) the structure of our future economic systems,

[9] This implies further human tampering with the global environment, which we may prefer to avoid. However, environmentally benign geoengineering options seem possible. Global warming could be counteracted by deliberately introducing fine particles – such as those thrown up naturally from volcanoes – into the upper atmosphere to scatter sunlight and heat back into space. Cooling caused by volcanic eruptions shows that this simple technique could work.

it is virtually impossible to assign a value to the carbon-seque services that forests provide. Enacted taxes tell us little about we attach to preventing carbon emissions, because the local b better air quality) far outweigh the potential global benefits. estimates using the "enumerative approach" are likely to ove costs of carbon emissions, since they ignore second-order eff also tend to ignore many beneficial effects, such as CO_2 fertilizatio causes plants to grow faster.

The fact that there is so much uncertainty associated with of carbon emissions implies that it is worthwhile to err on the caution. A large part of the value of carbon sequestration can th thought of as the insurance premium we are willing to pay to preserve forest until we get more information about the costs of carbon emissions.

For the 2 percent discount rate we thus choose \$10/tC, as that seems to be what people with relatively long time horizons would be willing to pay for the global benefits of reduced carbon emissions. For the 6 percent discount rate we choose \$5/tC, which we think is the maximum willingness of the more shortsighted people. Finally we choose \$1/tC for the 12 percent discount rate, as the adverse effects are likely to occur so late that they will have very little weight when applying such a high discount rate. These are NPV figures expressed per ton of carbon, not annual figures.

To arrive at NPV figures per hectare, we multiply these values by average direct carbon emissions per hectare as found in chapter 7 and add 3 percent to account for edge effects (carbon losses in fragmented forest). Rounding up, we assume total direct and indirect carbon emissions of 100tC/hectare, which results in values for the carbon-sequestration service of \$1500/hectare, \$750/hectare, and \$150/hectare, for the 2 percent, 6 percent, and 12 percent discount rate, respectively. These high values are mainly owing to the large amount of uncertainty surrounding carbon emissions. A large part of this value should be interpreted as an option value we are willing to pay until we get more accurate information about the actual costs of carbon emissions.

Biodiversity protection

Biodiversity has both an esthetic and a scientific benefit. The esthetic benefit can be expressed in the marketplace in the form of "eco-tourism" and market forces should allocate land to accommodate this kind of demand for biodiversity (Schneider 1991, p. 5). The scientific benefit of biodiversity arises from the provision of genetic material to be used for medical purposes or for genetic engineering of, for example, more pest-resistant crops. The scientific benefit of biodiversity is allocated poorly in the marketplace. This is primarily because the owner of the land which provides the habitat within which genetic information will flourish will usually not benefit from its discovery and eventual application[10] (Schneider 1991, p. 5).

The recreational value of the Amazon forest. World tourism is growing rapidly, representing about 12 percent of World Product and mobilizing close to 6.3 percent of total employment. Within this sector there is a shift towards ecological tourism, where the Amazon has great potential (SUDAM 1992, p. 36).

Because of its characteristics, tourism is a very clean and environmentally friendly economic activity, provided that the intensity does not exceed the carrying capacity of the eco-system. At present, Amazonia has an extremely modest tourist industry, with only half a million tourists visiting between 1984 and 1989 (SUDAM 1992, p. 37). Properly managed, this number could be multiplied many times without hurting the environment. It would at the same time be one of the most effective ways of earning foreign currency.

Suppose the number of tourists visiting the Amazon increased to 1 million per year and each person were willing to pay $800 in order to augment their vacation with a trip to the Amazon, then the total willingness to pay for experiencing the rainforest would amount to $0.8 billion/year or $1.6 per hectare per year. The net present recreational value would then be $80/hectare with a discount rate of 2 percent. Brazil would probably be able to appropriate only about half of this value, so we will divide this value evenly between local direct-use value in the form of revenues from tourism and global benefit in the form of recreational value.

The scientific value of Amazonian biodiversity. Because tropical organisms have evolved in a very species-rich environment, they have developed an astonishing variety of genetic features designed to enhance their survival chances. The genetic information available in tropical organisms may be of considerable commercial value if adapted to agricultural and pharmaceutical applications.

Many of the food products that we currently consume in vast amounts originate from tropical forests. This is the case with, for example, coffee, cocoa, bananas, pineapples, peanuts, rice, and avocados which are currently being produced in plantations, but still depend on regular infusions of new genetic material from their wild relatives in order to maintain

[10] At the 1992 UNCED conference in Rio, a treaty on biodiversity was proposed, which addressed the issue of patent rights to medicine derived from tropical plants. The economic importance of such rights are highlighted by the fact that George Bush refused to sign the contract because "it would undermine the patent rights acquired at great cost by US companies" (UNCED 1992, p. 43).

productivity, resist emergent types of diseases and pests, or even to improve in taste or nutritive content. Many of the drugs we use to improve or save lives also originate from tropical forests. Through scientific analysis of rainforest organisms, new and valuable products can be developed in both the pharmaceutical industry and in agriculture.

Simpson *et al.* (1996) has developed a model to estimate an upper bound of the value of the marginal species in biodiversity prospecting, taking into account the possibility of redundancy. They find that even under the most generous assumptions the maximum possible value of the marginal species is slightly less than $10,000. They also show that small variations in the optimal conditions and assumptions would lead to drastically lower estimates.

Applying the theory of island biogeography, Simpson *et al.* (1996) calculates that the maximum value of the marginal hectare for biodiversity prospecting is $20 for biodiversity hotspots like the Western Ecuador (when using a 10 percent discount rate). In the Uplands of Western Amazonia, which is considered another biodiversity hotspot by Myers (1988, 1990), the maximum value would be $2.59 per hectare. The authors emphasize that even these very low estimates arise under optimistic assumptions concerning the probability of discovery and expectations of profitability. Equally plausible conjectures concerning these parameters would yield radically lower values.

For our purposes we choose a biodiversity prospecting value of $2 per hectare, which according to Simpson *et al.* (1996) would be a very optimistic estimate. This is an upper limit on what pharmaceutical researchers and agricultural engineers would be willing to pay per hectare for the availability of tropical forest for biodiversity prospecting. Their willingness does not capture the full value to society, however, as market prices for drugs understate their true value. If we instead of market prices use the value of lives saved, the value may be two–three times higher (e.g. Pearce 1993; Andersen 1999). We will therefore assume that the value of biodiversity for biodiversity prospecting purposes is $5 per hectare if applying the 12 percent discount rate. This corresponds to $10 for the 6 percent discount rate and $30 for the 2 percent discount rate.

Existence value

People reveal a willingness to pay for the mere existence of environmental assets by contributing to wildlife and other environmental charities without taking direct use of the wildlife through recreation. Existence value is likely to be an important part of TEV in contexts where (a) the asset is unique and (b) many people are familiar with the attributes of the asset to be valued (Pearce 1993, p. 21).

The Amazon rainforest is certainly unique and many people know that it hosts an abundance of unique plant and animal species in its intricate and delicate eco-systems. They may therefore place quite a big existence value on the Amazon rainforest as a whole. Based on studies for other endangered species and natural assets, Pearce (1991) proposes as a willingness to pay for the conservation of the Amazon a conservative figure of \$8 per person per year for the 400 million richest people in the world. This would amount to \$3.2 billion/year or on average \$6.4 per hectare per year, given the approximately 500 million hectares of Amazon rainforest.

The existence value may not be as big for the first hectares to be removed, though, since people are not familiar with the uniqueness of each single hectare of Amazonian rainforest. 300 million hectares of undisturbed Amazon rainforest may yield almost the same existence value as 500 million hectares. Brown *et al.* (1993) provides an overview of the implicit global willingness to pay (WTP) for habitat (mainly rainforest) protection derived from debt-for-nature swaps. It is clear from this overview that the WTP values for relatively small, well-known, and unique areas, such as Madagascar, are much higher (hundreds of times higher) than for less unique parts of the Amazon, such as the Beni Park in Bolivia. We would therefore expect the existence value per hectare to be close to zero at relatively low levels of deforestation but be exponentially increasing with the level of deforestation. The implicit global WTP at the Beni park in Bolivia (the closest thing to the Brazilian Amazon) in 1987 was calculated at only \$0.01/hectare. We will adopt the value \$1/hectare as the annual existence value for the marginal piece of Amazon rainforest at the current level of deforestation. This implies a net present existence value of \$50/hectare if the discount rate is 2 percent.

The value of cleared land in the Amazon

This section will develop estimates of the value of cleared land in Legal Amazonia, and thus provide estimates for the opportunity costs of conserving natural forests. For comparison, we will use several different methods to estimate the values generated through land clearing in the Amazon. The first method is the easiest, since it is simply based on observed land prices. The second method is based on site studies of agriculture in Pará (Almeida and Uhl 1995) and Acre (Vosti *et al.* 2001). The third method is based on the aggregate levels of clearing and rural and urban GDP observed in Legal Amazonia at several points in time. The final estimate is based on simulations using the model estimated in chapter 6.

The exercise here, as with all our analyses, comes with some important caveats that limit the interpretation of the results. In particular, we can only observe the economic benefits as measured by GDP estimates in the Brazilian Census data that we are using. Thus, our definition of "benefit" is in value added terms. We cannot say that the economic activity observed in the Amazon was the best possible outcome to come from the inputs of labor and capital. In other words, we cannot say if even better outcomes would have occurred had those resources been directed elsewhere in the country. The fact that certain government policies might have resulted in increased economic activity in the Amazon does not imply that those policies were "good" in the sense that they resulted in the best overall result for Brazil. As we have discussed in other parts of this book, the approach that would probably be in the best position to answer such questions would be a fully specified CGE model with which it would be possible to examine counterfactuals. Within the constraints of our own methodology and data, however, such questions are beyond our reach.

The benefits of land clearing according to land prices and site studies

Estimates of the per hectare profits from agriculture in the Amazon vary greatly, not only because the success of farmers vary greatly across farmers, but also because very few farmers are actually trying to maximize profits per hectare. They are rather maximizing the returns to the two scarce input factors, labor and capital, while the returns per land area is of secondary importance as long as land is abundant and cheap.

The easiest way to estimate the value of agricultural land is to look at the price of agricultural land. If the social discount rate is equal to the land-owners' discount rate then the net present value of agricultural land should be equal to the price of that land. On p. 75, we saw that land prices averaged about US$300/hectare in Legal Amazonia in 1995. We can adopt that number as the NPV of agricultural land at a 12 percent discount rate, assuming that the discount rate that current farmers in the Amazon operate with is approximately 12 percent. The corresponding NPVs for discount rates of 6 and 2 percent would be $600/hectare and $1,800/hectare, respectively.

It is important to realize that the current low per hectare values of agricultural land in the Amazon is the result of abundant land, combined with scarce capital and labor. As the relative supply of these factors changes, the price of land will also change. Since land over time will become more scarce and labor and capital more abundant, land prices are expected to increase, as farmers adopt more and more intensive farming methods. Vosti *et al.* (2001) shows that a typical traditional-technology farm in

Acre yields a NPV profit stream of approximately US$400/hectare (using a 9 percent discount rate). If the farm were to adopt more intensive technologies, they could more than double this value, but it would require initial capital outlays and labor commitment that many farms cannot afford presently. Site research by Almeida and Uhl (1995) in Pará show that the NPV of land with sustainably grown perennial crops is about $5,000/hectare (using a 6 percent discount rate).

The benefits of land clearing according to Legal Amazonia-wide data

Table 8.2 shows the development of rural, urban, and total GDP in Legal Amazonia as well as the amount of cleared land in 1970, 1985, and 1995. Assuming that a constant level of deforestation would have caused a constant level of GDP, it is possible to calculate how much additional GDP is caused by the additional clearing. For example, the extra clearing of 334,563 km^2 between 1970 and 1995 was accompanied by additional rural GDP of US$8,275 million in the year 1995. This corresponds to extra annual rural GDP of $25 per hectare. At the 2 percent discount rate this implies a NPV of $1,236 per hectare. This value includes only the rural incomes generated. In addition to rural incomes there has been a dramatic increase in urban GDP, some of which was directly related to the rural activities, for example the income from timber processing, mineral processing, and the processing of agricultural goods. If we include the full increase of urban GDP as a benefit of land clearing, the NPV of cleared land increases to $5,676 per hectare.

While average urban benefits per hectare of cleared land has remained approximately constant over time, the rural benefits have increased substantially, indicating that agriculture in the Amazon has become more intensive over time. It is highly likely that the very aggressive development policies at work during the 1970s encouraged an inefficient use of land. This has been partly corrected with the general reduction in subsidies to forest clearing, and we believe that the benefits observed during the 1985–1995 period are more representative for the future than the benefits experienced in the 1970s and early 1980s. The very high urban GDPs generated in the earlier period was to a large extent explained by government subsidies and activities like the MFZ, which were unrelated to the extent of cleared land. These subsidies, as well as the industrial income generated from the MFZ have decreased dramatically over time, and the remaining urban GDP is now much more directly related to the amount of cleared land. We therefore think that it is most appropriate to evaluate the benefits of cleared land based on the developments between 1985 and 1995 only. Based on the data from this period we conclude

Table 8.3. *NPV of cleared land in Legal Amazonia, according to Agricultural Census data*

Discount rate (%)	2	6	12
1970–1985			
Rural benefits (1995-US$/ha)	758	253	126
Urban benefits (1995-US$/ha)	4,091	1,363	782
Total benefits (1995-US$/ha)	4,849	1,616	808
1985–1995			
Rural benefits (1995-US$/ha)	2,424	804	402
Urban benefits (1995-US$/ha)	5,288	1,767	883
Total benefits (1995-US$/ha)	7,712	2,571	1,285

Source: Author's calculations based on data from IBGE Agricultural Censuses, 1970, 1985, and 1995.

that the NPV of rural benefits of cleared land amounts to $2,424 per hectare and the NPV of total benefits of cleared land amounts to $7,712 per hectare (using the 2 percent discount rate). Table 8.3 summarizes this information for the three alternative discount rates.

The value of cleared land as estimated by observed land prices falls somewhere in between the rural benefits estimated based on 1970–1985 data and those estimated using 1985–1995 data.

Whether urban benefits should be counted as part of the overall benefits of deforestation is open to discussion. If rural and urban activities in the Amazon are so closely linked that rural development would not be possible without corresponding urban development, and vice versa, then both rural and urban benefits should count as benefits of developing the Amazon. However, if there is no link between rural and urban activities in the Amazon, the urban benefits would be completely unrelated to the amount of land clearing taking place, and thus only the rural benefits should count as a benefit of clearing. The truth is to be found somewhere between those two extremes, and the strength of the link between rural and urban activities is likely to vary between municipalities. Municipalities with important mineral deposits, for example, can theoretically generate a lot of urban GDP (mining is counted as an urban activity) that is not associated with land clearing. In practice, however, the jobs and income created through mining will attract farmers who wish to supply this urban market with food products and this will cause clearing. Most of the agricultural production in the Amazon is destined for local markets, which means that rural output is highly dependent on local urban markets. Conversely, it is quite unlikely that the urban population in the Amazon would grow as rapidly as it actually does if there were not a local food supply; it would be extremely expensive to have all food flown in from outside the region. Most industrial activities in the Amazon build naturally on the availability of local rural inputs (e.g. wood processing and food processing) while the electronics industry in Manaus was a freak case based on preferential tax treatments. This means that rural and urban development tends to go hand in hand, although there is not a fixed relationship between the two across time.

We report rural and urban benefits separately so that the reader can judge for her/himself how much of the urban benefits s/he considers to be part of the total benefits of deforestation and how much s/he thinks would have been possible without associated clearing.

The benefits of land clearing according to the estimated model

The calculations in the previous section relied on the simple assumption that a constant level of clearing would imply a constant level of GDP, and vice versa. This need not necessarily be so. If all development effort in the region was suddenly halted, aggregate clearing could either fall if farmers decided to abandon the region in the absence of government support, or it might increase if there was sufficient local momentum and local demand to justify further clearing. The same holds for rural and urban GDP: they may either fall or increase in the absence of active development policies in the region. A model that captures the relationship between clearing and rural and urban GDP could give us a more precise estimate of the trade-offs between clearing and GDP growth, without making the simplistic assumption that a constant level of clearing implies a constant level of GDP. In addition, it could give us estimates of the trade-offs for different policies, which would be very useful for policy recommendations.

In this section we therefore use the model estimated in chapter 6 to calculate the NPV of cleared land. We do that by simulating the aggregate values of rural GDP, urban GDP, and accumulated deforestation in 1995 for different policy scenarios. According to our model, unpaved and paved roads were the only policy variables that had a significant impact on any of our dependent variables. The scenarios we will analyze are therefore the following:

1. Predicted values of endogenous variables using actual levels of both paved and unpaved roads
2. Assume that paved roads in 1975 are half their actual values, and that paved road growth proceeds at half the actual rate
3. Assume that unpaved roads in 1975 are half their actual values, and that unpaved road growth proceeds at half the actual rate

Table 8.4. *Simulated rural GDP, urban GDP, and cleared area in Legal Amazonia, 1995*

Scenario	Accumulated clearing (km^2)	Rural GDP (million 1995-US$)	Urban GDP (million 1995-US$)
0. Actual values	485,809	9,882	33,948
1. Base scenario	475,862	9,519	34,457
2. Less paved roads	525,980	8,913	30,277
3. Less unpaved roads	451,910	9,466	35,504
4. Less total roads	499,670	8,913	30,763

Source: Authors' calculations based on the model estimated in chapter 6.

4. Assume that both paved and unpaved roads in 1975 are half their actual values, and that their growth proceeds at half the actual rates.

The results are given in table 8.4. Line 0 shows the actual values of accumulated clearing, rural GDP, and urban GDP in 1995. Line 1 shows what our model predicts for 1995, using actual values of all exogenous variables including paved and unpaved roads. This does not exactly coincide with the actual values owing to the fact that we predict growth rates, rather than levels, which introduces some slight biases into the levels estimation, as discussed in chapter 6 and technical appendix (p. 214). Nevertheless the values indicate that our model produces reasonably unbiased aggregate predictions. Line 2 presents a counterfactual prediction of what would have been the levels of clearing and GDP in 1995 according to our model if there had been only half the actual paved roads and half the actual growth since 1975. Line 3 presents another counterfactual prediction of what would have been the levels of clearing and GDP in 1995 if there had been the same 50 percent cut in the level and growth of unpaved roads since 1975. Finally, line 4 presents the predictions for 1995 if there had been cuts in both paved and unpaved roads since 1975.

Comparing the predictions in line 2 and 3 with the predictions in line 1, we see that paved roads tend to cause increases in both rural and urban GDP, but a fall in accumulated clearing. Unpaved roads, on the other hand, cause additional clearing, but are actually associated with a fall in urban GDP and only a slight rise in rural GDP. These are extremely important findings. They indicate that construction of federal and state unpaved roads should be avoided, since they tend to cause a lot of clearing without any corresponding economic benefits. The likely mechanism for this relationship is that unpaved roads opens up access to new forest land, which suppresses the price of agricultural land and encourages wasteful land-use. The construction of paved roads works in exactly the

Table 8.5. *NPV of road building in Legal Amazonia, according to estimated model*

Discount rate (%)	2	6	12
Paved roads			
Rural benefits (000 1995-US$/km)	4,531	1,510	755
Total benefits (000 1995-US$/km)	35,786	11,929	5,964
Unpaved roads			
Rural benefits (000 1995-US$/km)	118	39	20
Total benefits (000 1995-US$/km)	−2,221	−740	−370

Source: Authors' calculations, based on the model estimated in chapter 6.

opposite way. By increasing land prices, it encourages a more efficient use of land, which adds to GDP without causing additional clearing. The results discussed in chapter 6 are consistent with this view, with the one extremely important caveat that the benefits from paved roads largely accrue to areas that are already highly cleared; there is no evidence that building paved roads through relatively virgin areas will decrease land clearing.

Since the model predicts that paved roads actually encourage less clearing, there is no trade-off between clearing and economic growth. We can simultaneously obtain economic growth and less clearing by paving roads, and the win–win possibilities are particularly pronounced in highly settled areas. The relevant comparison then becomes the benefits of constructing paved roads versus the direct construction costs. Table 8.5 therefore gives the NPV per km of road constructed rather than per hectare cleared. According to our estimated model, 1 additional km of paved road causes extra GDP every year of $715,717. This amounts to a NPV of 1 additional km of paved road of about $6.0 million using the 12 percent discount rate. This should be compared to the cost of constructing a km of paved road, which is in the order of $200,000–400,000 per km, depending on how many bridges are necessary.[11] Thus, from both an environmental and a project cost-benefit viewpoint, road paving – especially in the most settled areas – seem to be beneficial.

[11] According to Newton Rabello (personal communication):

1. Implantation of new non-paved road R$50,000 to R$80,000 per km
2. Implantation of new paved roads R$200,000 per km
3. Pavement of an implanted (nonpaved)road R$70,000 per km.

Figures are for 1998 in R$ (the average R$/US$ exchange rate was 1.1602 in 1998) and do not include costs of some infrastructure work (like bridges, tunnels etc.) nor losses due to corruption, which of course could be quite significant. Small bridges can cost you R$6.000/m in wood and three times that in concrete.

An extra km of unpaved roads, on the other hand, subtracts $44,419 from GDP every year. This amounts to a negative NPV of 1 extra km of unpaved roads of $370,155 (at the 12 percent discount rate), plus the direct cost of constructing this road.

There is, of course, considerable uncertainty associated with the size of the benefits of road construction, but various versions of our model have consistently predicted that paved roads cause less clearing and more GDP, especially when paving takes place in areas with relatively high levels of clearing. Unpaved roads (federal and state), on the other hand, tend to cause considerable clearing without an associated increase in GDP. It is thus clear that if Brazil wants economic growth in the Amazon while causing as little deforestation as possible, it should concentrate on infrastructure improvements in already relatively settled areas, while avoiding opening up new land by building roads through virgin forest.

Towards a better use of the Amazon rainforest

In order to encourage a beneficial combination of land-use in the Amazon, both the Brazilian government and the international community need to provide good incentives for local land-owners. So far, government policies have been successful in the first stage of attracting farmers and entrepreneurs to the Amazon region. But the current land-use pattern is far from optimal. The question now is: how to promote the intensification of land use?

The factor most directly affecting the intensity of land use is the price of land. The higher the land price (relative to labor) the more intensive the land use. The government has several policy measures available that affect land prices. Road building is one of them. Improvement of the road network in already settled areas will reduce transportation costs and thus increase farm profitability. This will put an upward pressure on land prices. New road building through virgin areas, on the other hand, will increase the supply of cheap land and therefore put a downward pressure on currently accessible land. The provision of health, educational, cultural, and recreational services in settled areas will further increase the attractiveness of settlement and push up land prices.

Land ownership policies and enforcement of property rights are other important instruments. Until recently, land titles were granted in proportion to the amount of land cleared. This policy, of course, promoted artificially extensive land uses. This could be corrected, and is being corrected. A lack of enforcement of property rights further promotes extensive land use, since land being kept as virgin forest is subject to encroachment by squatters who perceive the land as unoccupied.

One of the big barriers to intensification is the start-up capital needed and the three or more years it takes before returns start to arrive. Access to credit on reasonable terms would therefore promote intensification. Lower interest rates would make perennial cropping relatively more attractive because it is sustainable over a longer period.

While Brazil is responsible for not wasting its natural resources without sufficient economic benefits to the country, the international community is responsible for providing incentives for Brazil to take their preferences into account. Since Brazil's Amazon region provides several types of services to the international community (carbon storage, biodiversity protection, recreational value, and existence value), it would seem most reasonable if these incentives take the form of payments for services rather than punishment for the reduction of services. Brazil should not be punished because it happens to have preserved its natural forest much longer than any other region in the World.

The international institutions necessary to facilitate these payments are not yet in place, but when the cost of deforestation becomes large enough, they will undoubtedly emerge. Swanson (1995) makes a good analysis of how such an international institution must work in order to be able to provide the right incentives for conservation at the smallest cost. The most obvious mechanism would be an international parks agreement, where the international community pays the rental price of the land preserved, plus possibly the management costs as well, for each year that the park remains protected. If the international community wishes to maintain the area almost completely undisturbed, they would have to pay practically the full costs of forgone land development opportunities and management services. If they allow some economic activities, such as sustainable timber harvesting, the price they have to pay may be somewhat lower, deducting the local profits from timber harvesting. For such transfers from the international community to work in practice, an international institution responsible for the payments must be created and funded. This institution would have to develop a general global land-use plan that specifies how much rainforest, how much wetlands, etc. it wishes to conserve. If they decide they want as many 100,000 hectare chunks of Amazon forest as possible for at least thirty years, they may put a contract out to international tender stating the required limitations on land use. Host states can then bid on this contract, stating the per hectare annual rental payment required by the host state for the agreed restrictions. Once the bids are received, the international institution will have to decide which bids to accept, ranging from all to none. If a bid is accepted, the host country is responsible for adhering to the land-use restrictions of the contract, and as long as they do that they will be paid according to the agreement (see Swanson 1995 for details).

Conclusions

This chapter has collected estimates of the costs and benefits of clearing land in the Amazon. Both cost and benefit estimates are attached with substantial uncertainty and we offer only point estimates related to the current level of deforestation (10–15 percent). At this level, potential benefits of deforestation seem to be approximately equal to the likely global costs. As the level of deforestation increases, however, the global costs of deforestation will rise, and the costs will soon exceed the value of agricultural land, if they do not already do so.

The cost-benefit analysis made in this chapter is of a relatively simple form with a constant discount rate and with few considerations about uncertainty, irreversibility, equity, and ethics. Whether it is appropriate to reduce all the diverse effects of deforestation into a single dimension measured in monetary terms is both an ethical and practical issue. This approach could be biased or invalid if the dynamic evolution of biophysical processes examined here are non-linear and not well captured in a marginalist framework as discussed in the introduction to the chapter. There could be further biases if peoples' values and resource allocation would substantially change if there were actually markets for these public goods through which their actions could be perceived to have tangible effects.

It is also an ethical issue. Cost-benefit analyses are by definition homocentric and measure everything from the viewpoint of human utility. Other species get considered only to the extent that humans care about them or need them, and religion matters only by affecting the value humans put on different things. However, if one believes that flora and fauna (at either the individual or species level) have an instrinsic right to exist beyond their value to mankind, then the idea of putting a money value on them makes little sense and from the perspective of an extreme form of this view, society should absorb whatever costs are required to preserve those species (or individual creatures, if the idea is taken that far). A less extreme, and probably very common, version of this ethic would suggest a slightly less dramatic conclusion: that society should do whatever possible, within reason, to preserve natural habitat and wildlife. What constitutes "within reason" could be determined by voting or other democratic mechanisms and individuals could be swayed by either economic arguments or by their own gut feelings and ethics. This approach also has its drawbacks (captured by wealthy special interests, for example), so more discussion and open debate on these issues would be a very welcome development.

Given that most countries in the developed world have already cleared more than 95 percent of their primary forests and benefitted greatly from it, it is not clear how much forest Brazil should or should not clear. We believe that a cost-benefit analysis can add valuable information, but not stand alone as the only basis behind the clearing decision. A cost-benefit analysis can try to capture and express in a single dimension many of the effects arising from changes in land use, but it can never claim to have captured them all. Such analyses needs to be repeated and improved over time to add ever-more information to the decision makers' information set, and perhaps combined with other public policy objectives. The present analysis is only a sketchy start, and each component of the cost-benefit analysis could be expanded to fill several books.

9 Conclusions and recommendations

Deforestation in the Amazon has become an emotional topic and thus it is unlikely that scientific or economic research alone will be able to resolve the question of what the socially optimal combinations of end-uses in the Brazilian Amazon are. Agreement among people with diverse preferences and backgrounds is often difficult, and all the more so in this case owing to the underlying uncertainty regarding different choices. Many of the biophysical processes and feedback effects that connect forests with biological and climatic systems are not yet well understood, so within the bounds of normal scientific discourse people can have different beliefs about the probable biological and climatic risks associated with deforestation. Furthermore, even among those that share the same risk assessment, people will have varying degrees of risk aversion and may disagree on how to proceed.

Even if all the scientific controversies could be resolved, different people could still legitimately reach different conclusions. Some people might be relatively more concerned about the extinction of species and loss of natural habitat on either scientific or ethical grounds, while others may not care much about the extinction of animals that never were important to them in the first place. Some might prefer to champion the cause of indigenous cultural survival of native peoples, while others would promote the interests of poor landless peasants.

Indeed, as something like 85 percent of the Amazon forest has not yet been cleared, public policy set today will have a major impact on how the remaining area is managed. While many search for solutions that will satisfy as many perspectives as possible, ultimately there will be trade-offs to be made. Attempting to provide a better understanding of some of those trade-offs has been the purpose of the analyses presented in this book.

Conclusions

Let us first summarize the main facts about the status of clearing and development in the Brazilian Amazon. The area comprises roughly

5 million km^2, of which about 79 percent can be said to be naturally forested. By 1995, 9.6 percent of Legal Amazonia had been cleared and converted into agricultural land according to the Agricultural Census conducted that year. Since not all of the area cleared was originally forested, accumulated deforestation was somewhat less than that. The Agricultural Census of 1995 probably understates deforestation, for two main reasons. First, it does not count land that has recently been cleared but subsequently abandoned (secondary re-growth). Second, the Census was conducted after the main harvest period, which means that some of the most transitory farmers and their impact may not have been counted in the Census. According to INPE satellite estimates, 9.8 percent of the total area had been deforested by 1995. However, the satellite estimates from INPE tend to exaggerate the amount of deforestation, because it counts even old secondary forest as deforested. Despite their discrepancies, satellite and land survey data agree that around 90 percent of Legal Amazonia remains with its natural vegetation cover more or less intact.

Both measures, however, ignore forest degradation that has only partly affected the original vegetation cover. A field study by FAO/UN (1993) indicates that in Brazil, most changed area is converted directly into non-wooded land, while degraded and fragmented areas account for only about 15 percent of changed area. This is in contrast to areas in Africa and Asia, where degradation and fragmentation appear to play a major role as preliminary stages to deforestation (Downton 1994). Thus, when counting both deforested areas and degraded areas generously, it still leaves at least 85 percent of Legal Amazonia with its natural vegetation intact.

The consequences of deforestation and clearing were both positive and negative. Of positive effects we can mention the impressive growth of both rural and urban GDP in the region. Over the twenty-five-year period from 1970 to 1995, rural GDP *per capita* grew at an average annual rate of 5.8 percent in real terms. Cleared area "only" increased by 4.8 percent annually, which suggests that the productivity of land has been increasing over time. Rural GDP per hectare cleared increased steadily by about 2.6 percent per year in real terms from $106/hectare in 1970 to $203/hectare in 1995 (all measured in fixed 1995-US$).

Urban GDP *per capita* grew rapidly (5.7 percent annually) between 1970 and 1985 when the federal government was subsidizing the Amazon region most heavily, but fell slightly in *per capita* terms between 1985 and 1995 after many subsidies were withdrawn and the whole country suffered an economic recession. This suggests that urban development is more dependent on investment inflows and the general economic situation in the country than rural development. Towards the end of the sample period the Brazilian economy recovered but it remains to be seen how *per capita* growth in urban areas will fare with fewer subsidies, but amid a more robust national economy.

The steady growth of rural GDP was associated primarily with the rapid growth of local urban markets and improved access to these markets via paved roads. As we have shown, urban market size, as measured by urban population, increased dramatically from 2.7 million in 1970 to 10.8 million in 1995, corresponding to an average annual growth rate of 5.7 percent. The extent of paved roads also increased steadily at an annual rate of about 6 percent.

Beyond aggregate measures of economic growth, most indicators of the standard of living in the Amazon have also improved substantially since 1970. Average life expectancy in Legal Amazonia increased from fifty years in 1970 to sixty-one years in 1991. Average illiteracy rates dropped from 44 percent in 1970 to 28 percent in 1991. Most impressively, infant mortality fell by more than half from 124 deaths per 1,000 live births in 1970 to only 57 in 1991. Infant mortality in Legal Amazonia is now substantially lower than in the neighboring Northeast, and in the Amazonian state of Mato Grosso it is even well below the national average. The overall mortality rates (deaths per 1,000 inhabitants) in 1997 in the states of Legal Amazonia were among the lowest in Brazil. Only the rate for Maranhão was higher than the national average.[1] The social indicators for Legal Amazonia thus show that the developments in the Amazon have benefitted large parts of the population, not only a few rich speculators.

The primary negative consequence of concern has been the conversion of approximately 335,000 km^2 of land with natural vegetation and wildlife into agricultural land, mainly pasture. As a result natural habitats have been reduced and fragmented in many areas, and emissions of around 3.3 billion tons of carbon have been poured into the atmosphere over the twenty-five-year period 1970–1995. The consequences of these emissions are highly uncertain, but the amount corresponds to the carbon released from fossil fuel burning in the United States every two years.

The number of species that have gone extinct owing to clearing in Legal Amazonia is unknown, but so far it is probably very small. Brazil's Atlantic rainforest has been cleared much more heavily (about 90 percent) than the Amazon, and even there it has been difficult for botanists and zoologists to identify any species that have gone extinct. However, even if few species have actually gone extinct, the genetic diversity within the barely surviving species have been reduced substantially. This may lead

[1] The Institute of Brazilian Business and Public Management Issues at the George Washington University (http://www.gwu.edu/~ibi/database/Mortality˙Rate.pdf).

to inbreeding problems, such as reduced fertility, increased susceptibility to disease, and other negative effects (Brown *et al.* 1993).

Given that 85–90 percent of Legal Amazonia remains undisturbed, there has probably been very little loss of existence value. Deforestation may actually have increased the existence value of Legal Amazonia rather than decreased it, as global environmental concerns have raised awareness about the uniqueness of the region. One of the worst consequences of clearing may be the loss of protection against wildfires. Old rainforest works as a very effective firewall, but once it has been disturbed or fragmented through logging and slash-and-burn agriculture, its effectiveness as firewall decreases dramatically, and farmers in heavily disturbed areas are more likely to lose their crops to wildfires than farmers with isolated plots in the rainforest.

Our econometric analysis indicates that the processes of deforestation and development in the Amazon have changed character over time. Until the early 1980s these processes were to a large extent driven by government policies, such as road building, subsidized credit, tax breaks, settlement schemes, and land titling policies. Since the 1980s, however, the process has become much more endogenous. Agricultural activities are increasingly being driven by local urban demand rather than government incentives. Urban population growth and urban income growth were found to be important explanatory variables for the growth of cleared land, the growth of rural GDP, and the growth of cattle herds. Federal transfers, on the other hand, were highly significant in the early model of urban GDP growth (1980–1985), but not significant at all in the later model (1985–1995).

Road building is still very important, but even the expansion of federal and state roads has become an increasingly endogenous process. Urban population growth, for example, was found to be one of the most robust variables affecting the construction of paved roads in the later model (1985–1995), while it was not significant at all in the earlier model (1980–1985). The construction of unpaved roads also tends to be endogenously driven in the latter period, driven by rural variables such as the growth of the cattle herd and the level of rural GDP.

Policy implications

Given that there are substantial negative externalities associated with forest clearing, basic economic theory suggests that forest clearing should be taxed in order to compensate for the missing market for forest services. Brazil has in fact been doing exactly the opposite. Since the late 1960s they have been subsidizing forest conversion heavily through federal road building, subsidized rural credit, and various tax exemptions for economic activities involving forest clearing. It is interesting to reflect on the possible causes of such an apparent contradiction between recommended and actual policies, because it will highlight potential flaws or oversimplifications in the analysis.

There are two main reasons why Brazil may have ignored the negative externalities associated with forest clearing. The first reason is that forest services benefit all world citizens both now and in the future, and the Brazilian part of the benefits is relatively small. At least until the early 1990s there was little hope that Brazil would ever receive payments for those forest services, so ignoring them was the rational response. The second reason is that there might be positive externalities associated with forest clearing. In the 1960s, for example, development in the Amazon was encouraged on the grounds of national security, and in the 1970s Amazon colonization was hoped to provide an escape valve for increasing social unrest among landless rural peasants. More recently, with the *Avança Brasil* plan, Amazon development has been encouraged in order to create a more united and homogeneous Brazil. Thus, other motives than pure growth maximization clearly play a role.

Before the initiation of "Operation Amazonia," only 0.5–2 percent of Brazil's Amazon rainforest had been cleared. With about 99 percent left it must have seemed reasonable to believe that Brazil would not forgo much benefit by clearing a little more. Some types of sustainable income actually increase with incipient development/deforestation. Eco-tourism, for example, would be extremely limited if there were not some urban centers that could host travel agencies and supply local labor in the form of nature guides, hotel staff, boat operators, etc.

The marginal value of a standing forest increases, though, as the forest is reduced and agricultural land takes its place: the capacity for fire protection is reduced at the same time as it becomes more important that crops and timber are not lost; sustainable timber becomes more important as infrastructure develops and it becomes economically sensible to harvest timber; biodiversity will be squeezed together in a shrinking area, implying increased loss per hectare; and existence value will be concentrated on a smaller area, implying a higher value per hectare when the forest is smaller.

If we have not already reached the point where the total economic value (TEV) of standing forest exceeds the value of converted forest, we soon will. Brazil is not likely to halt deforestation at that point, however, because some of the benefits of a standing forest accrue to the rest of the world, and Brazil has no incentive to take this into account. Incentives can be provided, though. The most obvious method would be an "international parks agreement," where the international community pays the rental price of land, plus possibly the management costs as well, for each year that the park remains protected. If the international community wishes to maintain the area almost completely undisturbed, they would have to pay practically the full cost of forgone land development opportunities and management services. If they allow some economic activities, such as sustainable timber harvesting, the price they have to pay may be somewhat lower, deducting the local profits from timber harvesting.

It is important that international payment schemes provide the right incentives. If, for example, the international community intends to pay only for the preservation of areas that are under immediate threat of conversion and not for areas that are well protected by their natural remoteness, then tropical forest countries will be encouraged to threaten more of their forest in order to increase their eligibility for international payments in the future. This would clearly be a counterproductive strategy. In order to provide the right incentives for preservation of forest services, the international community will have to pay for all the services they receive, not only for those that are under threat of being eliminated. In practice an efficient arrangement could work as follows: each year, the international community invites the Amazon countries to submit tenders for protected chunks of Amazon forest. Brazil could, for example, offer to protect 200 million specific hectares of forest at the low cost of $2/hectare/year. It could add another 100 million hectares, but at the higher price of $5/hectare/year because the opportunity costs and the costs of protection are higher in these less remote areas. It could continue setting a price on each part of the Amazon, and so could the other countries that hold Amazonian rainforest within their borders. They could also offer different degrees of protection at different prices. The international community could then rank the offers they have received, and decide how much forest they were willing to pay to protect. They could then sign agreements with those countries that have provided the most attractive bids, and by the end of the year, after compliance had been confirmed, they would have to pay the agreed amount. This procedure, repeated every year, would result in the largest amount of forest being protected at the lowest cost, and the procedure would not provide bad incentives. It requires, of course, that an international institution authorized to make these negotiations is created and funded in a credible manner, so that the rainforest countries can count on the payments being made both now and in the future.

While the international community is responsible for incentives to take their preferences into account, Brazil is responsible for managing the process of land clearing in the most sensible way. For better or for worse Brazil initiated the development process in the Amazon through aggressive and effective settlement policies. These policies have drawn people to the Amazon and helped build cities, towns, and rural communities with local governments and a social infrastructure. The development process has now taken on a life of its own and cannot be undone, so the emphasis must be on policies that are consistent with sustainable development. Current policies do not yet measure up to this challenge; they need to be adjusted and fine-tuned to a new situation with a substantial population and local development momentum.

Roads were initially planned in a bold fashion with little regard to soil conditions, topography, and local needs. Extensive road building tends to reduce land prices by increasing the supply of cheap, accessible land. This can be good for poor people because it gives them the opportunity to earn money through slash-and-burn agriculture with very little initial investment. But it does not encourage a sustainable use of land. Road building can promote sustainability, however, if it improves infrastructure conditions in already cleared areas and thus pushes land prices upwards. Detailed information and careful, probably decentralized, planning is necessary for roads to have that effect.

The road building plans contemplated in the *Avança Brasil* plan are good in the sense that they focus almost exclusively on the paving of existing unpaved roads while virtually no new roads are being planned. This should help push land prices up and encourage more intensive and less wasteful land uses. However, compared to previous road paving, the paving projects listed in *Avança Brasil* tend to go through less settled areas, and our econometric analysis shows that the clearing caused by paved roads tend to be much bigger when paving is done in relatively virgin areas rather than in more settled areas. In addition, our econometric model shows that the economic benefit of paved roads tend to be bigger in already highly settled areas. Thus, in order to reap maximum economic benefits at minimum environmental costs, Brazil should concentrate their road paving efforts in the most highly settled areas and stay away from more virgin areas.

Paved roads in highly settled areas provide the additional benefit of lowering the prices of food products in urban areas. This is important given that most of the poor Amazonians now live in urban areas.

Public investment in schools, health systems, marketing facilities, etc. in old frontier areas also improves living conditions for people in the Amazon while at the same time relieving the pressure on intact forest.

Public investment in proper agricultural methods for the region also has great potential for improving yields and benefitting Amazonian farmers. The identification of suitable and profitable crops and crop combinations would tend to reduce current wasteful land uses like extensive cattle ranching. It will not necessarily reduce deforestation, but at least it will make deforestation more justifiable. A good example of this situation is the rapidly increasing soybean production in the *cerrado* areas of Mato Grosso. The Brazilian Agricultural Research System (EMBRAPA) is the world leader in soybean research, which has helped turn farmers in Mato Grosso into some of the most competitive soybean producers in the world, rapidly gaining market share from the traditional producers in the United States. Improved market access through the infrastructure projects (especially waterways) contemplated in *Avança Brasil* will help make these farmers even more competitive in the rapidly growing world market for soybeans, and this will encourage more clearing in the *cerrado* areas to which the soybeans have been adapted. Unlike most other tropical countries, Brazil actually has the research capacity, the funds, and the necessary entrepreneurial spirit to vastly improve the technology behind tropical agriculture. Accompanied by a lower degree of protection and subsidization of Northern agriculture, this research could potentially improve the lots of many tropical farmers, and at the same time benefit consumers world-wide.

When the probability of international payments for forest services increases, the perceived value of intact forest in Brazil should also increase. This, in turn, should encourage more investment in environmental protection. This is indeed what we observe: apart from having set aside more than 100 million hectares of forest for conservation units and indigenous reserves, Brazil is currently setting up very extensive and expensive environmental monitoring and data gathering programs. Not only will this help to reduce the degree of lawlessness and private exploitation in the Amazon and improve Brazil's basis for making sound policy decisions, but it will also improve Brazil's bargaining position towards the rest of the world by showing that it can control the developments in the Amazon. The institutional capacity to monitor and control activities in the Amazon will be essential for the implementation of payments for forest services as the international community will need some evidence that their payments have the desired impact.

As one of the biggest and economically most powerful tropical forest countries, Brazil should take a leading role in the negotiations on international payments for forest services. Until a fair system of payments is implemented with appropriate long-run incentives for preservation, tropical deforestation is likely to continue much too quickly. Regardless of one's particular perspective on the issue, it is in everybody's interest that well-functioning markets and international agreements on the use of forest services are created. International environmental lobbying alone is unlikely to be sufficient to adequately protect the forest against powerful economic interests. Like all sovereign nations, Brazil has the right to choose how to allocate its resources; a set of incentive-compatible and internationally-based agreements has the best chance of producing outcomes that are acceptable to a broad range of interests.

Technical appendix

In the following sections we detail the econometric methodology employed in this book. While most of the econometrics are fairly standard procedures, several of the techniques have been developed by the authors, in some cases specifically for the purpose of analyzing the kind of data we have in the DESMAT data set. These include the panel model evaluation technique developed by Granger and Huang (1997), the random reduction estimation strategy developed by Weinhold (2001) and the ideas of "thick" modeling presented in Granger (2000). We provide a fairly comprehensive description here but for a complete technical discussion we refer the interested readers to the academic working papers cited above.

The technical appendix proceeds as follows:

- Section A1 addresses the overall modeling philosophy and discusses some of the econometric work that preceded the models presented in this book.
- Section A2 describes the technical detail behind the Granger and Huang (1997) model evaluation technique frequently utilized in writing this book.
- Section A3 outlines in detail the random reduction strategy employed in the estimation of the main models and reviews some of Granger's ideas of "thick" modeling.
- Section A4 discusses some technical details of how the models were used to produce the roads and *Avança Brasil* simulations.
- Section A5 includes a table of variables and the full model results for both the 1985 and 1995 models.

A1 Econometric philosophy

The process by which any model is derived is of critical importance in evaluating the policy implications that result, and thus we provide a general outline of our modeling philosophy here. A primary guiding principle that has permeated the analysis is that the empirical model be derived in as objective a manner as possible. To that end we have made extensive use of new model evaluation techniques developed in Granger and Huang (1997) (see section A2 below) and employed the ideas of random reduction and "thick" modeling (see section A3 below) as explored in Weinhold (2001) and Granger (2000), respectively, in both model selection and interpretation. In particular, Granger and Huang propose a method to use the out-of-sample forecasting performance of competing models to select the "best" model. This approach is superior in many respects to some of the more traditional techniques for choosing a model. Quite frequently models which have the best in-sample fit (i.e. R^2, AIC or other goodness of fit measure) do not produce forecasts as accurate as models with lower R^2. This is because these models can be overfit in sample, while the simpler model may actually better capture the underlying true data generating process. In section A2 we outline the specific technical details of the Granger–Huang approach. In what follows we simply outline how the technique was utilized to create as objective a modeling strategy as possible.

The first and most basic decision was to use a data-based model rather than a more theory-driven approach. There are some compelling theoretical arguments for choosing a data-based model, especially given our data set, and these are outlined in chapter 6. Even so, we endeavored to make the choice based on objective criteria rather than instinct so we compared the out-of-sample forecasting ability of different models including both data-generated models and a theory-based model proposed by Lykke Andersen, based on her extensive knowledge of theories of land clearing. Using these model evaluation techniques we found that all of the data-based models outperformed the theory-based model in out-of-sample forecasting performance and thus we believe that for our purposes the data-based approach is preferable.

A similar approach was taken when choosing the functional form for the regression models. We examined both static and dynamic models of the growth rates of the key variables of interest and, based on model evaluation results, chose to include past growth rates of both the independent and dependent variables as possible explanatory variables in the general model.

Given our specification, we then turn to specifying a "general" model including the variables that we feel could be important. The set of initial explanatory variables is discussed in chapter 6. We did face a decision about how best to capture the spatial dependence of the processes under study. Spatial variables are created by calculating weighted averages of neighbors' variables (or the log of the weighted average in the case of GDP). Several weighting schemes are possible; weighting by whether the municipalities share a border or not, by the length of the border, or by the distance between them. In Granger–Huang model evaluation exercises the distance-weighted spatial variables did best and were thus adopted.

The research design we have adopted is meant to be "open." We have developed an objective criterion via which to evaluate competing models and thus we can use this approach to test our own model against any competitor which claims to explain the data generating process better. Of course, someone might argue with our criterion, but then the burden would fall on them to propose and defend an alternative measure with which to discriminate between two models. Either way, our purpose is not to defend one particular "pet" model but to find the best model possible of the complex processes occurring in the Amazon. We recognize that the hard work in this field is really just beginning and we are very hopeful that many researchers (perhaps even ourselves) will improve upon the models we have presented here. How will we know when a better model comes along? Not just because it yields different implications which we may or may not like better, but because it can predict the future state of important variables out of sample with greater accuracy.

A2 Panel model evaluation

Granger and Huang (1997) suggest a method for evaluating panel data models on the basis of how well they forecast out of sample. Their methodology is especially useful for panel data models with short time periods, and, as discussed above, has been extensively utilized by the authors of this book throughout the process of investigation for choosing among competing model specifications at different stages of the analysis. The approach has also been used for causality testing with the data set in Weinhold (2001).

For two competing models, A and B, of growth from 1985 to 1995 that condition on a lagged information set (i.e. data from 1985 and earlier) the procedure goes as follows:

- First we estimate each model using N–1 observations (in our case, 256) leaving out the jth observation.
- Using the coefficient estimates from the previous step, we use the 1985 and earlier data for our omitted jth observation to generate two predicted values for 1995 growth (one for each model), $\hat{\gamma}_A$ and $\hat{\gamma}_B$.
- We repeat steps 1 and 2 for all N observations, thus generating N predicted values of 1995 growth for each model A and B.
- Subtracting our N predicted growth rates from the N true values of 1995 growth rate from the data set we generate N forecast errors for each model, $\hat{\upsilon}_A$ and $\hat{\upsilon}_B$.

- The model with the lowest mean-squared forecast error, $\hat{\nu}^2$, is superior if the difference in mean-squared forecasting error is statistically significantly different between the two models. In order to test whether the difference is in fact statistically different we use a SUM-DIFFERENCE test, described in Granger and Huang (1997) as well as in Mincer and Zarnowitz (1969), Granger and Newbold (1986), and more recently in Diebold and Mariano (1995).

To conduct the SUM-DIFFERENCE test we first calculate the sum and the difference of the two forecast errors:

$$SUM_{AB} = \hat{\nu}_A + \hat{\nu}_B \; DIFF_{AB} = \hat{\nu}_A - \hat{\nu}_B \tag{A2.1}$$

A test of the null hypothesis $HO: \hat{\nu}_A^2 = \hat{\nu}_B^2$ is equivalent to a test of whether $\hat{\beta}$ is statistically different from zero in the regression:

$$SUM_{AB} = \alpha + \beta * DIFF_{AB} + \varepsilon \tag{A2.2}$$

This test can be done using a variety of robust form of t-test. If HO is rejected, the model with the lowest error variance should be accepted as being significantly superior to the other model.

A3 Random reduction estimation strategy

Having chosen our preferred general to simple methodology and settled on a functional form and set of initial variables for our general model we now turn to the question of estimation. As we have discussed in chapter 6, the basic estimation strategy upon which our methodology is based is a Hendry model reduction procedure in which a general model is initially estimated and variables found not to be statistically significant are sequentially deleted, keeping an eye on model performance, until a final, parsimonious model is obtained. However, in general models generated in this manner face a major problem in that the actual sequence of reduction can be somewhat arbitrary, such that several different but equally "good" models could legitimately be derived from the same starting point. Furthermore at this point there is quite a bit of room for discretionary actions by the researcher in terms of the reduction sequence as well as deletion criteria. Even with the best of intentions subtle biases can enter the process.

In order to avoid these problems we develop an approach which we call "random reduction" estimation (see Weinhold 2001). For each endogeneous variable we start with an original set of fifty-five possible explanatory variables. This set includes time-invariant characteristics such as soil and land characteristics, rainfall and temperature data, distance to markets, land area, length of rivers, area set aside in reserves, and state-level dummy variables. Time-varying variables include lags of growth rates of other endogenous variables, and levels lagged twice (the level of the endogenous left-hand-side variable is lagged once). In addition we include past growth of paved and unpaved roads, and levels of paved and unpaved roads lagged two periods, and a number of spatial variables (discussed above and in chapter 6). The full set of starting explanatory variables that was used for the present analysis is presented in table A.1; all the tables of the model (tables A.1–A.9) are at the end of the technical appendix (pp. 217–240). Thus we have a general functional form that looks like:

$$gY_{ki,t} = \alpha + \beta_1 lY_{ki,t-1} + \beta_{2z} \sum_{z \neq k} gY_{zi,t-1} + \beta_{3z} \sum_{z \neq k} lY_{zi,t-2} + \beta_{4q} \sum_{q} X_q + \epsilon \quad \text{(A3.1)}$$

where gY_z are the endogenous variables $z = 1 \ldots 7$, lY_z are log-level endogenous variables, and X_q are a set of q exogenous and/or time-invariant variables.

The model selection procedure is as follows:

- The model is estimated and heteroskedasticity and autocorrelation consistent standard errors are calculated. In the case of a single time observation these are simple Huber–White standard errors. Where we have more than one time period we use a HAC estimator suggested by Den Haan and Levin (1999).
- First we delete observations for which the error term in the unreduced model is more than three standard deviations from the mean so that these outliers do not unduly impact the estimation.
- Then the program finds the three lowest robust t-statistics that are under 2.0 in absolute value. It then selects *randomly* between these three t-statistics and deletes the corresponding variable from the right-hand side of the equation. In the case that there are only two t-statistics under 2.0 (in absolute value), the program randomly chooses one of these. If there is only one t-statistic under 2.0 then the corresponding variable is deleted. The model is then re-estimated as per the first step.
- This process continues until a specification is found which fulfills some criteria of a "good" model. In our case the criteria we have selected is that all variables have Huber–White robust t-statistics of at least 2.0. One could legitimately question this criterion as the true size of the final t-statistics is unknown because they are the result of a purposeful search, not a one-off hypothesis test. An alternative approach would be to search over different model specifications and select variables not on the basis of individual t-statistics but of some overall model selection criteria such as adjusted R^2, AIC, BIC and/or other selection

criterion. However, starting from a very general specification and using this approach to reduce the number of explanatory variables is very computer-intensive as the number of possible alternative models is enormous. Given that our methodology already relies on computer-intensive iteration this approach was deemed to be computationally infeasible.

- The whole process is repeated again from the start, resulting in another final functional form that, because of the randomization of the reduction process, may be quite different from the first one. We continue to repeat the whole process 100 times so that we have 100 "final" models.
- We then count how many times each variable appears in a final model. In addition we can observe the lowest and highest value that each variable's coefficient takes. This gives us a sense of how stable the coefficient value is across the different patterns of reduction that could occur.
- Finally, the selection of a final model to be used for policy simulations requires some rule of thumb for selecting among all the variables which made it at least once to the final model stage. For the policy analyses presented in the book, that rule was that any variable which had made it at least 50 percent of the time (i.e. had a count of 50 or higher) was included in the utilized model.

A4 Technical issues with simulations

As our model has six interdependent equations with spatial and dynamic interactions (eight when we endogenize paved and unpaved roads), the only way to work out what the effects are of some policy change on different municipalities is to observe how the model evolves after we have manually made the change. However, while the approach is straightforward we have faced several issues which we discuss here, and welcome comments or suggestions on how to improve the methodology.

The first issue is a general one that is faced by all models that estimate growth rates. The regression procedure produces unbiased estimates of the growth rates. However, for the purposes of the simulation we are also interested in the corresponding *levels* of variables such as cleared land and GDP. We need to have these levels values because they will in turn feed back into the model as it is iterated into the future (i.e. predicted cleared land today will become (log) cleared land lagged twice in two periods forward). In addition, we would like to calculate the "final" predicted levels of our variables of interest. The problem arises as follows: take the example of urban GDP. Although the predicted growth rates of urban GDP may themselves be unbiased on average (in the sense that a prediction error of 0.3 for one municipality will be cancelled out by errors summing to −0.3 elsewhere), urban GDP itself varies considerably from one municipality to the next. Thus, 0.3 percent of urban GDP in one municipality may not cancel out with −0.3 percent of urban GDP from other municipalities. Thus, even in-sample the model may produce predicted 1995 levels whose average is not the true average of the sample.

Generally, these errors will in fact more or less cancel each other out and the final difference will be small. However, if there is a relationship between the magnitude of the level of urban GDP and the sign or magnitude of the error term (i.e. certain forms of heteroskedasticity) then this bias can be large. Generally we consider heteroskedasticity to be a problem of the standard errors and of tests of hypotheses only because our coefficient estimates remain unbiased. However, in the case we have explained heteroskedasticity also becomes a problem for the main model itself. Although we correct for heteroskedasticity in the standard errors for our hypotheses testing, this does not change the coefficient estimates and does not affect this bias.

A solution for this kind of problem is to model the heteroskedasticity directly in the model specification. Thus, if municipalities with extremely large urban GDP levels tend to have a large and negative error term, we include either a threshold dummy or another variable (such as GDP squared) that will capture this effect and thus eliminate the systematic relationship with the error term. In the models used for this book we encountered this problem with both the HERD model as well as the urban GDP model. By including a large GDP dummy as well as a GDP squared term (both defined using lagged level of GDP) in the urban GDP model and two dummies for large and small values in the HERD model this bias was virtually eliminated in the urban GDP model and considerably reduced in the HERD model. Nevertheless, in generating simulation results we have always compared our simulated policy outcome to a baseline outcome generated using the same iteration process so that any biases should, in theory, be present in both simulations and thus cancel each other out when comparing the difference between them.

The second question is what periodicity to adopt for the simulations. As the preferred 1995 model estimates average annual growth over ten years but conditions on average annual growth over five years, it is not immediately obvious if it would be better to assume ten-year or five-year increments. This question becomes even more important when we take into account that the levels bias described above is compounded every time we increase this interval. For example, for a five-year interval the predicted growth rate (and error) is taken to the fifth power. In order to investigate the effects of paved and unpaved roads, for example, we have tried to avoid this issue all together by simply keeping our simulations "in-sample" and predicting 1995 values while restricting in-sample road building. However, for the *Avança Brasil* and land restriction simulations we have to project the model into the future. For these we have chosen a five-year periodicity in order to keep any levels bias as small as possible given the periodicity of the underlying data. Actually, iterating one year at a time would minimize the levels bias most effectively, but as the model is estimated with (mostly) five-year intervals, a five-year forecast periodicity seems more appropriate. In any case, owing to this problem the results should not be taken as a direct prediction for a particular time frame but more as a general indication of the relative magnitudes of benefits and costs over a medium-term horizon.

A5 Full model results

Table A.1. *List of variables*

Amapá dummy	Growth cleared land (−1)
Amazonas dummy	Log cleared land (−2)
Goiás dummy	Neighbors' cleared land intensity (−1)
Maranhão dummy	Growth urban pop. (−1)
Mato Grosso dummy	Log urban pop. (−2)
Pará dummy	Neighbors' urban pop. density (−1)
Rondônia dummy	Growth rural pop. (−1)
Roraima dummy	Log rural pop. (−2)
Log (area)	Neighbors' rural pop. density (−1)
Log (dist. to state capital)	Log (1985 FINAM credit)
Log (dist. to federal capital)	Growth rural GDP (−1)
Log (km nav. river)	Log rural GDP (−2)
City dummy	Neighbors' rural GDP (−1)
Share Arbustiva/Arborea	Growth urban GDP (−1)
Share Campos	Log urban GDP (−2)
Share Floresta Aluvial	Neighbors' urban GDP (−1)
Share Floresta Baixa	Growth cattle herd (−1)
Share Floresta Alta	Log cattle herd (−2)
Share Floresta Semidecidual	Neighbors' herd density (−1)
Share other	Growth land price (−1)
Share soil = ARSOL1	Log land price (−2)
High rain dummy	Neighbors' av. land price (−1)
Av. temp. (Mar.)	Growth paved roads (−1)
Av. temp. (Jun.)	Log paved roads (−2)
Av. temp. (Sep.)	Neighbors' paved roads density (−1)
Av. temp. (Dec.)	Growth non-paved roads (−1)
Share Indian reserve	Log non-paved roads (−2)
Share protected	Neighbors' non-paved roads density (−1)

Table A.2. *Full estimation results: growth of cleared land*

Variable	1980–1985	1985–1995
Intercept	63.446 (100) (40.330 84.468)	−5.697 (100) (−12.50 6.335)
City dummy		−12.01 (100) (−13.87 −9.351)
Amapá dummy		−8.620 (100) (−10.24 −6.181)
Amazonas dummy	−6.560 (87) (−7.452 −5.866)	−12.55 (100) (−14.17 −10.61)
Maranhão dummy	4.258 (20) (4.197 4.503)	−4.296 (100) (−5.471 −3.458)
Mato Grosso dummy	8.618 (98) (3.929 12.783)	
Pará dummy		−7.150 (100) (−8.421 −5.645)
Rondônia dummy		4.706 (4) (3.338 5.541)
Roraima dummy	33.226 (100) (30.707 37.798)	−10.91 (95) (−13.80 −7.106)
Log (area)	3.301 (100) (2.766 3.582)	2.036 (100) (1.714 2.310)
Log (dist. to capital)		−0.198 (3) (−0.198 −0.198)
Log (dist. to capital2)		−1.678 (30) (−2.187 −1.527)
Log (km nav. river)	−0.747 (100) (−0.821 −0.670)	−0.219 (47) (−0.249 −0.200)
Share Arbustiva/Arborea	−0.442 (100) (−0.497 −0.418)	
Share Campos	−0.376 (100) (−0.427 −0.351)	
Share Floresta Aluvial	−0.510 (100) (−0.573 −0.472)	0.099 (100) (0.061 0.108)
Share Floresta Baixa	−0.398 (100) (−0.455 −0.384)	
Share Floresta Alta	−0.375 (100) (−0.428 −0.354)	
Share Floresta Semidecidual	−0.699 (100) (−0.802 −0.575)	
Missing Bohrer dummy	−36.20 (100) (−40.07 −35.08)	−1.440 (100) (−2.178 −0.377)
Share good soil		−0.030 (100) (−0.034 −0.023)
High rainfall dummy	3.419 (78) (2.487 4.601)	−2.061 (10) (−2.300 −1.869)
Av. temp. (Mar.)	−2.026 (80) (−2.736 −1.526)	

Table A.2. (*cont.*)

Variable	1980–1985	1985–1995
Av. temp. (Jun.)	1.547 (73) (1.381 1.927)	
Av. temp. (Sep.)	1.727 (7) (1.714 1.808)	
Missing temp. dummy	−12.12 (100) (−25.76 6.151)	0.626 (100) (−0.542 0.876)
Share protected		20.995 (60) (18.681 23.813)
Log (1985 FINAM credit)	−0.121 (34) (−0.121 −0.118)	
Dummy for missing federal transfer	−29.43 (100) (−31.92 −28.28)	7.348 (100) (2.679 8.943)
Growth cleared land (−1)	−0.301 (100) (−0.312 −0.279)	−0.340 (100) (−0.364 −0.311)
Growth cleared land (−2)		−0.202 (100) (−0.214 −0.176)
Log cleared land (−2)	−2.971 (100) (−3.217 −2.546)	
Log cleared land (−3)		−2.731 (100) (−2.946 −1.934)
Neighbors' cleared land intensity (−1)	8.699 (100) (7.727 9.421)	15.662 (100) (13.662 17.143)
Growth urban pop. (−1)		0.259 (100) (0.199 0.311)
Neighbors' urban pop. density (−1)		4.499 (97) (4.212 4.890)
Growth rural pop. (−1)	0.383 (100) (0.314 0.495)	0.367 (100) (0.275 0.460)
Growth rural pop. (−2)		0.158 (6) (0.153 0.165)
Log rural pop. (−2)	−3.127 (100) (−3.739 −2.872)	
Neighbors' rural pop. density (−1)		−13.86 (100) (−15.21 −10.37)
Neighbors' rural GDP (−1)		−1.360 (3) (−1.395 −1.289)
Neighbors' urban GDP (−1)		0.855 (3) (0.816 0.874)
Growth cattle herd (−1)		0.072 (100) (0.039 0.079)
Growth cattle herd (−2)		0.059 (99) (0.057 0.065)
Log cattle herd (−3)		0.907 (99) (0.810 0.951)
Neighbors' herd density (−1)		−17.98 (100) (−20.82 −13.49)

Table A.2. (*cont.*)

Variable	1980–1985	1985–1995
Growth land price (−1)	0.111 (100) (0.093 0.123)	
Log land price (−2)	3.403 (100) (3.216 3.853)	
Log land price (−3)		0.827 (99) (0.735 0.903)
Neighbors' av. land price (−1)	−3.017 (100) (−3.273 −2.586)	
Growth paved roads (−1)		0.423 (79) (0.327 0.492)
Log paved roads (−3)		4.276 (100) (3.323 4.873)
Growth non-paved roads (−1)		0.047 (89) (0.041 0.051)
Log non-paved roads (−2)	−6.095 (100) (−6.606 −5.221)	
Log non-paved roads (−3)		0.523 (97) (0.420 0.579)
Interaction of growth unpaved roads and cleared land (−1)		0.004 (8) (0.004 0.004)
Interaction of growth paved roads and cleared land (−1)		−0.036 (88) (−0.047 −0.001)
Interaction of growth paved roads and cleared land (−2)		−0.001 (7) (−0.001 −0.001)
Interaction of paved roads and cleared land (−2)		−0.399 (100) (−0.450 −0.309)
Interaction of unpaved roads and cleared land (−2)	0.588 (100) (0.505 0.639)	0.048 (1) (0.048 0.048)

Table A.3. *Full estimation results: growth of rural GDP*

Variable	1980–1985	1985–1995
Intercept	78.209 (100)	58.994 (100)
	(63.488 126.75)	(42.521 67.780)
City dummy	−17.33 (100)	−17.86 (100)
	(−22.34 −14.41)	(−18.81 −12.68)
Amazonas dummy	9.532 (100)	−3.760 (88)
	(8.257 11.073)	(−4.987 −3.591)
Goiás dummy	−11.97 (100)	−4.943 (30)
	(−16.57 −10.39)	(−7.625 −4.142)
Maranhão dummy		−5.855 (100)
		(−7.527 −5.257)
Mato Grosso dummy		−14.82 (100)
		(−15.35 −12.75)
Pará dummy	7.546 (100)	
	(5.932 8.623)	
Roraima dummy	9.726 (89)	−51.51 (100)
	(6.465 16.324)	(−52.49 −48.59)
Log (area)		2.756 (100)
		(2.341 3.176)
Log (dist. to capital)	−0.524 (85)	
	(−0.613 −0.483)	
Log (dist. to capital2)	5.896 (89)	
	(4.588 6.566)	
Share Arbustiva/Arborea		0.078 (96)
		(0.065 0.090)
Share Campos		0.106 (99)
		(0.036 0.130)
Share Floresta Aluvial		0.162 (100)
		(0.088 0.177)
Share Floresta Baixa		0.060 (96)
		(0.059 0.072)
Share Floresta Alta	0.099 (100)	−0.060 (4)
	(0.085 0.127)	(−0.061 −0.059)
Share Floresta Semidecidual	−0.234 (100)	
	(−0.263 −0.179)	
Missing Bohrer dummy	10.486 (100)	−0.953 (100)
	(9.678 11.930)	(−8.503 4.606)
Share good soil	−0.043 (95)	−0.034 (99)
	(−0.053 −0.029)	(−0.039 −0.032)
Av. temp. (Jun.)	−1.468 (99)	
	(−1.575 −1.261)	
Av. temp. (Sep.)		−1.765 (99)
		(−1.866 −1.542)
Av. temp. (Dec.)	−2.020 (1)	1.269 (99)
	(−2.020 −2.020)	(1.070 1.334)
Missing temp. dummy	−35.35 (100)	−14.90 (100)
	(−51.77 −28.98)	(−17.86 −1.196)

Table A.3. (*cont.*)

Variable	1980–1985	1985–1995
Share protected	37.156 (35) (35.498 46.713)	
Dummy for missing federal transfer	−9.880 (100) (−14.85 0.025)	26.642 (100) (24.148 27.716)
Growth cleared land (−1)	0.123 (100) (0.096 0.146)	
Growth cleared land (−2)		0.131 (100) (0.125 0.147)
Log cleared land (−2)	4.666 (100) (3.489 5.144)	
Log cleared land (−3)		3.371 (100) (3.123 3.765)
Neighbors' cleared land intensity (−1)		11.717 (100) (9.455 12.022)
Growth rural GDP (−1)	−0.570 (100) (−0.596 −0.518)	−0.351 (100) (−0.368 −0.332)
Growth rural GDP (−2)		−0.273 (100) (−0.283 −0.246)
Log rural GDP (−2)	−11.93 (100) (−12.24 −10.80)	
Log rural GDP (−3)		−8.011 (100) (−8.337 −7.063)
Growth urban GDP (−1)	0.110 (50) (0.100 0.137)	
Log urban GDP (−2)	1.977 (11) (1.667 2.261)	
Log urban GDP (−3)		1.005 (93) (0.871 1.085)
Growth urban pop. (−1)	0.589 (100) (0.482 0.661)	0.312 (100) (0.258 0.325)
Log urban pop. (−2)	−1.340 (36) (−2.167 −1.049)	
Growth rural pop. (−2)		0.323 (100) (0.272 0.457)
Log rural pop. (−2)	4.678 (100) (3.986 5.611)	
Neighbors' rural pop. density (−1)	11.135 (100) (9.079 13.718)	
Neighbors' rural GDP (−1)		−3.002 (100) (−3.311 −2.800)
Neighbors' urban GDP (−1)	−0.778 (1) (−0.778 −0.778)	1.982 (100) (1.858 2.102)
Growth cattle herd (−1)		0.035 (92) (0.030 0.039)
Log cattle herd (−2)	1.047 (100) (0.838 1.252)	

Table A.3. (*cont.*)

Variable	1980–1985	1985–1995
Growth land price (−1)	0.062 (25) (0.062 0.070)	0.072 (7) (0.041 0.077)
Growth land price (−2)		0.063 (6) (0.063 0.063)
Log land price (−2)	1.788 (80) (1.334 2.570)	
Log land price (−3)		2.760 (100) (2.534 3.807)
Growth paved roads (−1)		0.091 (100) (0.073 0.101)
Growth paved roads (−2)		−0.126 (77) (−0.135 −0.121)
Neighbors' paved roads density (−1)	−101.7 (88) (−123.6 −61.66)	
Neighbors' non-paved roads density (−1)		−96.92 (100) (−102.3 −77.86)
Interaction of growth paved roads and cleared land (−2)		0.010 (77) (0.010 0.011)

Table A.4. *Full estimation results: growth of urban GDP*

Variable	1980–1985	1985–1995
Intercept	86.662 (100) (9.492 115.51)	15.744 (100) (−25.96 54.658)
Amapá dummy	−9.672 (64) (−13.81 −7.288)	
Amazonas dummy		−5.648 (27) (−6.956 −4.526)
Goiás dummy	−18.84 (100) (−20.16 −14.51)	−13.33 (27) (−16.37 −7.611)
Maranhão dummy		−8.859 (100) (−16.37 −5.269)
Mato Grosso dummy	−9.679 (19) (−11.92 −6.195)	−12.59 (100) (−20.17 −8.304)
Pará dummy	5.041 (89) (3.217 6.562)	−5.339 (27) (−6.359 −3.105)
Roraima dummy	−28.30 (100) (−34.42 −18.50)	
Log (area)	2.426 (100) (1.162 3.022)	1.114 (1) (1.114 1.114)
Log (dist. to capital)	−0.896 (100) (−0.970 −0.440)	
Log (dist. to capital2)		−4.292 (28) (−5.307 −2.813)
Log (km nav. river)		−0.356 (13) (−0.433 −0.296)
Share Floresta Baixa	0.071 (75) (0.055 0.079)	
Share Floresta Alta	0.104 (99) (0.071 0.119)	
Share Floresta Semidecidual		−0.169 (1) (−0.169 −0.169)
Share other	31.367 (97) (23.615 51.608)	
Missing Bohrer dummy	9.894 (100) (2.499 12.072)	−6.825 (100) (−10.80 −3.582)
Share good soil		−0.049 (24) (−0.059 −0.046)
High rainfall dummy		−4.914 (100) (−6.575 −2.722)
Av. temp. (Mar.)	−4.811 (100) (−5.898 −2.846)	
Av. temp. (Jun.)	−2.631 (2) (−2.765 −2.498)	−0.888 (1) (−0.888 −0.888)
Av. temp. (Sep.)	2.291 (92) (1.646 4.550)	−1.219 (83) (−1.458 −1.041)
Missing temp. dummy	−72.02 (100) (−97.32 −50.33)	−24.06 (100) (−36.99 4.148)

Table A.4. (*cont.*)

Variable	1980–1985	1985–1995
Share Indian reserve		−5.666 (80) (−6.708 −3.350)
Share protected		−31.92 (1) (−31.92 −31.92)
Ratio of federal transfers to GDP (−1)	45.862 (100) (34.178 55.150)	
Dummy for missing federal transfer	25.199 (100) (17.337 28.505)	2.220 (100) (0.767 5.140)
Growth cleared land (−1)	−0.120 (2) (−0.122 −0.119)	
Log cleared land (−2)	−2.133 (2) (−2.282 −1.984)	
Neighbors' cleared land intensity (−1)		7.648 (9) (7.203 7.812)
Growth rural GDP (−2)		0.076 (8) (0.070 0.084)
Growth urban GDP (−1)	−0.265 (100) (−0.314 −0.227)	−0.284 (100) (−0.295 −0.266)
Growth urban GDP (−2)		−0.202 (100) (−0.223 −0.191)
Log urban GDP (−2)	−2.404 (99) (−3.315 −1.898)	
Log urban GDP (−3)		−3.985 (100) (−4.487 −3.475)
Growth urban pop. (−1)		0.699 (100) (0.590 0.735)
Growth urban pop. (−2)		0.497 (100) (0.448 0.555)
Log urban pop. (−3)		5.667 (100) (5.216 6.114)
Neighbors' urban pop. density (−1)	6.692 (81) (5.865 7.179)	6.451 (100) (5.615 7.130)
Growth rural pop. (−1)	0.396 (1) (0.396 0.396)	
Log rural pop. (−2)	−3.158 (88) (−4.547 −2.561)	
Neighbors' rural pop. density (−1)	15.397 (16) (13.331 18.616)	
Neighbors' rural GDP (−1)	2.077 (9) (1.989 2.717)	
Growth cattle herd (−1)	0.092 (3) (0.078 0.104)	
Log cattle herd (−2)	0.892 (97) (0.612 1.506)	
Log cattle herd (−3)		1.729 (100) (1.047 1.928)

Table A.4. *(cont.)*

Variable	1980–1985	1985–1995
Neighbors' herd density (−1)		−17.60 (73) (−23.47 −12.10)
Log land price (−2)	2.061 (97) (1.705 2.517)	
Log land price (−3)		1.581 (1) (1.581 1.581)
Neighbors' av. land price (−1)		3.898 (100) (3.242 4.420)
Growth paved roads (−1)	0.037 (4) (0.031 0.043)	0.115 (74) (0.099 0.127)
Growth paved roads (−2)		0.090 (14) (0.035 0.229)
Log paved roads (−3)		1.147 (95) (0.859 1.351)
Neighbors' paved roads density (−1)	−101.2 (5) (−120.7 −96.28)	51.159 (22) (47.496 60.882)
Growth non-paved roads (−1)	0.044 (2) (0.044 0.044)	
Log non-paved roads (−2)	0.777 (13) (0.719 1.037)	
Log non-paved roads (−3)		3.066 (93) (2.370 3.768)
Neighbors' non-paved roads density (−1)		−92.77 (47) (−119.7 −59.36)
Interaction of growth unpaved roads and cleared land (−1)	0.004 (14) (0.003 0.004)	
Interaction of growth paved roads and cleared land (−1)	0.003 (58) (0.003 0.004)	0.011 (12) (0.009 0.011)
Interaction of growth paved roads and cleared land (−2)		−0.017 (4) (−0.017 −0.016)
Interaction of paved roads and cleared land (−2)		0.094 (5) (0.091 0.105)
Interaction of unpaved roads and cleared land (−2)		−0.283 (94) (−0.349 −0.014)

Table A.5. *Full estimation results: growth of cattle herd*

Variable	1980–1985	1985–1995
Intercept	15.716 (100) (−26.44 30.121)	−1.150 (100) (−8.212 26.301)
City dummy		−34.75 (100) (−37.10 −32.46)
Amapá dummy		−4.039 (5) (−4.039 −4.039)
Goiás dummy	−7.125 (3) (−7.974 −6.700)	
Maranhão dummy		−2.665 (16) (−3.458 −1.805)
Mato Grosso dummy	5.603 (88) (4.277 10.242)	−3.719 (13) (−4.662 −2.785)
Pará dummy		−2.647 (22) (−3.566 −1.513)
Rondônia dummy	10.765 (6) (10.475 12.082)	11.350 (100) (8.202 14.253)
Roraima dummy		−30.42 (100) (−32.39 −29.57)
Log (dist. to capital2)		−2.102 (16) (−2.732 −1.031)
Log (km nav. river)		−0.469 (100) (−0.512 −0.381)
Share Arbustiva/Arborea	−0.069 (79) (−0.073 −0.047)	
Share Campos		0.027 (1) (0.027 0.027)
Share Floresta Aluvial	−0.221 (100) (−0.269 −0.147)	0.114 (100) (0.105 0.129)
Share Floresta Semidecidual	−0.189 (94) (−0.224 −0.087)	
Share other	−32.90 (99) (−38.98 −12.90)	
Missing Bohrer dummy	−1.925 (100) (−4.475 4.538)	0.131 (100) (−3.156 1.335)
Share good soil	−0.037 (11) (−0.046 −0.025)	
High rainfall dummy	4.171 (13) (2.615 6.395)	
Av. temp. (Mar.)	4.408 (93) (2.638 5.370)	
Av. temp. (Jun.)	−0.948 (1) (−0.948 −0.948)	0.513 (4) (0.456 0.684)
Av. temp. (Sep.)		−0.788 (9) (−0.940 −0.761)

Table A.5. (*cont.*)

Variable	1980–1985	1985–1995
Av. temp. (Dec.)	−4.718 (96) (−5.898 −1.294)	0.882 (5) (0.805 1.001)
Missing temp. dummy	−8.538 (100) (−27.99 7.896)	1.121 (100) (−7.331 6.515)
Dummy for missing federal transfer	−6.449 (100) (−10.55 −5.002)	28.829 (100) (27.287 29.915)
Growth cleared land (−1)		−0.106 (100) (−0.114 −0.088)
Growth cleared land (−2)		−0.056 (100) (−0.062 −0.041)
Neighbors' cleared land intensity (−1)		4.282 (5) (2.153 5.956)
Log rural GDP (−2)	3.524 (100) (2.184 4.967)	
Growth urban GDP (−1)	0.158 (97) (0.092 0.181)	0.043 (51) (0.039 0.050)
Growth urban GDP (−2)		0.084 (100) (0.066 0.109)
Log urban GDP (−2)	−1.466 (84) (−1.616 −1.226)	
Log urban GDP (−3)		0.510 (8) (0.501 0.516)
Growth urban pop. (−1)	0.361 (100) (0.307 0.399)	0.234 (100) (0.202 0.284)
Growth urban pop. (−2)		−0.140 (61) (−0.172 −0.121)
Growth rural pop. (−2)		0.248 (99) (0.198 0.336)
Log rural pop. (−2)	−2.593 (2) (−2.765 −2.421)	
Neighbors' rural pop. density (−1)		−10.32 (100) (−12.02 −8.995)
Neighbors' rural GDP (−1)		−1.151 (21) (−1.367 −1.046)
Neighbors' urban GDP (−1)		0.925 (100) (0.726 1.443)
Growth cattle herd (−1)	−0.134 (90) (−0.143 −0.110)	
Log cattle herd (−2)	−3.500 (100) (−4.160 −2.707)	
Log cattle herd (−3)		−1.192 (100) (−1.405 −0.965)
Neighbors' herd density (−1)	15.919 (10) (12.556 20.563)	11.209 (95) (6.807 13.654)

Table A.5. (*cont.*)

Variable	1980–1985	1985–1995
Neighbors' av. land price (−1)	−1.131 (1) (−1.131 −1.131)	
Neighbors' paved roads density (−1)	−120.5 (7) (−152.3 −110.9)	
Growth non-paved roads (−2)		0.036 (86) (0.031 0.040)
Log non-paved roads (−2)	−3.533 (84) (−4.512 0.079)	
Log non-paved roads (−3)		1.001 (100) (0.864 1.074)
Neighbors' non-paved roads density (−1)		−48.38 (93) (−57.10 −43.97)
Interaction of growth unpaved roads and cleared land (−2)		0.003 (14) (0.003 0.004)
Interaction of unpaved roads and cleared land (−2)	0.365 (80) (0.286 0.436)	

Table A.6. *Full estimation results: growth of urban population*

Variable	1980–1985	1985–1995
Intercept	−5.226 (100)	0.550 (100)
	(−24.42 5.055)	(−4.739 4.133)
City dummy	5.622 (81)	
	(4.974 7.435)	
Amapá dummy	4.346 (11)	2.542 (100)
	(3.430 5.571)	(1.670 2.892)
Amazonas dummy	3.140 (2)	
	(3.140 3.140)	
Goiás dummy	4.419 (2)	1.339 (99)
	(4.419 4.419)	(1.000 1.596)
Maranhão dummy	1.439 (39)	
	(0.944 4.224)	
Mato Grosso dummy	4.653 (2)	−1.453 (26)
	(4.653 4.653)	(−1.754 −1.123)
Pará dummy	2.459 (4)	
	(1.200 3.718)	
Rondônia dummy		−0.783 (1)
		(−0.783 −0.783)
Roraima dummy	10.403 (100)	−10.96 (100)
	(4.985 12.794)	(−11.81 −10.37)
Log (area)		0.284 (100)
		(0.204 0.396)
Log (km nav. river)	−0.140 (4)	
	(−0.140 −0.140)	
Share Arbustiva/Arborea	0.077 (96)	0.007 (1)
	(0.064 0.093)	(0.007 0.007)
Share Campos	0.080 (96)	
	(0.070 0.087)	
Share Floresta Aluvial	0.079 (96)	0.015 (88)
	(0.062 0.098)	(0.009 0.021)
Share Floresta Baixa	0.074 (96)	0.006 (1)
	(0.063 0.090)	(0.006 0.006)
Share Floresta Alta	0.102 (100)	0.011 (1)
	(0.034 0.121)	(0.011 0.011)
Share Floresta Semidecidual	0.112 (96)	
	(0.076 0.161)	
Missing Bohrer dummy	7.058 (100)	−0.009 (100)
	(−0.112 8.737)	(−0.205 0.834)
Share good soil	−0.019 (69)	
	(−0.026 −0.014)	
High rainfall dummy	−1.528 (8)	−0.476 (19)
	(−1.646 −1.293)	(−0.558 −0.433)
Av. temp. (Mar.)	0.802 (7)	0.410 (100)
	(−0.590 1.578)	(0.315 0.728)
Av. temp. (Sep.)		−0.267 (99)
		(−0.374 −0.162)

Table A.6. *(cont.)*

Variable	1980–1985	1985–1995
Av. temp. (Dec.)	−0.514 (80) (−1.698 −0.272)	−0.611 (1) (−0.611 −0.611)
Missing temp. dummy	−8.551 (100) (−15.94 1.097)	3.804 (100) (0.794 7.309)
Share protected		−6.804 (88) (−9.171 −5.586)
Ratio of federal transfers to GDP (−1)	6.222 (60) (5.394 7.367)	
Dummy for missing federal transfer	−6.096 (100) (−7.686 −1.339)	11.760 (100) (11.019 12.429)
Growth cleared land (−1)	−0.031 (93) (−0.048 −0.024)	
Growth cleared land (−2)		−0.009 (49) (−0.015 −0.007)
Log cleared land (−2)	−0.538 (12) (−0.738 −0.345)	
Log cleared land (−3)		−0.173 (5) (−0.276 −0.138)
Neighbors' cleared land intensity (−1)	−2.499 (1) (−2.499 −2.499)	0.812 (8) (0.683 1.073)
Growth rural GDP (−2)		0.008 (1) (0.008 0.008)
Growth urban GDP (−1)	0.069 (100) (0.055 0.081)	
Log urban GDP (−2)	1.268 (100) (0.984 1.675)	
Growth urban pop. (−1)	−0.103 (9) (−0.108 −0.098)	0.503 (100) (0.490 0.514)
Log urban pop. (−2)	−2.204 (100) (−2.565 −1.867)	
Log urban pop. (−3)		−0.358 (100) (−0.470 −0.258)
Neighbors' urban pop. density (−1)	3.824 (100) (2.626 4.609)	1.001 (1) (1.001 1.001)
Growth rural pop. (−1)	0.151 (92) (0.115 0.210)	
Log rural pop. (−2)	0.876 (86) (0.425 1.372)	
Log rural pop. (−3)		0.289 (48) (0.246 0.432)
Neighbors' rural pop. density (−1)	−4.667 (40) (−5.507 −3.465)	1.709 (79) (1.104 2.148)
Neighbors' rural GDP (−1)	0.832 (61) (0.207 1.276)	
Neighbors' urban GDP (−1)	−0.579 (53) (−0.726 −0.422)	−0.120 (62) (−0.157 −0.116)

Table A.6. (*cont.*)

Variable	1980–1985	1985–1995
Growth cattle herd (−1)	0.053 (100) (0.047 0.061)	
Neighbors' herd density (−1)	4.310 (2) (4.310 4.310)	1.064 (6) (1.057 1.100)
Growth land price (−2)		−0.009 (83) (−0.013 −0.007)
Neighbors' av. land price (−1)	−0.639 (11) (−0.814 −0.489)	−0.562 (98) (−0.814 −0.234)
Growth paved roads (−1)	0.012 (1) (0.012 0.012)	
Neighbors' paved roads density (−1)		11.190 (90) (8.732 13.477)
Growth non-paved roads (−1)		−0.099 (92) (−0.126 −0.088)
Log non-paved roads (−2)	−0.701 (16) (−1.262 0.255)	
Log non-paved roads (−3)		−0.351 (21) (−0.526 −0.062)
Neighbors' non-paved roads density (−1)	25.776 (6) (16.485 44.438)	
Interaction of growth unpaved roads and cleared land (−1)		0.009 (93) (0.000 0.012)
Interaction of unpaved roads and cleared land (−2)	0.055 (35) (0.016 0.135)	0.036 (16) (−0.008 0.046)

Table A.7. *Full estimation results: growth of rural population*

Variable	1980–1985	1985–1995
Intercept	−7.271 (100) (−12.91 −2.155)	−5.180 (100) (−9.897 1.342)
City dummy		−10.41 (100) (−11.13 −8.537)
Amazonas dummy		−1.056 (1) (−1.056 −1.056)
Maranhão dummy	2.445 (100) (1.642 2.967)	
Pará dummy	2.687 (100) (2.243 2.949)	
Rondônia dummy	3.058 (99) (1.614 5.071)	
Roraima dummy	2.103 (7) (1.320 3.856)	−1.254 (1) (−1.254 −1.254)
Log (area)	0.948 (100) (0.601 1.415)	−0.291 (90) (−0.352 −0.207)
Log (dist. to capital2)	1.078 (25) (0.892 1.304)	
Share Arbustiva/Arborea	0.018 (79) (0.014 0.023)	
Share Campos	−0.026 (10) (−0.034 −0.017)	
Share Floresta Aluvial	0.019 (5) (0.019 0.020)	0.013 (2) (0.013 0.013)
Share Floresta Baixa	−0.017 (6) (−0.020 −0.014)	
Share Floresta Alta	0.021 (91) (0.013 0.027)	
Share Floresta Semidecidual		−0.054 (96) (−0.057 −0.042)
Missing Bohrer dummy	0.949 (100) (−1.319 1.867)	−1.424 (100) (−1.814 −1.085)
Share good soil	−0.015 (43) (−0.017 −0.011)	
Av. temp. (Mar.)	1.216 (51) (1.077 1.457)	0.241 (1) (0.241 0.241)
Av. temp. (Dec.)	−0.903 (82) (−1.493 −0.230)	0.221 (98) (0.194 0.311)
Missing temp. dummy	−3.534 (100) (−7.551 0.235)	6.820 (100) (0.832 9.294)
Share Indian reserve		1.797 (91) (0.895 1.985)
Share protected	13.060 (82) (8.807 19.340)	

Table A.7. (*cont.*)

Variable	1980–1985	1985–1995
Dummy for missing federal transfer	6.000 (100) (3.393 6.685)	
Growth cleared land (−1)	0.021 (2) (0.019 0.022)	
Growth cleared land (−2)		−0.018 (94) (−0.026 −0.017)
Log cleared land (−3)		−0.292 (3) (−0.321 −0.267)
Neighbors' cleared land intensity (−1)	−1.893 (59) (−2.264 −1.208)	−1.534 (94) (−1.780 −0.914)
Growth rural GDP (−1)	−0.034 (81) (−0.044 −0.026)	0.026 (6) (0.021 0.028)
Log rural GDP (−2)	−1.048 (100) (−1.453 −0.712)	
Growth urban GDP (−1)	−0.026 (2) (−0.026 −0.026)	
Growth urban pop. (−1)	0.063 (67) (0.051 0.078)	
Growth urban pop. (−2)		0.051 (9) (0.051 0.055)
Log urban pop. (−3)		0.332 (94) (0.225 0.488)
Neighbors' urban pop. density (−1)	−2.093 (100) (−2.313 −1.840)	
Growth rural pop. (−1)		0.668 (100) (0.632 0.688)
Neighbors' rural pop. density (−1)	14.963 (100) (14.132 15.998)	
Neighbors' rural GDP (−1)	0.490 (99) (0.325 0.697)	
Growth cattle herd (−1)	0.022 (36) (0.021 0.024)	
Log cattle herd (−2)	−0.188 (2) (−0.221 −0.155)	
Neighbors' herd density (−1)		−2.440 (3) (−2.858 −2.144)
Growth land price (−1)		−0.013 (14) (−0.013 −0.012)
Log land price (−2)	0.458 (68) (0.354 0.573)	
Neighbors' av. land price (−1)	0.529 (22) (0.430 0.643)	
Growth paved roads (−1)	0.008 (1) (0.008 0.008)	−0.015 (22) (−0.025 −0.012)

Table A.7. (*cont.*)

Variable	1980–1985	1985–1995
Log paved roads (−3)		−0.173 (3) (−0.178 −0.170)
Neighbors' paved roads density (−1)		8.777 (1) (8.777 8.777)
Growth non-paved roads (−1)	−0.060 (2) (−0.063 −0.056)	
Growth non-paved roads (−2)		−0.006 (1) (−0.006 −0.006)
Log non-paved roads (−2)	−0.831 (4) (−0.882 −0.783)	
Interaction of growth unpaved roads and cleared land (−1)	0.003 (5) (0.001 0.007)	
Interaction of growth unpaved roads and cleared land (−2)		−0.000 (1) (−0.000 −0.000)
Interaction of growth paved roads and cleared land (−1)		0.001 (96) (0.001 0.001)
Interaction of unpaved roads and cleared land (−2)		0.086 (4) (0.080 0.092)

Table A.8. *Full estimation results: growth of paved roads*

Variable	1980–1985	1985–1995
Intercept	−13.49 (100)	−2.915 (100)
	(−35.93 3.127)	(−33.73 19.311)
City dummy	−7.146 (71)	
	(−10.83 −4.466)	
Amapá dummy	−3.093 (1)	
	(−3.093 −3.093)	
Mato Grosso dummy		−5.860 (1)
		(−5.860 −5.860)
Roraima dummy	−7.595 (1)	
	(−7.595 −7.595)	
Log (area)	0.515 (1)	−1.338 (49)
	(0.515 0.515)	(−1.545 −1.129)
Log (dist. to capital)	−0.371 (16)	
	(−0.406 −0.364)	
Log (km nav. river)	−0.343 (95)	
	(−0.437 −0.163)	
Share Campos		0.135 (89)
		(0.103 0.149)
Share Floresta Aluvial	−0.061 (79)	
	(−0.074 −0.046)	
Share Floresta Semidecidual	0.106 (95)	0.137 (1)
	(0.060 0.122)	(0.137 0.137)
Share other		−20.13 (5)
		(−24.20 −14.90)
Missing Bohrer dummy	−0.140 (100)	−7.246 (100)
	(−0.541 0.724)	(−9.363 −5.068)
Share good soil	−0.052 (70)	
	(−0.066 −0.044)	
High rainfall dummy	3.630 (95)	
	(1.538 4.806)	
Av. temp. (Mar.)		4.680 (83)
		(3.754 5.495)
Av. temp. (Jun.)	−1.055 (1)	
	(−1.055 −1.055)	
Av. temp. (Sep.)	0.492 (1)	
	(0.492 0.492)	
Av. temp. (Dec.)	1.174 (1)	−4.518 (91)
	(1.174 1.174)	(−5.718 −0.668)
Missing temp. dummy	−3.102 (100)	−8.396 (100)
	(−5.660 11.413)	(−39.91 13.632)
Share protected		93.751 (76)
		(65.226 104.71)
Log (1985 FINAM credit)	−0.131 (87)	0.269 (6)
	(−0.143 −0.105)	(0.267 0.275)

Table A.8. (*cont.*)

Variable	1980–1985	1985–1995
Ratio of federal transfers to GDP (−1)	−7.820 (1) (−7.820 −7.820)	
Dummy for missing federal transfer	6.396 (100) (2.520 9.746)	3.904 (100) (0.830 8.160)
Log cleared land (−2)	0.846 (75) (0.437 1.073)	
Log cleared land (−3)		1.604 (5) (1.335 1.805)
Neighbors' cleared land intensity (−1)	−7.400 (69) (−11.56 −4.374)	
Growth rural GDP (−2)		0.134 (63) (0.121 0.149)
Log rural GDP (−2)	0.948 (32) (0.749 0.981)	
Growth urban pop. (−2)		0.415 (100) (0.356 0.541)
Log urban pop. (−2)	1.012 (44) (0.802 1.184)	
Neighbors' urban pop. density (−1)	−5.662 (99) (−6.373 −4.065)	
Log rural pop. (−3)		2.503 (72) (1.740 2.776)
Neighbors' rural pop. density (−1)	12.882 (95) (6.288 15.004)	
Neighbors' rural GDP (−1)	−0.840 (1) (−0.840 −0.840)	
Growth cattle herd (−1)	0.024 (34) (0.020 0.027)	
Growth paved roads (−1)	0.518 (100) (0.466 0.611)	−0.706 (100) (−0.764 −0.695)
Growth paved roads (−2)		0.331 (77) (0.194 0.387)
Log paved roads (−2)	−8.199 (95) (−9.296 −0.677)	
Log paved roads (−3)		11.729 (76) (9.242 13.367)
Neighbors' paved roads density (−1)		159.06 (100) (121.62 187.29)
Growth non-paved roads (−1)	−0.035 (10) (−0.039 −0.030)	−0.883 (78) (−1.241 −0.170)
Growth non-paved roads (−2)		0.057 (66) (0.050 0.062)
Log non-paved roads (−3)		−13.27 (100) (−16.16 −6.604)

Table A.8. (*cont.*)

Variable	1980–1985	1985–1995
Neighbors' non-paved roads density (−1)	124.14 (48) (100.90 159.65)	110.61 (94) (78.807 152.45)
Interaction of growth unpaved roads and cleared land (−1)	−0.003 (81) (−0.004 −0.003)	0.097 (52) (0.087 0.100)
Interaction of growth unpaved roads and cleared land (−2)		0.006 (9) (0.006 0.007)
Interaction of growth paved roads and cleared land (−1)	−0.031 (100) (−0.037 −0.027)	
Interaction of growth paved roads and cleared land (−2)		−0.032 (100) (−0.044 −0.007)
Interaction of paved roads and cleared land (−2)	0.687 (94) (0.529 0.801)	−1.076 (100) (−1.493 −0.224)
Interaction of unpaved roads and cleared land (−2)	−0.071 (91) (−0.090 −0.037)	1.321 (100) (0.700 1.576)

Table A.9. *Full estimation results: growth of unpaved roads*

Variable	1980–1985	1985–1995
Intercept	14.142 (100)	−103.2 (100)
	(1.398 34.326)	(−154.2 −55.10)
City dummy	10.351 (72)	
	(9.114 11.854)	
Amazonas dummy		−12.67 (100)
		(−13.94 −8.849)
Maranhão dummy	−4.320 (98)	−7.893 (100)
	(−4.982 −2.038)	(−10.17 −5.494)
Mato Grosso dummy	−6.029 (82)	
	(−6.850 −3.991)	
Pará dummy	1.829 (1)	
	(1.829 1.829)	
Rondônia dummy		−10.41 (87)
		(−15.12 −7.181)
Roraima dummy	33.444 (100)	17.818 (86)
	(26.874 37.359)	(13.723 22.221)
Log (area)		1.906 (59)
		(1.245 2.290)
Log (km nav. river)		−0.603 (41)
		(−0.638 −0.444)
Share Arbustiva/Arborea		0.138 (100)
		(0.114 0.229)
Share Floresta Aluvial		−0.129 (10)
		(−0.150 −0.112)
Share Floresta Baixa	0.034 (3)	0.084 (4)
	(0.033 0.037)	(0.078 0.089)
Share Floresta Alta		0.094 (19)
		(0.079 0.137)
Share other		−17.52 (1)
		(−17.52 −17.52)
Missing Bohrer dummy	0.612 (100)	10.994 (100)
	(−0.712 4.546)	(8.183 18.059)
High rainfall dummy		5.127 (51)
		(4.600 5.848)
Av. temp. (Mar.)	−2.076 (2)	
	(−2.084 −2.067)	
Av. temp. (Jun.)	1.426 (2)	−2.467 (74)
	(1.348 1.504)	(−3.807 −0.547)
Av. temp. (Sep.)		2.780 (68)
		(2.306 3.266)
Av. temp. (Dec.)		2.344 (10)
		(2.344 2.344)
Missing temp. dummy	1.668 (100)	9.956 (100)
	(−17.54 2.772)	(−18.86 42.437)
Share Indian reserve		11.229 (2)
		(11.025 11.433)

Table A.9. (*cont.*)

Variable	1980–1985	1985–1995
Log (1985 FINAM credit)	−0.114 (88) (−0.156 −0.092)	
Ratio of federal transfers to GDP (−1)	−19.24 (18) (−20.60 −18.92)	
Dummy for missing federal transfer	−29.71 (100) (−32.90 −22.86)	−12.29 (100) (−15.98 −1.949)
Growth cleared land (−1)		0.155 (4) (0.124 0.184)
Growth cleared land (−2)		0.106 (2) (0.106 0.106)
Growth rural GDP (−1)	0.076 (26) (0.074 0.076)	
Log rural GDP (−2)	1.130 (54) (0.758 1.892)	
Log rural GDP (−3)		5.308 (100) (4.355 6.300)
Log urban GDP (−2)	−1.444 (88) (−1.847 −0.929)	
Log urban GDP (−3)		−1.957 (27) (−2.534 −0.430)
Growth urban pop. (−1)	−0.415 (100) (−0.480 −0.387)	
Log urban pop. (−3)		2.133 (50) (1.405 2.980)
Neighbors' urban pop. density (−1)	−4.408 (83) (−4.870 −3.562)	
Neighbors' rural pop. density (−1)		−10.71 (100) (−14.08 −9.231)
Growth cattle herd (−1)		0.070 (75) (0.052 0.083)
Growth cattle herd (−2)		0.160 (100) (0.124 0.180)
Growth paved roads (−1)	−0.030 (1) (−0.030 −0.030)	1.041 (65) (0.835 1.228)
Log paved roads (−2)	7.501 (100) (6.367 8.486)	
Log paved roads (−3)		7.331 (67) (4.739 8.478)
Growth non-paved roads (−1)	0.194 (100) (0.188 0.198)	
Growth non-paved roads (−2)		−0.095 (43) (−0.380 −0.060)
Log non-paved roads (−2)	−10.92 (100) (−11.48 −9.418)	
Log non-paved roads (−3)		−2.729 (100) (−3.471 −1.927)

Table A.9. (*cont.*)

Variable	1980–1985	1985–1995
Neighbors' non-paved roads density (−1)	108.25 (72) (85.252 117.90)	
Interaction of growth unpaved roads and cleared land (−1)		−0.078 (100) (−0.083 −0.074)
Interaction of growth unpaved roads and cleared land (−2)		0.024 (5) (−0.006 0.033)
Interaction of growth paved roads and cleared land (−1)	−0.003 (6) (−0.004 −0.003)	−0.099 (67) (−0.122 −0.001)
Interaction of paved roads and cleared land (−2)	−0.665 (100) (−0.811 −0.551)	−0.699 (67) (−0.806 −0.457)
Interaction of unpaved roads and cleared land (−2)	1.005 (100) (0.846 1.074)	

References

Allegretti, M. H. (1990), Extractive reserves: an alternative for reconciling development and environmental conservation in Amazonia, in A. B. Anderson, ed., *Alternatives to Deforestation: Steps toward Sustainable Use of the Amazon*, New York: Columbia University Press

(1994), Policies for the use of renewable natural resources: the Amazonian region and extractive activities, in M. Glüsener-Godt and I. Sachs, eds., *Extractivism in the Brazilian Amazon: Perspectives on Regional Development*, Paris: UNESCO

Allen, E. (1990), Calha Norte: military development in Brazilian Amazonia, Occasional Paper 52, Institute of Latin American Studies, University of Glasgow

Almeida, A. d. (1992a), A colonização sustentável da Amazônia, Texto Para Discussão 266, IPEA/DIPES, Rio de Janeiro, Brazil

(1992b), Deforestation and turnover in Amazon colonization, Discussion Paper (Draft), Washington, DC: World Bank

Almeida, L. d. and Campari, J. S. (1995), *Sustainable Settlement in the Brazilian Amazon*, New York and Oxford: IBRD and Oxford University Press

Almeida, O. T. d. and Uhl, C. (1995), Developing a quantitative framework for sustainable resource-use planning in the Brazilian Amazon, *World Development* 23, 1745–1764

Alston, Lee J., Libecap Gary D. L. and Mueller, Bernado (1999), A model of rural conflict: violence and land reform policy in Brazil, *Environment and Development Economics* 4(2), 135–160

(2000), Land reform policies, the sources of violent conflict and implications for deforestation in the Brazilian Amazon, *Journal of Environmental Economics and Management* 39(2), 162–188

Alston, Lee J., Libecap Gary D. L. and Schneider, R. (1996), The determinants and impact of property rights: land titles on the Brazilian frontier, *Journal of Law, Economics and Organization* 1

Alves, D. S. (1999), An analysis of the geographical patterns of deforestation in Brazilian Amazonia in the 1991–1996 period, Paper prepared for the 48th annual conference of the Center for Latin American Studies, University of Florida, March 23–26, 1999, Instituto Nacional de Pesquisas Especiais

(2002), An analysis of the geographical patterns of deforestation in Brazilian Amazonia in the 1991–1996 period, in C. H. Wood and R. Porro, eds., *Land*

Use and Deforestation in the Amazon, Gainesville, Florida: University Press of Florida, in press

Amsberg, J. v. (1994), Economic parameters of deforestation, Policy Research Working Paper 1350, Washington, DC: World Bank

Andersen, L. E. (1997), A cost-benefit analysis of deforestation in the Brazilian Amazon, Texto Para Discussão 455, IPEA/DIPES, Rio de Janeiro, Brazil

(1998), Uma análise de custo-benefício do desflorestamento na Amazônia Brasileira, in IPEA, ed., *A Economia Brasileira em Perspectiva – 1998*, vol. I, Rio de Janeiro: IPEA, chapter 22, pp. 823–866

(1999), Deforestation and economic growth in the Brazilian Amazon, PhD thesis, Department of Economics, University of Aarhus, Denmark

Andersen, L. E., Granger, C. W. J. and Reis, E. J. (1997), A random coefficient VAR transition model of the changes in land-use in the Brazilian Amazon, *Brazilian Review of Econometrics* 17, 1–13

Andersen, L. E., Granger, C. W. J., Reis, E. J., Huang, L.-L. and Weinhold, D. (1996), Report on Amazon deforestation, Discussion Paper 96–40, Department of Economics, University of California, San Diego

Anderson, A. B., ed. (1990), *Alternatives to Deforestation: Steps Toward Sustainable Use of the Amazon Rain Forest*, New York: Columbia University Press

Anderson, A. B. and Ioris, E. M. (1992), The logic of extraction: resource management and income generation by extractive producers in the Amazon estuary, in K. Redford and C. Padoch, eds., *Conservation of Neotropical Forests: Working from Traditional Resource Use*, New York: Columbia University Press

Anderson, A. B. and Jardim, M. A. G. (1989), Costs and benefits of floodplain forest management by rural inhabitants in the Amazon estuary: a case study of Açaí palm production, in J. Browder, ed., *Fragile Lands of Latin America: Strategies for Sustainable Development*, Boulder, CO: Westview Press

Anderson, A. B., May, P. H. and Balick, M. J. (1991), *The Subsidy from Nature: Palm Forests, Peasantry, and Development on an Amazonian Frontier*, New York: Columbia University Press

Arima, E. Y. and Uhl, C. (1997), Ranching in the Brazilian Amazon in a national context: economics, policy and practice, *Society and Natural Resources* 10, 433–451

Assies, W. (1997), The extraction of non-timber forest products as a conservation strategy in Amazonia, *European Review of Latin American and Caribbean Studies* 62

Aylward, B. (2000), Economic analysis of land-use change in a watershed context, Conference Paper presented at a UNESCO Workshop on Forest-Water-People in the Humid Tropics, Kuala Lumpur, Malaysia, July 31–August 4

Barbier, E. B. and Burgess, J. C. (2001), The economics of tropical deforestation, *Journal of Economic Surveys* 15(3), 413–433

Barbosa, L. C., ed. (2000), *The Brazilian Amazon Rain Forest: Global Ecopolitics, Development, and Democracy*, New York: University Press of America

Barreto, P., Amaral, P., Vidal, E. and Uhl, C. (1998), Costs and benefits of forest management for timber production in the eastern Amazon, *Forest Ecology and Management* 108, 9–26

Bierregaard, R. O., Gascon, C., Lovejoy, T. E. and Mesquita, R. C. G. (2001), *Lessons from Amazonia: The Ecology and Conservation of a Fragmented Forest*, New Haven and London: Yale University Press

Bilsborrow, R. E. (1994), Population, development and deforestation: some recent evidence, Report ST/ESA/SER.R/129, chapter X, New York: United Nations

Binswanger, H. P. (1991), Brazilian policies that encourage deforestation in the Amazon, *World Development* 19, 821–829

Bohrer, C. B. A. (1993), Base de dados municipais sobre o volume de madeira e a biomassa florestal da Amazônia Legal, Memo, IPEA/Rio

Bojanic, A. and Echeverría, R. G. (1990), Retornos a la Inversión en Investigació Agrícola en Bolivia: El Caso de la Soya, ISNAR Staff Notes number 90–94, International Service for National Agricultural Research (ISNAR), The Hague

Brandão, A. S. P. (1988), Mercado da terra e estrutura fundiária, in A. S. P. Brandão, ed., *Os Principais Problemas da Agricultura Brasileira: Análise e Sugestões*, Rio de Janeiro: IPEA /PNPE

Breton, B. L. (1993), *Voices from the Amazon*, West Hartford, CT: Kumarian Press

Broekhoven, G. (1996), *Non-Timber Forest Products. Ecological and Economic Aspects of Exploitation in Colombia, Ecuador and Bolivia*, Gland: IUCN, The World Conservation Union

Browder, J. O. (1985), *Subsidies, Deforestation, and the Forest Sector of the Brazilian Amazon*, Washington, DC: World Resources Institute

(1988), The social costs of rainforest destruction: a critique of the "hamburger debate", *Interciencia* 13, 115–120

(1989a), Development alternatives for tropical rainforests, in H. J. Leonard, ed., *Environment and the Poor: Development Strategies for a Common Agenda*, Oxford: Transaction Books

(1989b), Introduction, in J. O. Browder, ed., *Fragile Lands of Latin America: Strategies for Sustainable Development*, Boulder, CO: Westview Press, pp. 1–8

(1992), Social and economic constraints on the development of market oriented extractive reserves in Amazon rain forests, *Advances in Economic Botany* 9, 33–41

Brown, I. F., Martinelli, L. A., Thomas, W. W., Moreira, M. Z., Ferreira, C. A. C. and Victoria, R. A. (1995), Uncertainty in the biomass of Amazonian forests: an example from Rondônia, Brazil, *Forest Ecology and Management* 75, 175–189

Brown, K. S. and Brown, G. G. (1992), Habitat alteration and species loss in Brazilian forests, in T. C. Whitmore and J. A. Sayer, eds., *Tropical Deforestation and Species Extinction*, London: Chapman and Hall, pp. 119–142

Brown, K., Pearce, D., Perrings, C. and Swanson, T. (1993), Economics and the conservation of global biological diversity, Working Paper no. 2, Global Environment Facility

Brown, K. and Pearce, D. W. (1994), The economic value of carbon storage in tropical forests, in J. Weiss, ed., *The Economics of Project Appraisal and the Environment*

Brown, S., Gillespie, A. J. R. and Lugo, A. E. (1989), Biomass estimation methods for tropical forests with applications to forest inventory data, *Forest Science* 35, 881–902

Brown, S. and Lugo, A. E. (1984a), Biomass estimates for tropical forests: a new estimate based on forest volumes, *Science* 223, 1290–1293

(1984b), The storage and production of organic matter in tropical forests and their role in the global carbon cycle, *Biotropica* 14, 161–187

(1992a), Aboveground biomass estimates for tropical moist forest of the Brazilian Amazon, *Interciencia* 17, 8–18

(1992b), Biomass estimates for Brazil's Amazonian moist forests, in 'Forests '90: Annals of the First International Symposium on Environmental Studies on Tropical Rain Forests', Manaus, pp. 46–52

Bruijnzeel, L. A. (1990), *Hydrology of Moist Tropical Forests and Effects of Conversion: A State of the Knowledge Review*, Amsterdam: Netherlands Committee for the International Hydrological Programme of UNESCO

Buarque de Holanda, A. (1978), *Raízes do Brasil*, Rio de Janeiro: José Olympio

Bunker, S. (1985), *Underdeveloping the Amazon: Extraction, Unequal Exchange, and the Failure of the Modern State*, Chicago: University of Illinois Press

Cannell, M. G. R. (1982), *World Forest Biomass and Primary Production Data*, London: Academic Press

Carvalho Jr., J. A., Santos, J. C., Santos, J. M. and Higuchi, N. (1994), Estimate of combustion efficiency in a forest clearing experiment in the Manaus region, *Revista Brasileira da Geofísica* 12, 45–48

CBO (1990), Carbon charges as a response to global warming: the effects of taxing fossil fuels, Congressional Budget Office, Congress of the United States

CCSIVAM (1997), Politicas florestais e desenvolvimento sustentável na Amazônia, Workshop, July 14, 1997, Ministério da Aeronáutica

Chomitz, K. M. and Gray, D. A. (1996), Roads, land-use and deforestation: a spatial model applied to Belize, *World Bank Economic Review* 10(3), 487–512

Chomitz, K. M. and Kumari, K. (1996), The domestic benefits of tropical forests: a critical review emphasizing hydrological functions, Policy Research Working Paper no. 1601, Washington, DC: World Bank

(1998), The domestic benefits of tropical forests: a critical review, *World Bank Research Observer* 13(1), 13–35

Chomitz, K. M. and Thomas, T. S. (2000), Geographic patterns of land-use and land intensity in the Brazilian Amazon, Policy Research Working Paper no. 1601, Washington, DC: World Bank

Clay, J. W. (1997), *Brazil Nuts. The Use of a Keystone Species for Conservation and Development*, Baltimore and London: Johns Hopkins University Press

Cline, W. R. (1992), *The Economics of Global Warming*, Washington, DC: Institute for International Economics

Cline-Cole, R. A., Main, A. C. and Nichol, J. E. (1990), On fuelwood consumption, population dynamics and deforestation in Africa, *World Development* 18, 513–527

Cochrane, M. A. (2000), Forest fire, deforestation and landcover change in the Brazilian Amazon, in L. F. Neuenschwander, K. C. Ryan, G. E. Gollberg and J. D. Greer, eds., *Crossing the Millennium: Integrating Spatial Technologies and Ecological Principals for a New Age in Fire Management*, Proceedings from the

Joint Fire Science Conference and Workshop, June 15–17, 1999, Moscow, Idaho: University of Idaho and the International Association of Wildland Fire, pp. 170–176

Cochrane, M. A., Alencar, A., Schulze, M. D., Souza, C. M., Jr., Nepstad, DC, Lefebvre, P. and Davidson, E. A. (1999), Positive feedbacks in the fire dynamic of closed canopy tropical forests, *Science* 284, 1832–1835

Colinvaux, P. (1989), Ice-age Amazon revisited, *Nature* 340, 188–189

Coppen, J. J. W., Gordon, A. and Green, C. L. (1994), The development potential of selected Amazonian non-wood forest products: an appraisal of opportunities and constraints, Paper presented at the FAO Expert Consultation on Non-Timber Forest Products in Latin America and the Caribbean, Santiago de Chile, June

Costanza, R., *et al.* (1997), The value of the world's ecosystem services and natural capital, *Nature* 387, 253–260

Cummings, B. J. (1990), *Dam the Rivers, Damn the People: Development and Resistance in Amazonian Brazil*, London: Earthscan Publications

Daly, J. L. (2001), The "hockey stick": a new low in climate science, Technical report, http://www.vision.net.au/ daly/hockey/hockey.htm

Deacon, R. T. (1995), Assessing the relationship between government policy and deforestation, *Journal of Environmental Economics and Management* 28, 1–18

Den Haan, W. J. and Levin, A. T. (1997), A practitioner's guide to robust covariance matrix estimation, in G. Maddala and C. Rao (eds.), *Robust Inference, Handbook of Statistics*, 15, Amsterdam, New York and Oxford: Elsevier Science/North-Holland, 299–342

Diebold, F. and Mariano, R. (1995), Comparing predictive accuracy, *Journal of Business and Economic Statistics* 13, 253–264

Downton, M. W. (1994), Measuring tropical deforestation: development of the methods, Draft, Boulder, CO: National Center for Atmospheric Research

Dubois, J. C. L. (1990), Secondary forests as a land-use resource in frontier zones of Amazonia, in A. B. Anderson, ed., *Alternatives to Deforestation: Steps Toward Sustainable Use of the Amazon Rain Forest*, New York: Columbia University Press, pp. 183–194

Ekins, P. (1996), The secondary benefits of CO_2 abatement: how much emissions reduction do they justify?, *Ecological Economics* 16, 13–24

Eltahir, E. A. B. and Bras, R. L. (1992), On the response of the tropical atmosphere to largescale deforestation, *Quarterly Journal of the Royal Meteorological Society* 119, 779–793

Enters, T. (1995), The economics of land degradation and resources conservation in Northern Thailand, in J. Rigg, ed., *Counting the Costs: Economic Growth and Environmental Change in Thailand*, Singapore: Institute of Southeast Asian Studies, pp. 90–110

FACE (1993), *Jaarverslag*, Arnhem: The FACE Foundation

Faminow, M. D. (1998), *Cattle, Deforestation and Development in the Amazon: An Economic, Agronomic and Environmental Perspective*, New York: CAB International

Fankhauser, S. (1994), *Valuing Climate Change: The Economics of the Greenhouse Effect*, London: Earthscan

FAO (1994), The state of food and agriculture 1994, FAO Agriculture Series no. 27

FAO/UN (1993), Forest resources assessment 1990: tropical countries, FAO Forestry Paper 112

(1997), State of the world's forests – 1997, FAO report

FAO/UNDP/MARA (1992), Principais indicadores sócio-econômicos dos assentamentos de reforma agrária, Project BRA-87/022, Ministerio da Agricultura e Reforma Agrária

Fearnside, P. M. (1985a), Brazil's Amazon forest and the global carbon problem, *Interciencia* 10(4), 179–186

(1985b), Brazil's Amazon forest and the global carbon problem: reply to Lugo and Brown, *Interciencia* 11, 58–64

(1987), Summary of progress in quantifying the potential contribution of Amazonian deforestation to the global carbon problem, in D. Athié, T. E. Lovejoy and P. de M. Oyens, eds., Proceedings of the Workshop on Biogeochemistry of Tropical Rain Forests: Problems for Research, Piracicaba, São Paulo: Universidad de São Paulo, pp. 75–82

(1989a), Brazil's Balbina Dam: environment versus the legacy of the pharaohs in Amazonia, *Environmental Management* 13, 401–423

(1989b), Extractive reserves in Brazilian Amazonia, *BioScience* 39

(1990), The rate and extent of deforestation in Brazilian Amazonia, *Environmental Conservation* 17, 213–226

(1992a), Forest biomass in Brazilian Amazonia: comments on the estimate by Brown and Lugo, *Interciencia* 17, 19–27

(1992b), Greenhouse gas emissions from deforestation in the Brazilian Amazon, in W. Makundi and J. Sathaye, eds., *Tropical Forestry and Global Climate Change: Land-use Policy, Emission and Sequestration*, Proceedings of an International Workshop held at the Lawrence Berkeley Laboratory, Berkeley, California, May 29–31, 1991

(1993), Deforestation in Brazilian Amazon: the effect of population and land tenure, *Ambio* 22, 537–545

(1995a), Hydroelectric dams in the Brazilian Amazon as sources of "greenhouse" gases, *Environmental Conservation* 22, 7–19

(1995b), Potential impacts of climatic change on natural forests and forestry in Brazilian Amazonia, *Forest Ecology and Management* 78, 51–70

(1996), Deforestation in Brazilian Amazon: comparison of recent Landsat estimates, Manaus, National Institute for Research in the Amazon

Fearnside, P. M., Leal Jr., N. and Moreira Fernandes, M. (1993), Rainforest burning and the global carbon budget: biomass, combustion efficiency, and charcoal formation in the Brazilian Amazon, *Journal of Geophysical Research* 98, 16733–16743

Fellner, W. (1967), Operational utility: the theoretical background and a measurement, in W. Fellner, ed., *Ten Economic Studies in the Tradition of Irving Fisher*, New York: John Wiley

Ferraz, C. (2001), Measuring the causes of deforestation, agriculture land conversion and cattle ranching growth: evidence from the Amazon, Draft, Part of the World Bank Project "Making Long-Term Economic Growth More Sustainable," Rio de Janeiro: IPEA

Freese, C. H. (1998), *Wild Species as Commodities. Managing Markets and Ecosystems for Sustainability*, Washington, DC and Covelo: Island Press

Freyre, G. (1977), *Casa Grande and Senzala. Formação da família brasileira sob o regime da economia patriarcal*, 18th edn., Rio de Janeiro: José Olympio

FUNATORA (1992), Cost of implementation of Conservation Units in Legal Amazonia, annexes N.3 and N.4, Brasília: FUNATURA-SCT/PR-PNUD

Furtado, C. (1970), *Formação econômica do Brasil*, 10th edn., São Paulo: Editora Nacional

Geist, H. J. and Lambin, E. F. (2001), What drives tropical deforestation: a meta-analysis of proximate and underlying causes of deforestation based on subnational case studies evidence, Lucc Report Series no. 4, Land Use and Land Cover Change Project, University of Louvain

German Bundestag, ed. (1990), *Protecting the Tropical Forests: A High Priority International Task*, Bonn: Bonner Universitäts-Buchdruckerei

Glüsener-Godt, M. and Sachs, I., eds. (1994), *Extractivism in the Brazilian Amazon: Perspectives on Regional Development*, Paris: UNESCO, MAB Digest 18

Godoy, R., Lubowski, R. and Markandya, A. (1993), A method for the economic valuation of nontimber tropical forest products, *Economic Botany* 47, 220–233

Goldin, I. and Rezende, G. (1993), *A agricultura brasileira na decada de 80: crescimento numa economia em crise*, Brasília, IPEA

Granger, C. W. J. (2000), Thick modeling, Draft, Department of Economics, University of California, San Diego

Granger, C. W. J. and Huang, L.-L. (1997), Evaluation of panel data models: some suggestions from time series, Draft, Department of Economics, University of California, San Diego

Granger, C. W. J. and Newbold, P. (1986), *Forecasting Economic Time Series*, 2nd edn., San Diego: Academic Press

Graves, P. E. (2001), Valuing public goods, unpublished manuscript, University of Colorado at Boulder

Gregersen, H. M., Arnold, J. E. M., Lundgren, A. L. and Contreras-Hermosilla, A. (1995), Valuing forests: context, issues and guidelines, Forestry Paper 127, Rome: FAO

Hamilton, L. S. and King, P. N. (1983), *Tropical Forested Watersheds: Hydrologic and Soils Response to Major Uses or Conversions*, Boulder, CO: Westview Press

Harcourt, C. and Sayer, J. A. (1996), *The Conservation Atlas of Tropical Forests. The Americas*, New York: Simon and Schuster

Harrison, S. (1991), Population growth, land-use and deforestation in Costa Rica, 1950–1984, *Interciencia* 16, 83–93

Hecht, S. B. (1986), Environment, development and politics: capital accumulation and the livestock sector in Eastern Amazônia, *World Development* 13, 663–684

Hecht, S. B. and Cockburn, A. (1989), *The Fate of the Forest: Developers, Destroyers and Defenders of the Amazon*, New York: Verso

Hecht, S., Norgard, R. R. and Possio, G. (1988), The economics of cattle ranching in Eastern Amazonia, *Interciencia* 13, 233–240

Helfand, S. M. and Brunstein, L. F. (1999), The 1995–96 Agricultural Census in Brazil: fact or fiction?, Paper prepared for the NeMESIS Seminar in Rio de Janeiro, December 6–7, Rio de Janeiro: IPEA

Henderson-Sellers, A. *et al.* (1993), Tropical deforestation: modeling local to regional-scale climate change, *Journal of Geophysical Research* 98, 7289–7315

Hendry, D. (1995), *Dynamic Econometrics*, Oxford: Oxford University Press

Hoeller, P. and Coppel, J. (1992), Energy taxation and price distortions in fossil fuel markets: some implications for climate change policy, in OECD, ed., *Climate Change: Designing a Practical Tax System*, Paris: OECD, pp. 185–212

Hoffman, R. (1988), Distribuição da renda na agricultura, in A. Brandão, ed., *Os Principais Problemas da Agricultura Brasileira: Análise e Sugestões*, Rio de Janeiro: IPEA /PNPE

Homma, A. K. O. (1994), Plant extractivism in the Amazon: limitations and possibilities, in M. Glüsener-Godt and I. Sachs, eds., *Extractivism in the Brazilian Amazon: Perspectives on Regional Development*, Paris: UNESCO, MAB Digest 18

(1996), Modernization and technological dualism in the extractive economy in Amazonia, in M. R. Pérez and J. E. M. Arnold, eds., *Current Issues in Non-Timber Forest Products Research*, Bogor, Indonesia: Center for International Forestry Research

ed. (1993), *Extractivismo Vegetal na Amazônia: Limites e Oportunidades*, Brasília: Embrapa-SPI

Hoppe, A. (1992), Mining in the Amazonian rainforests, *Nature* 355, 593–594

Houghton, R. A., Hobbie, J. E., Melillo, J. M., Moore, B., Peterson, B. J., Shaver, G. R. and Woodwell, G. M. (1983), Changes in the carbon content of terrestrial biota and soils between 1860 and 1980: a net release of CO_2 to the atmosphere, *Ecological Monographs* 53, 235–262

Houghton, R. A., Boone, R., Fruci, J. *et al.* (1987), The flux of carbon from terrestrial ecosystems to the atmosphere in 1980 due to changes in land-use: geographic distribution of the global flux tellus 39b, Technical Report, pp. 122–139

Houghton, R. A., Skole, D. L. and Lefkowitz, D. S. (1991), Changes in the landscape of Latin America between 1850 and 1985. II. net release of CO_2 to the atmosphere, *Forest Ecology and Management* 38, 173–199

IBGE (1950), Censos econômicos Brasil 1940, v. 3, Rio de Janeiro

(1997), *Contagem da Populaçăo – 1996*, Rio de Janeiro: IBGE

(1998), Censo agropecuário 1995–1996, Rio de Janeiro

(no year), Manual do recenseador. conso agropecuário, ce 2.06, Rio de Janeiro

Idso, S. B. and Kimball, B. A. (1993), Tree growth in carbon dioxide enriched air and its implications for global carbon cycling and maximum levels of atmospheric CO_2, *Global Biogeochemical Cycles* 7, 537–555

Intergovernmental Panel on Climate Change (IPCC) (1990), *Scientific Assessment of Climate Change: Report Prepared for IPCC by Working Group I*, New York: World Meteorological Organization and United Nations Environmental Programme, June

(2001), Third assessment report of working group 1: summary for policymakers, http://www.ipcc.ch/pub/spm22-01.pdf, New York: IPCC

Johanssen, P. (1990), Valuing environmental damage, *Oxford Review of Economic Policy* 6

Jones, D. W. *et al.* (1992), *Farming in Rondonia*, Blacksburg, Virginia: Oak Ridge National Laboratory for the US Department of Energy and Department of Urban and Regional Planning, Virginia Polytechnic Institute and State University

Jordan, C. and Heuneldop, J. (1981), The water budget of an Amazonian rainforest, *Acta Amazonica* 11, 87–92

Kaimowitz, D. (2001), Amazon deforestation revisited, Draft, Center for International Forestry Research, San Jose, Costa Rica

Kaimowitz, D. and Angelsen, A. (1997), What can we learn from economic models of tropical deforestation?, Draft, September 1997, Bogor, Indonesia: Center for International Forestry Research

(1998), *Economic Models of Tropical Deforestation: A Review*, Bogor, Indonesia: Center for International Forestry Research

(2001), *Agricultural Technologies and Tropical Deforestation*, Wallingford: CABI Publishing

Kaimowitz, D. and Smith, J. (2001), Soybean technology and the loss of natural vegetation in Brazil and Bolivia, in D. Kaimowitz and A. Angelsen, eds., *Agricultural Technologies and Tropical Deforestation*, Wallingford: CABI Publishing

Kemfert, C. (2001), Economy–energy–climate interaction: the model WIAGEM, Working Paper no. 71/2001, Fundazione Eni Enrico Mattei, Milan

Kohlhepp, G. (1980), Analysis of state and private regional development projects in the Brazilian Amazon basin, *Applied Geography and Development* 16, 53–79

Kolk, A. (1996), *Forests in International Environmental Politics: International Organisations, NGOs and the Brazilian Amazon*, Utrecht: International Books

Körner, C. and Arnone III, J. A. (1992), Responses to elevated carbon dioxide in artificial tropical ecosystems, *Science* 257, 1672–1675

Kurtze, K. and Springer, K. (1999), Modeling the economic impact of global warming in a general equilibrium framework, Kiel Working Paper 922, Kiel Institute of World Economics

Laurance, W. F., Cochrane, M. A., Bergen, S., Fearnside, P. M. *et al.* (2001a), The future of the Brazilian Amazon, *Science* 291, 438–439

(2001b), Supplementary Material, www.sciencemag.org/cgl/content/full/291/5503/438/dc1

Laurance, W. F., Delamônica, P., Laurance, S. G., Vasconcelos, H. L. and Lovejoy, T. E. (2000), Rainforest fragmentation kills big trees, *Nature* 404, 836

Laurance, W. F., Laurance, S. G. and Delamônica, P. (1998), Tropical forest fragmentation and greenhouse gas emissions, *Forest Ecology and Management* 110, 173–180

Laurance, W. F., Laurance, S. G., Ferreira, L. V., Rankin-de Merona, J. M., Gascon, C. and Lovejoy, T. E. (1997), Biomass collapse in Amazonian forest fragments, *Science* 278, 1117–1118

Lean, J. and Rowntree, P. R. (1993), A GCM simulation of the impact of Amazonian deforestation on climate using an improved canopy representation, *Quarterly Journal of the Royal Meteorological Society* 119, 509–530

Lele, U., Viana, V., Verissimo, A., Vosti, S., Perkins, K. and Husain, S. A., eds. (2000), *Brazil. Forests in the Balance: Challenges of Conservation with Development*, Washington, DC: World Bank

Leopoldo, P., Franken, W., Matsui, E. and Salati, E. (1982), Estimativa da evapotranspiração de foresta Amazônica de terra firme, *Acta Amazonica* 12, 23–28

Lettau, H., Lettau, K. and Molion, L. (1979), Amazonia's hydrological cycle and the role of atmosphere recycling in assessing deforestation effects, *Monthly Weather Review* 107, 227–238

Liu, D. S., Iverson, L. R. and Brown, S. (1993), Rates and patterns of deforestation in the Philippines: application of Geographic Information System analysis, *Forest Ecology and Management* 57, 1–16

Lopes, A. S. (1996), Soils under *cerrado*: a success story in soil management, *Better Crops International* 10, 9–15

Ludeke, A. K., Maggion, R. C. and Reid, L. M. (1990), An analysis of anthropogenic deforestation using Logistic Regression and GIS, *Journal of Environmental Management* 31, 247–259

Lugo, A. E. and Brown, S. (1992), Tropical forests as sinks of atmospheric carbon, *Forest Ecology and Management* 54, 239–255

MacMillan, G., ed. (1995), *At the End of the Rainbow? Gold, Land and People in the Brazilian Amazon*, London: Earthscan Publications

Mahar, D. J. (1979), *Frontier Development Policy in Brazil: A Study of Amazonia*, New York: Praeger

(1989), Government policies and deforestation in Brazil's Amazon region, Technical Report, World Bank, A World Bank Publication in cooperation with World Wildlife Fund and The Conservation Foundation

Maia Gomes, G. and Vergolino, J. R. (1997), Trinta e cinco anos de crescimento econômico na Amazônia (1960/1995), Texto para Discussão, Instituto de Pesquisa Econômica Aplicada, Brasília, no. 533

Mann, M. E., Bradley, R. S. and Hughes, M. K. (1999), Northern hemisphere temperatures during the past millennium: inferences, uncertainties, and limitations, *Geophysical Research Letters* 26, 759–771

Mares, M. A. (1992), Neotropical mammals and the myth of Amazonian biodiversity, *Science* 255, 976–979

Marques, J., Salati, E. and Santos, J. (1980), Calculo de evapotranspiração real na bacia Amazônica através do metodo aerológico, *Acta Amazonica* 10, 357–361

Martine, G. (1989), *Migrações internas no Brasil – Tendências e perspectivas*, Brasilia: IPEA

Mattos, M. M. and Uhl, C. (1994), Economic and ecological perspectives on ranching in the Eastern Amazonia, *World Development* 22, 145–158

Mattos, M. M., Uhl, C. and de Almeida Goncalves, D. (1992), Economic and ecological perspectives on ranching in eastern Amazon in the 1990s, Paper submitted to World Development, Instituto do Homen e Meio Ambiente da Amazonia, Brazil: EMBRAPA/Penn State University

May, P. and Reis, E. J. (1993), The user structure of Brazil's tropical rainforest, Working Paper 565, Kiel Institute of World Economics

Meher-Homji, V. M. (1988), Effects of forests on precipitation in India, in E. R. C. Reynolds and F. B. Thompson, eds., *Forests, Climate, and Hydrology: Regional Impacts*, Tokyo: United Nations University

Mertens, B. and Lambin, E. F. (1997), Spatial modeling of deforestation in southern Cameroon, *Applied Geography* 17, 1–19

Mincer, J. and Zarnowitz, V. (1969), The evaluation of economic forecasts, in J. Mincer, ed., *Economic Forecasts and Expectations*, New York: National Bureau of Economic Research

Moore, P. (2000), *Green Spirit: Trees are the Answer*, Ontario: Hushion House Publishing Ltd

Moran, E. F. (1989), Government-directed settlement in the 1970s: an assessment of the Transamazon Highway colonization, in D. Schumann and W. Partridge, eds., *The Human Ecology of Tropical Land Settlement in Latin America*, Boulder, CO: Westview Press

Murrieta Ruiz, J. and Rueda Pinzón, M. (1995), *Extractive Reserves*, Gland, Switzerland and Cambridge: IUCN

Myers, N. (1988a), The biodiversity challenge: expanded hot-spots analysis, *Environmentalist* 10, 243–256

(1988b), Threatened biotas: "hot spots" in tropical forests, *Environmentalist* 8, 187–208

(1989), Deforestation rates in tropical countries and their climatic implications, Technical Report, Friends of the Earth Report

(1990), The biodiversity challenge: expanded hot-spots analysis, *Environmentalist* 110(4), 243–256

(1993), Tropical forests: the main deforestation fronts, *Environmental Conservation* 20, 9–16

National Academy of Sciences (1991), *Policy Implications of Greenhouse Warming*, Washington, DC: National Academy Press

Nelson, G. and Hellerstein, D. (1995), Do roads cause deforestation? Using satellite images in econometric analysis of land-use, Staff Paper 95-E488, Department of Agricultural Economics, University of Illinois, Urbana-Champaign

Nepstad, D., Capobianco, J. P., Barros, A. C., Carvalho, G., Moutinho, P., Lopes, U. and Lefebvre, P. (2001), *Avança Brasil*: the environmental costs for Amazonia, Draft, Instituto de Pesquisa Ambiental da Amazônia, IPAM

Nepstad, D., McGrath, D., Alencar, A., Barros, A. C., Carvalho, G., Santilli, M. and Vera Diaz, M. del C. (2002), Frontier governance in Amazonia, *Science* 295, 629–630

Nepstad, D. C. and Schwarzman, S., eds. (1992), *Nontimber Products from Tropical Forests: Evaluation of a Conservation and Development Strategy. Advances in Economic Botany, vol. 9*, New York: The New York Botanical Garden

Nordhaus, W. D. (1991), A survey of estimates of the costs of controlling greenhouse gases, *Energy Journal* 12, 37–66

(1994), *Managing the Global Commons: The Economics of Climate Change*, Cambridge, MA: MIT Press

Nordhaus, W. D. and Boyer, J. (2000), *Warming the World: Economic Models of Global Warming*, Cambridge, MA: MIT Press

O'Brien, K. L. (1995), Deforestation and climate change in the Selva Lacadona of Chiapas, Mexico, *Nordisk Geografisk Tidsskrift*

Odum, E. P. (1988), *Ecologia*, Rio de Janeiro: Guanabara SA

Otsuki, T. and Reis, E. (1998), Temporal and spatial evolution of the logging sector in the Brazilian Amazon: evidence from census, survey and export data in 1975–95, Draft, Rio de Janeiro: IPEA

Parker, E., Posey, D., Frechione, J. and da Silva, L. F. (1983), Resource exploitation in Amazonia: ethnoecological examples from four populations, *Annals of the Carnegie Museum* 52, 163–203

Pearce, D. (1991), Deforesting the Amazon: toward an economic solution, *Ecodecision* 1, 40–49

(1993), *Economic Values and the Natural World*, Cambridge, MA: MIT Press

Pearce, D. W., Barbier, E. and Markandya, A. (1990), *Sustainable Development: Economics and Environment in the Third World*, Aldershot: Edward Elgar

Peters, C. M. (1994), Sustainable harvest of non-timber plant resources in tropical moist forests: an ecological primer, Technical Report, Biodiversity Support Program, Washington, DC: WWF/TNC/WRI

Peters, C. M., Gentry, A. H. and Mendelsohn, R. O. (1989), Valuation of an Amazonian rainforest, *Nature* 339, 655–656

Pfaff, A. S. (1996), What drives deforestation in the Brazilian Amazon? Evidence from satellite and socioeconomic data, Global Change Report no. 16, MIT Joint Program on the Science and Policy of Global Change

Pinedo-Vasquez, M., Zarin, D. and Jipp, P. (1992), Economic returns from forest conversion in the Peruvian Amazon, *Ecological Economics* 6, 163–173

Pinedo-Vasquez, M. *et al.* (2001), Post boom logging in Amazonia, Draft, University of Columbia

Pires, M. O. and Scardua, F. P., eds. (1998), *Extractivismo Vegetal não Madeireiro no Cerrado*, Brasília: ISPN

Poterba, J. M. (1993), Global warming policy: a public finance perspective, *Journal of Economic Perspectives* 7, 47–63

Prado Júnior, C. (1978), *História Econômica do Brasil*, 21st edn., São Paulo: Brasiliense

Rasch, H. (1994), Mapping of vegetation, land cover, and land-use by satellite – experience and conclusions for future project applications, *Programmetric Engineering and Remote Sensing* 60, 265–271

Reis, E. J. (1996), Padrões geográficos de incidência dos efeitos econômicos e ambientais do programa Grande Carajás, in R. Varsano, ed., *Perspectivas da Economia Brasileira – 1996*, Rio de Janeiro: IPEA

Reis, E. J. and Andersen, L. E. (1997), Carbon emissions from deforestation in the Brazilian Amazon, Texto para Discussão, Rio de Janeiro: IPEA/DIPES

Reis, E. J. and Blanco, F. A. (1996a), The causes of Brazilian Amazon's deforestation, UNU/WIDER Project, Preliminary Draft, Rio de Janeiro: IPEA

(1996b), The expansion of the Brazilian agricultural frontier: a survey of the literature, UNU/WIDER Project, Preliminary Draft, Rio de Janeiro: IPEA

Richards, M. (1993), The potential of non-timber forest products in sustainable natural forest management in Amazonia, *Commonwealth Forestry Review* 27

Rivas, A. (1998), The Manaus Free Trade Zone: economic growth and deforestation in the state of Amazonas, NEMESIS Research Paper, April, Universidade do Amazonas

Rochefort, L. and Bazzaz, F. A. (1992), Growth response to elevated CO_2 in seedlings of four co-occurring birch species, *Canadian Journal of Forestry Research* 22, 1583–1587

Rudel, T. K. and Rober, J. (1997), The paths to rainforest destruction: crossnational patterns of tropical deforestation, 1975–1990, *World Development* 25, 53–65

Ruíz, M. and Pinzón, R. (1995), *Reservas Extrativistas*, Gland: IUCN, The World Conservation Unit

Saldarriaga, J. G. and West, D. C. (1986), Holocene fires in the northern Amazon Basin, *Quaternary Research* 26, 358–366

Sanchez, P. A., Palm, C. A., Szott, L. T., Cuevas, E. and Lal, R. (1989), Organic input management in tropical agroecosystems, in D. C. Colema *et al.*, eds., *Dynamics of Soil Organic Matter in Tropical Ecosystems*, Honolulu: University of Hawaii Press

Sanford, R. L., Saldarriaga, J. G., Clark, K., Uhl, C. and Herrera, R. (1985), Amazon rainforest fires, *Science* 227, 53–55

Santos, R. A. de Oliveira (1980), *História ecônomica da Amazonia (1800–1920)*, São Paulo: T. A. Queiroz

Sawyer, D., van der Ree, M., Pires, M. and Oliveira, M., eds. (1997), *Comercialização de Espécies Vegetais Nativas do Cerrado*, Brasília: ISPN

Schimel, D. S. (1995), Terrestrial ecosystems and the carbon cycle, *Global Change Biology* 1, 77–91

Schmink, M. (1988), Big business in the Amazon, in J. S. Denslow and C. Padoch, eds., *People of the Tropical Rain Forest*, Berkeley, CA.: University of California Press, pp. 163–174

Schneider, R. R. (1991), An analysis of environmental problems and policies in the Amazon, Paper presented at a ACT seminar in Caracas, Washington, DC: World Bank

(1992), An economic analysis of environmental problems in the Amazon, Draft, Washington, DC: World Bank

(1993), The potential for trade with the Amazon in greenhouse gas reduction, Laten Dissemination Note II, from http://www.worldbank.org/html/lat/english/-papers/env/note-2.pdf, World Bank

(1995), Government and the economy on the Amazon frontier, World Bank Environment Paper 11, Washington, DC: World Bank

Schneider, R. R., Arima, E., Veríssimo, A. V., Barreto, P. and Souza Jr., C. (2000), *Sustainable Amazon: Limitations and Opportunities for Rural Development*, Brasília: World Bank and IMAZON

Schroeder, P. E. and Winjum, J. K. (1994a), Assessing Brazil's carbon budget: I. Biotic carbon pools, Working Paper, US EPA Environmental Research Laboratory, Oregon

(1994b), Assessing Brazil's carbon budget: II. Biotic fluxes and net carbon balance, Working Paper, US EPA Environmental Research Laboratory, Oregon

Schuh, G. E. (2001), Reclaiming marginal lands and exploiting tropical soils: the *cerrado* in Brazil and its future role in international trade, Paper presented at The World Food Prize Symposium, Des Moines, October 18–19, 2001

Scott, M. (1989), *A New View of Economic Growth*, Oxford: Clarendon Press

Seiler, W. and Crutzen, P. J. (1980), Estimates of gross and net fluxes of carbon between the biosphere and the atmosphere from biomass burning, *Climatic Change* 2, 207–247

Serôa da Motta, R. (1993), Past and current policy issues concerning tropical deforestation in Brazil, Kiel Working Paper 566, The Kiel Institute of World Economics

Shah, A. and Larson, B. (1992), Carbon taxes, the greenhouse effect and developing countries, World Development Report 1992, New York: United Nations

Simpson, R. D., Sedjo, R. A. and Reid, J. W. (1996), Valuing biodiversity for use in pharmaceutical research, *Journal of Political Economy* 104, 163–185

Singh, J. S. and Joshi, M. C. (1979), Primary production, in R. T. Coupland, ed., *Grassland Ecosystems of the World: Analysis of Grasslands and their Uses*, Cambridge: Cambridge University Press

Smith, N. J. H. (1980), Anthrosols and human carrying capacity in Amazonia, *Annals of the Association of American Geographers* 70, 553–566

Smith, N. J. H., Serrão, E. A. S., Alvim, P. T. and Falesi, I. C. (1995), *Amazonia: Resiliency and Dynamism of the Land and its People*, Tokyo: United Nations University Press

Sombroek, W. (1992), Biomass and carbon storage in the Amazon ecosystems, *Interciencia*

Sombroek, W. and Sousa Carvalho, A. (2000), Macro and micro ecologic economic zoning in the Amazon region: some results and research needs, Paper Presented at the German–Brazilian Workshop on Neotropical Ecosystems – Achievements and Prospects of Cooperative Research, Hamburg, September 3–8

Southgate, D. (1998), *Tropical Forest Conservation. An Economic Assessment of the Alternatives in Latin America*, New York and Oxford: Oxford University Press

Springer, K. (2001), The economic implications of international climate policy in a globalizing world: a computable general equilibrium model with capital mobility and trade, PhD thesis, Christian-Albrechts-Universität zu Kiel, Kiel

Stone, S. W. (1996), Economic trends in the timber industry of the Brazilian Amazon: evidence from Paragominas, CREED Working Paper Series no. 6

SUDAM (1992), Sustainable development of the Amazon: development strategy and investment alternatives, Rio de Janeiro June

Suzuki, D. (2001), Weakened ocean currents could cause climate flip, http://www.enn.com/news/enn-stories/2001/06/06292001/smclimateflip44129.asp?site = seacoast, Environmental News Network

Swanson, T. M. (1995), The theory and practice of transferring development rights: the institutions for contracting for biodiversity, Paper presented at the Workshop on Financing Biodiversity Conservation, Harare, 13–15 September

Szultc, T. (1986), Brazil's Amazon frontier, in A. Maguire and J. W. Brown, eds., *Bordering on Trouble: Resources and Politics in Latin America*, Bethesda, MD: Adler and Adler, pp. 191–234

Tangtham, N. and Sutthipibul, V. (1989), Effects of diminishing forest area on rainfall amount and distribution in North-Eastern Thailand, Technical Report, Paper presented at the FRIM-IHP-UNESCO Regional Seminar on Tropical Forest Hydrology, Kuala Lumpur, September 4–9

Tol, R. S. J. (2002a), New estimates of the damage costs of climate change, part I: Benchmark estimates, *Environmental and Resource Economics*, 21(1), pp. 47–73

(2002b), New estimates of the damage costs of climate change, part II: dynamic estimates, *Environmental and Resource Economics*, 21(2), pp. 135–160

Toniolo, A. and Uhl, C. (1995), Economic and ecological perspectives on agriculture in Eastern Amazon, *World Development* 23, 959–973

Turcq, B., Sifeddine, A., Martin, L., Absy, M. L., Soubles, F., Suguio, K. and Volkmer-Ribeiro, C. (1998), Amazonia rainforest fires: a lacustrine record of 7000 years, *Ambio* 27, 139–142

Uhl, C. (1987), Factors controlling succession following slash-and-burn agriculture in Amazonia, *Journal of Ecology* 75, 377–407

Uhl, C., Bezerra, O. and Martini, A. (1993), An ecosystem perspective on threats to biodiversity in Eastern Amazonia, in C. S. Potter, J. I. Cohen and D. Janczewski, eds., *Perspectives on Biodiversity: Case Studies of Genetic Resource Conservation and Development*, New York: AAAS Press

Uhl, C. H., Buschbacher, R. and Serrão, E. A. S. (1988), Abandoned pastures in Eastern Amazonia: patterns of plant succession, *Journal of Ecology* 76, 663–681

Uhl, C. H., Jordan, C. F. and Herrera, R. (1982), Amazon forest management for wood production: an assessment of limitations and potentials based on field studies at San Carlos de Rio Negro, Venezuela, in E. G. Hallsworth, ed., *Socioeconomic Effects and Constraints in Tropical Forest Management*, Chichester: John Wiley, pp. 143–157

UNCED (1992), *Earth Summit 1992*, London: The Regency Press

UNESCO (1978), Tropical forest ecosystems, a state of knowledge report, Technical Report, Natural Resource Series, vol. 14, Pans: UNESCO

Veríssimo, A., Barreto, P., Mattos, M., Tarifa, R. and Uhl, C. (1992), Logging impacts and prospects for sustainable forest management in an old Amazonian frontier: the case of Paragominas, *Forest Ecology and Management* 55, 169–199

Veríssimo, A., Cochrane, M. A., Jr., Souza, C., Jr. and Salomão, R. (2002), Priority areas for establishing national forests in the Brazilian Amazon, *Conservation Ecology* 6, 4

Villa Nova, N., Salati, E. and Matsui, E. (1976), Estimativa da evapotranspiração na bacia Amazônica, *Acta Amazonica* 6, 215–228

Vincent, J. R. (1997), Economic considerations pertaining to the expansion of logging in the Amazon, *Cadernos FBDS* 2, 15–24

Vincent, J. R., Kaosa-ard, M. *et al.*, eds. (1995), *The Economics of Watershed Protection: A Case Study of the Mae Teng River*, Bangkok: Thailand Development Research Institute

von Thünen, J. H. (1966), Der isolierte staat in beziehung der landwirtschaft und nationalokonomie, in P. Hall, ed., *Von Thünen's Isolated State*, Oxford: Pergamon Press

Vosti, S. A., Carpentier, C. L., Witcover, J. and Valentim, J. F. (2001), Intensified small-scale livestock systems in the Western Brazilian Amazon, in A. Angelsen and D. Kaimowitz, eds., *Agricultural Technologies and Tropical Deforestation*, Wallingford: CABI Publishing

Weinhold, D. (1999), An estimation of land degradation in the Amazon, *Ecological Economics* 1, 63–76

(2001), Iterative general to simple estimation, Draft, London School of Economics

World Bank (1989), *Brazil: Agricultural Data*, Washington, DC: World Bank

(1998), *World Development Indicators*, Washington, DC: World Bank

Wunder, S. (1999), Value determinants of plant extractivism in Brazil, Discussion Paper no. 682, Rio de Janeiro: IPEA

(2000), *The Economics of Deforestation: The Example of Ecuador*, London: Macmillan

Wyman, R. L., ed. (1991), *Global Climate Change and Life on Earth*, New York: Chapman & Hall

Yokomizo, C. (1989), Incentivos financeiros e fiscais na Amazônia: Fatos, problemas e soluções, Symposium: "Amazonian Facts: Problems and Solutions," Brasília: USP-INPE, June

Young, C. E. F. (1995), Public policy and deforestation in the Brazilian Amazon, Report for CREED/IIED, International Institute for Environment and Development, London, July

Young, C. E. F. and Fausto, J. R. F. (1997), Valoração de recursos naturais como instrumento de análisie da expansão da fronteira agrícola na Amazônia, Discussion Paper no. 490, Rio de Janeiro: IPEA

Index

abandoned land, 41
açaí belt, 90, 98
agricultural
  census, 45, 94
  frontier, 64
  research, 207
aluminium processing, 99, 53
Avança Brasil, 33–34, 138, 140–141, 145, 206–207

babaçu belt, 98
Balbina dam, 86
bauxite mining, 53
benefits of clearing
  owing to unpaved roads, 196
biodiversity, 186
biomass content, 163
  steady-state assumption, 165
boom-bust cycles, 23, 82

Calha Norte, 18
Carajás, 17–19, 84
carbon
  content in different vegetation types, 153
  dynamics, 155
  emissions, 152, 202
  emission estimates, 160
  inventory model, 153
  tax, 181
carbon content
  climax, 156
cattle, 70
  and government subsidies, 71
  herd growth, 54, 70
  and land speculation, 74
  liquid investment, 77
  local urban demand, 76
  low-risk, 77
  not labor intensive, 77
  prestigious activity, 77
  useful by-products, 77
cerrado, 11–12, 71, 78
Cerrado Research Center, 78
clearing vs. deforestation, 6
Companhia Vale do Rio Doce, 53
computable general equilibrium model (CGE), 184
Conservation Units, 19, 62
conservationists, 1, 3
credit, 60
crops
  annual, 77
  perennial, 78

dams, 85
  Balbina, 86
  Tucurui, 85
deforestation
  accumulated: by INPE, 41; from land surveys, 111
  cross-country models, 111
  definition of: inclusive, 6; purist, 6
  farm-level studies, 112
  gross, 41
  measured by satellite, 41
  measures: sources of error, 44
  models, 111
  net, 41
  owing to dams, 86
  owing to mining, 85
  regional models, 112
degradation, 201
  forest, 201
developmentalists, 1, 2
discount rate, 171

econometric
  methodology, 209
  philosophy, 209
economic
  growth, 201
  valuation, 168
EMBRAPA, 78, 207
environmental protection, 207

ethics, 3
existence value, 188, 203
exports, 53
externalities, 203
extraction values, 96, 100
extractivism, 91, 93

fallow lands, 158
FINAM, 72
flooding
  owing to dams, 85
forest degradation, 201
fragmentation, 201
frontier effect, 64

GDP, 50
  rural 52, 127: *per capita*, 51
  urban 52, 53, 129: *per capita*, 51
genetic diversity, 202
Gini index, 73
global warming, 182
gold mining, 84
government subsidies, 72
Greater Carajás Program, 84
greenhouse gases, 184
growth poles, 15, 84

hydroelectric projects, 85
hydro-power, 85

illiteracy rates, 29, 202
import protection, 53
income distribution, 22
indigenous people, 4
Indigenous Reserves, 19, 62
industry, 52, 53
inequality, 31
infant mortality, 29, 202
inflation, 60
interest rates, 61
Intergovernmental Panel on Climate Change, 182
international parks agreement, 197, 205

Jari project, 79

Kyoto Protocol, 184

land
  distribution, 31, 32
  prices, 54, 74–75, 129, 190: and subsidized credit, 75
  speculation, 74
Legal Amazonia, 11
licensing, 20

life expectancy, 28, 202
local markets, 76
logging, 61, 80
  boom–bust cycles, 82
  even–flow harvesting, 82
  pulse harvesting, 82
  sustainable, 81

macroeconomic changes, 46
managed timber extraction, 82
Manaus Free Zone (MFZ), 51, 53
migrants, 23
mineral processing, 53
Minimum Comparable Areas (MCAs), 36
mining, 83
  large-scale, 83
  placer, 84
model evaluation, 211
modeling
  cattle herd growth, 133
  data based, 114
  general-to-simple, 114
  growth of cleared land, 124
  population growth, 129
  random reduction, 115
  rural GDP growth, 127
  theory-based, 113
  urban GDP growth, 129
monitoring, 20
  environmental, 207

National Forests, 82–83
National System of Rural Credit, 60
natural
  forest share, 39
  vegetation, 38, 45
neighbor variables, 64
non-wood forest products, 92
North region, 11
Nossa Natureza, 17

old deforestation, 44
Operation Amazonia, 15

Paragominas, 81
placer mining, 84
PLANAFLORO, 19
planted forest, 79
policy implications, 203
POLOCENTRO, 78
Polonoroeste Development Program, 17
population
  density, 48
  urban, 50

poverty
  indicators, 30
  rates, 27
  rights, 86

rainfall, 61, 149
random reduction, 212
reference period, 46
reforestation, 19
research
  tropical agriculture, 207
rivers, 59
road building, 55
roads
  Cuiaba-Porto Velho, 57
  federal, 56
  municipal, 56, 113
  paved, 56, 193
  state, 56
  Transamazonica, 57
  unpaved, 56, 127, 193
rubber boom, 13
rural population density, 49

secondary
  forest growth, 45, 88
  forest re-growth, 7
  forests, 89
silviculture, 79
slash-and-burn, 77, 88, 153
soil quality, 61
soybeans, 22, 71, 76, 78, 207
spatial variables, 64
species extinction, 202
squatting, 33
stumpage
  fees, 81
  values, 82
subsidized credit, 61
  and land values, 74
SUDAM, 16, 61, 72

temperature changes, 183
timber processing, 53
Total Economic Value (TEV), 169
  standing rainforest, 173
tourism, 187
trade liberalization, 46
Transamazonica, 57
trickle-down effects, 15
Tucurui dam, 86

urban centers, 50

value
  of agricultural land, according to: estimated model, 193; historical Legal Amazon-wide data, 191; land prices, 191; site studies, 191
value
  of cleared land, 189
  of intact forest, 173
  of standing forest: biodiversity protection, 186; carbon storage, 180; erosion control, 178; existence value, 188; fire control, 177; global benefits, 180; local private benefits, 173; local public benefits, 174; non-timber forest products, 173; nutrient recycling, 176; recreational value, 187; scientific value of biodiversity, 187; sustainable timber production, 173; water recycling, 175; watershed protection, 178
vegetation types, 39

wildfire, 203
World Bank, 84

zoning, 19